INDIA'S NEIGHBOURHOOD
Challenges in the Next Two Decades

INDIA'S NEIGHBOURHOOD

Challenges in the Next Two Decades

Editors

Rumel Dahiya

Ashok K Behuria

INSTITUTE FOR DEFENCE STUDIES & ANALYSES
NEW DELHI

AN IMPRINT OF PENTAGON PRESS

First Published in 2012

ISBN 978-81-8274-687-9

Copyright © Institute for Defence Studies and Analyses, New Delhi

All rights reserved. No part of this publication may be reproduced, stored in a retrieval system, or transmitted, in any form or by any means, electronic, mechanical, photocopying, recording, or otherwise, without first obtaining written permission of the copyright owner.

Disclaimer: The views expressed in this book are those of the authors and do not necessarily reflect those of the Institute for Defence Studies and Analyses, or the Government of India.

Published by
PENTAGON SECURITY INTERNATIONAL
An Imprint of
PENTAGON PRESS
206, Peacock Lane, Shahpur Jat,
New Delhi-110049
Phones: 011-64706243, 26491568
Telefax: 011-26490600
email: rajan@pentagonpress.in
website: www.pentagonpress.in

Maps: Geographic Information Systems (GIS) Lab, IDSA.
Cover Illustration: Map not to scale.

Printed at Avantika Printers Private Limited

CONTENTS

Foreword	vii
About the Contributors	ix
List of Abbreviations	xi
List of Tables, Figures, Maps	xvii
Introduction	xix

1. **Afghanistan**
   Likely Scenarios and India's Options 1
   Vishal Chandra

2. **Bangladesh**
   Illegal Migration and Challenges for India 19
   Sreeradha Datta

3. **Bhutan**
   India-Bhutan Relations in the Next Two Decades 35
   Medha Bisht

4. **China**
   Managing India-China Relations 55
   Prashant Kumar Singh and Rumel Dahiya

5. **Maldives**
   Harmonising Efforts to Mitigate Adverse Impacts of Climate Change and Achieve Growth 95
   Anand Kumar

6. **Myanmar**
   The Need for Infrastructure Integration 110
   Udai Bhanu Singh and Shruti Pandalai

7. **Nepal**
   Issues and Concerns in India-Nepal Relations 137
   Nihar Nayak

8. Pakistan
   Chronic Instability and India's Options 163
   Ashok K Behuria and Sushant Sareen

9. Sri Lanka
   Challenges and Opportunities for India 191
   Smruti S Pattanaik

   Conclusion 216

   Index 222

Foreword

The developments affecting India's neighbourhood over the past decade have led India to take a close look at her foreign and security policies. There is a widely shared belief that India has to formulate policy options to secure her national interests, keeping in view the changes occurring in her neighbourhood. This volume offers a well-rounded survey of India's relations with some of the important countries in her immediate neighbourhood, develops plausible scenarios for each of them, and proposes options for consideration by the policy establishment.

The chapters in the book take a prospective look at India's neighbourhood, as it may evolve by 2030. They underline the challenges that confront Indian policymakers, the opportunities that are likely to emerge, and the manner in which they should frame foreign and security policies for India, to maximise the gains and minimise the losses.

The key findings that emerge from this volume are: the geopolitical situation in the neighbourhood is likely to change significantly due to uncertainties in the global economy, chronic instability in the Af-Pak region, increasing salience of external factors in regional politics, continuing anti-India sentiments in some of the countries, demographic pressures, growth in illegal migration, and adverse consequences of climate change. However, there are also signs of greater desire for economic integration, strengthening of democratic institutions in some countries, and emphasis on regional cooperation. While India may face increasing security challenges due to instability in certain countries, there will be an opportunity for it to better integrate its economy with the region.

The authors in the volume argue that in order to deal with the uncertainties in an effective manner, India has to fine-tune its diplomatic apparatus to proactively deal with emerging realities in the neighbourhood, systematically pursue policies for inclusive and equitable economic growth at home, build networks of interdependence with all neighbouring countries, significantly improve the quality of the country's governance and take measures to deal with internal security situation effectively. In order to deal with the emerging challenges, policymakers will need to build a domestic consensus on key issues affecting India's neighbourhood policy. Sustained economic growth and cooperative security approaches will be needed to deal with a dynamic neighbourhood. The development of appropriate and robust defence capabilities to meet complex security challenges which lie ahead should also be given due priority, to make our neighbourhood policy more effective.

I commend the efforts of Brig. (Retd.) Rumel Dahiya and Dr Ashok Behuria for coordinating this project efficiently, and for taking special care to edit the manuscript and put together all the chapters in the present shape.

I compliment the efforts of IDSA scholars who have contributed chapters to this volume, as well as others—especially Dr R N Das, Dr G Balachandran and Dr Namrata Goswami—who participated in the discussions and offered their inputs while finalising the chapters. I will fail in my duty if I would not acknowledge the valuable efforts put in by anonymous referees for their comments and suggestions on the earlier drafts which helped the scholars in enriching the content.

I thank Ms Neha Kohli for patiently copyediting the draft, and Ms Gulbin Sultana for helping the editors in finalising the manuscript.

I hope this volume will be found useful by the wider strategic community and promote a more informed debate on the vital question of formulating policy options for India's neighbourhood in the coming years.

New Delhi
July 2012

Arvind Gupta
Director General, IDSA

About the Contributors

Dr Arvind Gupta is Director General, Institute for Defence Studies and Analyses (IDSA), New Delhi, India.

Vishal Chandra is Associate Fellow at IDSA.

Dr Sreeradha Datta, formerly Research Fellow at IDSA, is now Director, Maulana Abul Kalam Azad Institute of Asian Studies (MAKAIAS), Kolkata, India.

Dr Medha Bisht is Associate Fellow at IDSA.

Dr Prashant Kumar Singh is Associate Fellow at IDSA.

Brig (Retd.) Rumel Dahiya is Deputy Director General, IDSA.

Dr Anand Kumar is Associate Fellow at IDSA

Dr Udai Bhanu Singh is Senior Research Associate at IDSA.

Shruti Pandalai is OSD, Outreach and Research Analyst at IDSA.

Dr Nihar Nayak is Associate Fellow at IDSA.

Dr Ashok K Behuria is Research Fellow, and Coordinator, South Asia Centre at IDSA.

Sushant Sareen is Consultant, Pakistan Project at IDSA and Senior Fellow at Vivekananda International Foundation, New Delhi, India.

Dr Smruti S Pattanaik is Research Fellow, and Coordinator, Pakistan Project at IDSA.

LIST OF ABBREVIATIONS

AAI	Airports Authority of India
ADB	Asian Development Bank
Af-Pak	Afghanistan-Pakistan
AH	Asian Highway
AIS	Automatic Identification System
AITD	Asian Institute of Transport Development
AMHS	Automatic Message Handling System
ANA	Afghan National Army
ANI	Asian News International
ANSF	Afghan National Security Forces
ASEAN	Association of Southeast Asian Nations
ASIDE	Assistance to States for Developing Export Infrastructure and Allied Activities
BDCLIM	Bangladesh Climate
BIMSTEC	Bay of Bengal Initiative for Multi-Sectoral Technical and Economic Cooperation
BIPPA	Bilateral Investment Promotion and Protection Agreement
BJP	Bharatiya Janata Party
BoI	Board of Investment
BPO	Business Process Outsourcing
BRO	Border Roads Organisation
CA	Constituent Assembly
CBES	Chure Bhawar Ekta Samaj
CBM	Confidence Building Measures
CEO	Chief Executive Officer
CEPA	Comprehensive Economic Partnership Agreement
CIA	Central Intelligence Agency
CIRCL	Center for Islamic Research Collaboration and Learning

CPB	Communist Party of Bhutan
CPC	Communist Party of China
CPN-M	Communist Party of Nepal-Maoist
CSF	Competitiveness Support Fund
DCA	Department of Civil Aviation
DFID	Department for International Development
DPT	Druk Phuensum Tshogpa
DPR	Detailed Project Reports
EAS	East Asia Summit
EU	European Union
EXIM	Export Import
FATA	Federally Administered Tribal Areas
FDI	Foreign Direct Investments
FIA	Federal Investigation Agency
FICN	Fake Indian Currency Notes
FPAG	Foreign Policy Advisory Group
FTA	Free Trade Agreement
FY	Financial Year
GDP	Gross Domestic Product
GHQ	General Headquarters
GJM	Gorkha Janamukti Morcha
GLOF	Glacial Lake Outburst Floods
GNH	Gross National Happiness
GNI	Gross National Index
GoI	Government of India
GoSL	Government of Sri Lanka
GSP	Generalized System of Preferences
HCL	Hindustan Computers Limited
IB	Intelligence Bureau
ICAO	International Civil Aviation Organisation
ICICI	Industrial Credit and Investment Corporation of India
ICP	Integrated Check Post
IDSA	Institute for Defence Studies and Analyses
IED	Improvised Explosive Device
IFAD	International Fund for Agricultural Development

IGSC	Inter Governmental Sub-committee
IMDT	Illegal Migrants Determination by Tribunal
IMF	International Monetary Fund
IMTRAT	Indian Military Training Team
IRCON	Indian Railway Construction Company
ISAF	International Security Assistance Force
ISEAS	Institute of Southeast Asian Studies
ISI	Inter-Services Intelligence
IT	Information Technology
IWT	Inland Water Transport
IWT	Indus Water Treaty
J&K	Jammu & Kashmir
JVP	Janatha Vimukthi Peramuna
JWG	Joint Working Group
KKS	Kankesanthurai
KP	Khyber Pakhtunkhwa
km	kilometre
KVA	Kilo Volt Ampere
LAC	Line of Actual Control
LDC	Least Developed Countries
LDOF	Landslide Dam Outburst Floods
LEJ	Lashkar-e-Jhangvi
LEP	Look East Policy
LLRC	Lesson Learnt and Reconciliation Commission
LoC	Line of Control
L&T	Larsen & Toubro
LTTE	Liberation Tigers of Tamil Eelam
MEA	Ministry of External Affairs
MFN	Most Favoured Nation
MGC	Mekong-Ganga Cooperation
MHA	Ministry of Home Affairs
MJF	Madhesi Janadhikar Forum
MLM	Marxist-Leninist-Maoist
MP	Member of Parliament
MNC	Multi-National Companies

MoU	Memorandum of Understanding
MRP	Machine Readable Passport
MW	Megawatt
NATO	North Atlantic Treaty Organisation
NC	Nepali Congress
NDA	National Democratic Alliance
NDFB	National Democratic Front of Bodoland
NDN	Northern Distribution Network
NEFFA	Nepal Freight Forwarders Association
NER	Northeastern Region
NFC	National Finance Commission
NGO	Non-governmental Organisation
NH	National Highway
NHPC	National Hydroelectric Power Corporation
NHRC	National Human Rights Commission
NLD	National League for Democracy
NSG	Nuclear Suppliers Group
NTPC	National Thermal Power Corporation
Nu	Ngultrum (Bhutanese Currency)
ODA	Official Development Assistance
OLC	Official Languages Commission
ONGC	Oil and Natural Gas Commission
OPEC	Organisation of the Petroleum Exporting Countries
PBS	Performance Based Navigation
PDP	People's Democratic Party
PIL	Public Interest Litigation
PLA	People's Liberation Army
PML-N	Pakistan Muslim League-Nawaz
PNS	Pakistan Naval Station
PoK	Pakistan occupied Kashmir
PONM	Pakistan Oppressed Nationalities' Movement
PPP	Pakistan Peoples' Party
PRB	Population Research Bureau
PST	Pakistan Sunni Tehreek
PTI	Press Trust of India

PTI	Pakistan Tehrik-e-Insaf
RAW	Research and Analysis Wing
RGST	Reformed General Sales Tax
RTI	Right to Information
SAARC	South Asian Association for Regional Cooperation
SAFTA	South Asia Free Trade Agreement
SARDP-NE	Special Accelerated Road Development Programme for North East
SCO	Shanghai Cooperation Organisation
SDF	SAARC Development Fund
SF	Security Force
SIC	Sunni Ittehad Council
SL	Sri Lanka
SLFP	Sri Lanka Freedom Party
SLMC	Sri Lanka Muslim Congress
SME	Small and Medium Enterprises
SoFA	Status of Force Agreement
SPDC	State Peace and Development Council
SPS	Sanitary and Phyto-Sanitary
sq km	square kilometre
SSB	Sashastra Seema Bal
SSP	Sipah-e-Sahaba Pakistan
TAPI	Turkmenistan-Afghanistan-Pakistan-India
TAR	Tibet Autonomous Region
TAR	Trans Asian Railway
TERI	The Energy and Resources Institute
TK	Taka (Bangladesh Currency)
TMLP	Tarai-Madhesh Loktantrik Party
TNA	Tamil National Alliance
TTP	Tehrik-e-Taliban Pakistan
TYC	Tibetan Youth Congress
UAE	United Arab Emirates
UCPN	Unified Communist Party of Nepal
UK	United Kingdom
ULFA	United Liberation Front of Assam

UML	Communist Party of Nepal-Unified Marxist Leninist
UN	United Nations
UNDP	United Nations Development Programme
UNESCAP	United Nations Economic and Social Commission for Asia and the Pacific
UNFCCC	United Nations Framework Convention on Climate Change
UNMIN	United Nations Mission in Nepal
UNP	United National Party
UNSC	United Nations Security Council
UP	Uttar Pradesh
UPA	United Progressive Alliance
URFB	United Revolutionary Front of Bhutan
US	United States
USA	United States of America
USAID	United States Agency for International Development
USD	US Dollar
VHF	Very High Frequency
WEF	World Economic Forum
WFP	World Food Programme
WMD	Weapon of Mass Destruction
WTO	World Trade Organisation
WW	World War
YCL	Young Communist League
YMEC	Yunnan Machinery & Equipment Import & Export Company Limited

List of Tables, Figures and Maps

Tables

2.1	Population Growth Rate in Bangladesh	21
5.1	Climate Mitigation and Adaptation Measures Listed by Maldivian Government	99
6.1	Upgradation of Roads Linking Northeast India with Myanmar	128
8.1	Debt Forgiven or Reduced (1999-2004)	169
8.2	ODA Received by Pakistan (1999-2009)	171
9.1	Foreign Finance Commitments to Sri Lanka in 2010	193
9.2	Doing Business in Sri Lanka	194

Figures

8.1	GDP Growth, Net ODA (as % of GNI) and FDI (as % of GDP) (1960-2011)	170

Maps

5.1	Impact of One Meter Sea Level Rise on Various Maldivian Islands	108
5.2	Maldivian Islands where China has Shown its Interests	109
6.1	Stilwell Road (Ledo Road)	113
6.2	Proposed Rail Network	120
6.3	Kaladan Multimodal Project	122
6.4	Proposed Road Network	129

INTRODUCTION

The political, economic and social landscape in India's immediate neighbourhood has changed significantly since the end of the Cold War. A power transition is under way in the global order. The bipolar world has given way to a non-polar world in which several new powers have emerged. The centre of gravity of power is shifting towards the Asia-Pacific. The simultaneous rise of India and China is a development of great significance. The traditional concept of national security is being broadened gradually to include human security concerns. Non-military issues like climate change, energy security, competition for scarce resources, food and water security, pandemics, migrations, etc., are getting securitised. Globalisation, driven by technology, has created an unprecedented situation where borders are losing their relevance. People are able to connect with each other more easily and more quickly. At the same time, globalisation has also fostered the assertion of ethnic and linguistic identities. These massive changes, which are likely to further accelerate in the next 20 years, have also affected India and its neighbourhood.

Even a cursory glance at the developments of the last few years will show how significant the changes have been in India's neighbourhood. Who would have thought even a few years ago that the monarchy would disappear in Nepal; the LTTE would be militarily defeated; General Musharraf would be ousted and compelled to live in exile in London; a democratic government would be elected in Maldives; Sheikh Hasina would come back with a more than three-fourths majority; NATO would be fighting in South Asia; the Line of Control (LoC) in Kashmir would become a 'soft border'; insurgency in Kashmir would decline; insurgencies in the Northeast would be tamed; and China will become India's number one trading partner? The pace of change in the region will only intensify in the coming years.

What does this change mean for India's neighbourhood policy? While several new avenues for cooperation among countries of the region are likely to open up, fresh security challenges will also arise. Dominated by security concerns for the last six decades, India's policy towards its neighbourhood will require a makeover in the light of the great political, economic and social changes that are taking place. The concept of national security emerged largely because of the arbitrary borders drawn by the British colonial masters. The solution to the many security issues facing India lies in resolving the cross-border issues like migrations, water-sharing, transportation, trade, etc. Non-military concerns will need to be incorporated within a broader understanding of national security. The neighbourhood concerns will need to be integrated with India's overall security and developmental policies. This will be a major challenge for India's foreign and security policies in the coming decades.

The present volume, put together by researchers and analysts at IDSA, is an attempt to examine the emerging political, economic, social and security trends in the neighbouring countries and to identify those that are likely to endure in the future. Each chapter studies some key drivers of change that have high uncertainty as well as high degree of impact and some scenarios are created on the basis of these drivers. Each chapter then makes certain broad policy recommendations relevant to each scenario.

The future cannot be predicted precisely. The scenarios presented in the different chapters are not predictions. But they encapsulate a range of possibilities that might materialise depending upon how the key, high uncertainty–high impact drivers unfold. The scenario building exercise alerts the policy makers to the likely possibilities and prepares them better to meet these challenges.

In each scenario building exercise, one scenario represents business as usual. This is simply the linear extrapolation of the current trends. More interesting scenarios are envisaged by conjuring up drivers which may be less certain but whose impact is huge. For instance, in a business-as-usual scenario over the next 20 years, there will not be much change in the dynamics of India-Pakistan relations. But, in a scenario in which Pakistan might collapse as its economy continues to go downhill and religious fundamentalist forces take control of the government, a totally new situation might emerge. The probability of Pakistan's collapse may be small but it is not so insignificant that it can be ignored altogether. How will India deal with a collapsing or failing Pakistan? What will India's foreign policy be if such a scenario materialises. What will be the trigger point for such a scenario to materialise: a revolt in Balochistan or a war between Pakistan and Afghanistan over Pashtun regions? The policy maker is alerted to think of such low probability but high impact scenarios and think of policy options in advance. Many such examples can be imagined.

The volume covers Afghanistan, Bangladesh, Bhutan, China, Maldives, Myanmar, Nepal, Pakistan and Sri Lanka. The countries for study were carefully chosen after discussion with analysts and policy makers.

With regard to Pakistan, the question posed is: how will Pakistan's internal situation pan out and how will it impact India? With regard to China, it was important from the policy makers' point of view to understand the impact of China's rise on Sino-Indian relations. Sri Lanka is embarking on the path of high economic growth. Hence the question being posed here is: Will this be sustainable, and how will it impact Indo-Sri Lanka relations? Other questions being looked at in this study are: Is there anti-Indianism in Nepal? If so, how will it impact relations with India? How climate change would impact migration from Bangladesh and how India would cope with it? Likewise, in the case of Maldives, the issue was climate change, its impact on the country and relations with India. The Myanmar chapter seeks to look at the need for infrastructure development in India's Northeastern states and Myanmar, the rising influence of China in the country and its implications for India.

The authors have tried to answer these questions by drawing upon their own expertise, undertaking field trips to the respective countries and participating in several brainstorming sessions. The initial drafts of their chapters were reviewed by noted experts. The drafts were revised in the light of their comments and discussed further. Finally, the papers were put together and the entire volume was sent to two experts for final review.

In the backdrop of major uncertainties in the region, some interesting scenarios can be visualised.

AFGHANISTAN

What will the post-2014 Afghanistan look like? Most short-term scenarios for Afghanistan predict instability and even civil war. The foreign forces are leaving Afghanistan without having stabilised it. When they leave Afghanistan by 2014, their interest in the country will also decline. This will open up the field for the return of the Taliban. The prospects of national reconciliation are not bright. While there is still a question mark on whether the US will retain some troops even after 2014, it looks almost certain that these troops will perform a geo-strategic role for the US and would not necessarily take part in stabilising the country.

India, which has contributed significantly to Afghanistan's reconstruction, will face the question of whether to continue with these programmes if and when the Taliban return to power and instability increases. In the 10-year scenario, India should maintain contacts with all sides in Afghanistan, deepen people-to-people contacts but remain cautious about getting bogged down in the country. The prescription is wait and watch. An unstable Afghanistan will also have a destabilising impact on Pakistan whose Pashtun-dominated areas will become more restive and lawless. This will have implications for India's Pakistan policy also.

The game changing event that might occur after 2014 could be the beginning of a civil war in Afghanistan. It is unlikely that the continued presence of the US troops in Afghanistan will be tolerated by the Taliban who would need to be accommodated in the political settlement. The prospects of a regional solution to the Afghanistan problem are limited given the lack of capacities in the neighbouring countries as also the vastly different political agendas. Pakistan might get sucked into the Afghanistan imbroglio which could threaten its own stability. In such conditions India will have limited options.

BANGLADESH

Bangladesh is critical for India's security, the development of the Northeast and the success of its 'Look East Policy'. The two countries have had a troubled relationship since the assassination of Sheikh Mujibur Rehman in 1975. However, there are hopeful signs of a turnaround in bilateral relations initiated by Sheikh Hasina's visit to India in 2010 and Prime Minister Manmohan Singh's return visit to Dhaka in 2011. The challenge before the two countries is to ensure that the positive beginnings in bilateral relations are sustained.

One of the most important issues taken up for study in this volume is that of migration from Bangladesh into India. Bangladeshis are in denial mode and do not accept that there is any migration from their side. Yet, many well-informed Bangladeshis not only accept the facts on the ground but also warn that migration would intensify as Bangladesh faces the consequences of sea level rise, coastal erosion and shortened cycles of floods and droughts. India and Bangladesh have many issues to resolve including that of transit and connectivity, illegal smuggling, water sharing, trade, etc., but, migration will remain the major issue on the agenda. As connectivity between the two countries increases there will be demand for a more liberal visa regime. The next 20 years in Indo-Bangladesh relations will most likely be taken up with the issues of human security. The role of India's eastern states in Indo-Bangladesh relations will grow significantly. Bangladesh granting transit facilities to India, completion of the Asian highway and trans-Asian railways could be the game changing events in the region. Likewise a more liberal visa regime, which facilitates people-to-people connectivity, will change Indo-Bangladesh relations significantly.

BHUTAN

Bhutan is turning over a new leaf. It is transiting from a monarchical system to democracy. The process of debate and discussion on Bhutan's foreign and security policy has started in right earnest. So far, India has had a robust and comprehensive relationship with Bhutan. However, at the domestic level, issues of trade imbalance, disadvantages of overdependence on India and poor delivery mechanism are being debated in the media with increasing regularity. In the national assembly, the representatives are pushing for settling of border dispute with China and normalising relationship with China. With China extending rail link up to Yatung, economic relationship with Bhutan is likely to grow at a faster pace. Apart from Japan and India, China is likely to come up as a major economic player in Bhutan. On the ethnic front, the issue of Bhutanese refugees of Nepalese origin remains unresolved. This has the potential to strain Nepal-Bhutan relationship and complicate internal security situation in Bhutan. There is also the likelihood of Indian insurgent groups reusing Bhutanese territory against Indian interests.

In this context, there are several policy options for Bhutan. It may continue to strengthen its relationship with India and have a 'look south' policy, thereby establishing deeper linkages with India, Bangladesh and South East Asian counties. It may also use China as a balancer against India. There is also the possibility of Bhutanese popular concerns about increased migrations from India and Bangladesh translating into anti-India sentiments posing critical challenges for India-Bhutan relationship. India has to be mindful of the changing political discourse especially on India as democracy takes roots in Bhutan. It should be sensitive to local perceptions and encourage regular interactions at multiple levels, with an emphasis on greater people to people contact to dispel mutual misunderstandings and concerns.

CHINA

Most scenarios envisage the inexorable rise of China to superpower status. China has already overtaken Japan to become the second largest economy in the world. However, a more nuanced look at China's internal dynamic raises uncertainties about its rise. Will China be able to sustain its rise for the next 20 years or will its economic growth falter? Will China's one party system face internal challenges? Will Han nationalism in China accommodate the aspirations of the minorities? While fraught with uncertainties, political and social instability in China accompanied by economic decline in the next 20 years cannot be ruled out altogether.

For India, the main consequence of China's rise will be two-fold. First, India will have an unpredictable superpower at its borders. Cooperation and friendship with China cannot be taken for granted although that is the direction in which India's policy should move. The differential between India and China's national strengths might increase. This will restrict India's options in dealing with China. For instance, India will need to ensure that it does not get entangled in a military conflict with China. At the same time India will have to resist pressure from China on settling the border on unfavourable terms. If Tibet gets restive after the present Dalai Lama's exit, a new situation in Sino-Indian relations might arise. India will have to be on watch to see whether the post-Dalai Lama situation in Tibet offers any opportunities for India in dealing with China. On the whole, India will be compelled to increase its own economic and military strengths while improving governance in the areas bordering with China.

Could there be a military confrontation between India and China in the next 20 years? Both the countries have taken precautions to declare that they are in favour of developing a cooperative relationship. However, China's recent assertiveness vis-à-vis India cannot be ignored. There have been some incidents on the un-demarcated border; China's position on J&K appears to be changing; Chinese presence in Pakistan Occupied Kashmir (PoK) is increasing; China has expressed its disapproval regarding the presence of Indian oil companies in the South China Sea; it routinely describes Arunachal Pradesh as South Tibet; and its position on the diversion of the Brahmaputra waters is ambiguous. It has undertaken massive modernisation of infrastructure in Tibet and has constructed railway routes and airfields close to the borders with India.

The intentions behind Chinese action vis-à-vis India in the last two years are not fully understood. Are they aggressive or benign? In the context of uncertainty within China, it would be fair to expect the recurrence of crises in Sino-Indian relations over the next 20 years which will have to be managed by both sides. The game changer within China could be a slowdown of economic growth leading up to internal instabilities and changes in foreign policy behaviour. Likewise, the exit of the Dalai Lama could usher in a new phase in Sino-Indian relations as the Tibet issue assumes greater salience.

Second, with the rise of China, its influence in South Asia will grow. This is already visible, particularly in Nepal, Pakistan and Myanmar. India will come under pressure to restructure its neighbourhood policy to ensure that India does not get drawn into an unsavoury competition with China. The trajectory of Sino-Indian relations— will it be confrontationist or collaborative, or will it have an element of both?— will have a decisive influence in South Asia.

The analysis cautions against adopting a confrontationist approach towards China. At the same time, the chapter strongly recommends the strengthening of India's own capabilities as quickly as possible to reduce the capabilities differential.

MALDIVES

Maldives' strategic importance due to its location in the Indian Ocean, close to India's borders and en route to the major shipping highway in the ocean cannot be overestimated. Maldives is facing an existential threat. The sea level rise of up to 1 metre predicted in this century due to climate change can obliterate the country. One of the key challenges identified by the leadership of the country is how to adapt to the adverse consequences of climate change. The relocation of the population to other countries is a possibility and India will be involved. India can help Maldives in adapting to climate change; greater cooperation between India and Maldives will help India from the security perspective also. The policy option for India is to promote a comprehensive and deepen engagement with Maldives at all levels including on climate change.

MYANMAR

Unlike Bangladesh, Myanmar, despite its critical importance for India' security, India's 'Look East Policy' and the stability imperative for the Northeast does not receive as much attention as it should. Part of the reason is that Myanmar has undergone long periods of insurgency and has suffered international isolation. During its years of isolation, China's influence in the country has grown while India's engagement has reduced.

The next 20 years will see greater interaction between India and Myanmar. The political changes in Myanmar are slow but promising. In a marked departure from the past trends, the US Secretary of State, Hillary Clinton visited Myanmar in November 2011 and in April 2012, Aung San Suu Kyi participated in the fledgling democratic process in Myanmar and won the by-elections to become a member of the national legislature. Myanmar is rich in natural resources and has a superb geo-strategic location. China has invested considerably and rapidly in Myanmar and there is a perception that it may seek to push India out of Myanmar. The challenge before India in the next 20 years will be to ensure that it invests in Myanmar, contributes to its growth and draws it into the various regional cooperation projects. The development and connectivity of infrastructure projects between Northeast India and Myanmar is of critical importance. The game changing event that might occur in the not too distant future is the completion of the oil pipeline from the Bay of Bengal through Myanmar to China. India will have to deal with this situation. Myanmar will be more integrated with the world and its isolation will end. This will open up fresh avenues for Indo-Myanmar relations.

NEPAL

Will the present comprehensive political, economic and social transformation underway in Nepal have a positive impact on India-Nepal relations? Despite the current political crisis emanating from the inconclusive process of Constitution making, in the next 20 years, a new Nepal will emerge. It is likely to be republican and more democratic. This could pave the way for a deeper and friendlier relationship between India and Nepal. But uncertainties remain. The new political system has not yet crystallised as the Constitution has yet to be finalised. The Maoists have been mainstreamed to a considerable extent and have contributed two Prime Ministers in the last three years. However, the big questions relating to federalism, the form of the Constitution, language, economic system, etc., are still unresolved. The next 20 years will most likely be taken up by the long and complicated process of nation-building.

Anti-Indianism in Nepal, hydro-electricity and open borders are the three major issues studied in this volume. Because India is a major factor in the life of an ordinary Nepali, anti-Indianism is a fact of political life in Nepal. While millions of Nepalis benefit from close relations with India, the media and political parties routinely accuse India of interference in their country. It is unlikely that this tendency will disappear altogether.

Likewise, cooperation for the generation of hydro-electricity, which could benefit both Nepal and India, has become a symbol of mistrust rather than a catalyst for friendship. This is likely to continue as the Nepalese people regard water as their most important resource which they would not allow to be 'exploited' by India. Open borders, which bring so much benefit to India and Nepal and are a unique symbol of friendship between the two countries, have become criminalised. In the business as usual scenario, Indo-Nepal relations will continue to be bedevilled by these factors.

However, it is possible to imagine scenarios where India emerges as a key contributor to prosperity in Nepal. India will need to review its policies and take steps to correct the existing impression as an interfering neighbour. Indian assistance should go towards building Nepal's economy and society irrespective of which party or coalition is in power. India's role should be that of a trusted partner in Nepal.

On the negative side, continued uncertainty in Nepal could push it into a deep crisis. In such a scenario, China's influence might grow. The unrest in Tibet could also fuel instability in Nepal. India's endeavour should be to involve Nepal in regional cooperation projects. India will also need to shield its own Nepali speaking areas from instabilities in Nepal. India should avoid getting drawn into Nepal-Bhutan tensions. India will have to craft policies that would mitigate the negative effects of an unstable Nepal and the growing influence of China.

The game changing event that can be imagined in Nepal could be the inability of the political leaders to resolve the federal issue that is causing major and minor revolts, particularly in Madhesh, close to the Indian border. The federal question could result in fragmentation of Nepal. The growing influence of China in Nepal could be a major factor in Indo-Nepal relations. India might perceive Chinese presence in Nepal to be an acute security dilemma. India will need to prepare itself for meeting such eventualities which may have low probability but high impact.

PAKISTAN

Most scenarios paint a bleak picture for Pakistan. Instability in Pakistan is likely to increase further. A section of the Army might get radicalised reflecting the broad trend in the society. Parts of Pakistan might become ungovernable. The escalating violence in Karachi and the inability of the government to control it is a symptom of the deeper malaise in Pakistan. The military will continue to play an important role in Pakistan's governance. India will need to develop policy options to deal with such a Pakistan. The danger of terrorist attacks on India might increase. There is growing dissatisfaction within Pakistan over the way the country has been misgoverned in the past 60 years. But whether such disaffection translates into more rational approach towards India is still a question mark. The Pakistan government's decision to accord Most Favoured Nation (MFN) status to India is a positive step forward, but there are indications that spoilers are at work to stifle, if not reverse, the process of trade liberalisation with India. If India is able to stabilise its own part of J&K, the salience of Kashmir in Indo-Pak relations might diminish, making it easier for India to deal with Pakistan.

What are the game changing scenarios that can be envisaged? In the context of Pakistan's internal situation, the division within the Pakistan Army would radically change the internal situation in Pakistan. Pakistan's Army may not remain a monolith. A part of it may be radicalised. Will a section of Pakistan's Army favour rapprochement with India? The scenario has low probability but if it materialises, it would have a major impact on Pakistan's internal dynamics. Likewise, for Indo-Pak relations a direct or indirect dialogue with the Pakistani military could change the trajectory. The key adjustment in India's policy will require dealing with different segments of Pakistan's society and polity at both the official and the non-official level. India must deal with Pakistan beyond the government-to-government framework; India will need to build and nurture friendly constituencies in Pakistan.

SRI LANKA

With the defeat of the LTTE, Sri Lanka now has a unique opportunity to resolve the ethnic conflict and embark upon nation-building. It could potentially emerge as one of the major economies in the region. It is already registering impressive rates of growth. The India-Sri Lanka Free Trade Agreement has given a boost to the Sri Lankan economy. Sri Lanka has also diversified its foreign policy and now has a growing relationship with China, Pakistan and other countries. It could benefit from a comprehensive economic partnership with India.

Despite these positive developments, fundamental uncertainties which could block Sri Lanka's growth remain. The ethnic conflict has not been resolved. Sinhala nationalism is on the rise in the wake of LTTE's defeat. The Tamil minorities continue to feel discriminated. Sri Lanka's human rights record has also come under international scrutiny. This has seriously dented the country's international image. In light of these uncertainties, Sri Lanka's unhindered growth cannot be taken for granted.

Sri Lanka has strategic importance for India. What is the likely outlook for Indo-Sri Lankan relations over the next 20 years? India has contributed significantly to resettlement and rehabilitation efforts in Sri Lanka. If the two countries can conclude CEPA, the foundation for durable relations will be established. But, the non-resolution of the Tamil issue will continue to cast a shadow on bilateral relations. Thus on the political front, volatility in bilateral relations could be expected. The politics in Tamil Nadu could also affect Indo-Sri Lankan relations. Sri Lanka could also be tempted to play the China card when there is a souring of relations with India. India's policy towards Sri Lanka should be to pursue engagement at the political, economic and people-to-people levels. China's military presence in Sri Lanka could prove to be a game changer in Indo-Sri Lanka relations. The bilateral relationship should be depoliticised as much as possible.

NEIGHBOURHOOD POLICY

While the volume looks at India's neighbours one by one, it is apparent that India should also fashion a comprehensive neighbourhood policy. The South Asian region constitutes India's immediate neighbourhood and is vital for its security and prosperity. India must remain a pre-eminent military and economic power in the region without becoming a hegemon. India's growing economy presents an opportunity for regional integration and the building of connectivity to the benefit of all countries in the neighbourhood. At the same time, given India's numerous security challenges, military power will remain important in its overall foreign and security policy in future.

CONCLUSION

India's relations with its neighbours will depend upon developments in individual countries but also the broader trends which shape the region as a whole. Several critical drivers that may influence the South Asian situation can be identified. These drivers are uncertain but can have huge impact. They include demography, internal stability, economic growth, energy security, climate change, food and water security, terrorism, anti-India sentiments and external powers. Depending on how these drivers pan out, South Asia could see either a cooperative or a conflict scenario. For a cooperative scenario to materialise, the rising population must be turned into an asset and the demographic dividend must be exploited through creation of educational and employment opportunities. There would be a need to invest in social and physical infrastructure as well as greater regional cooperation. Energy shortages must be overcome through investment in renewable sources of energy. The emphasis must be on inclusive growth and regional cooperation.

However, a conflict scenario in South Asia can also materialise. This would happen if the security dilemmas faced by the countries of South Asia are not addressed. A slowdown in economic growth could also breed instability. The increasing population could create pressures on energy, food and water availability. India's policies might be seen as interference leading to rise in anti-India sentiments. Absence of meaningful regional cooperation could lead to tensions and conflicts.[1]

In the 20-year-scenario, India's relations with its neighbours will be dominated by human security concerns. While Pakistan, its nuclear weapons and its nexus with China will continue to present national security dilemmas, for which India should be prepared at all times, India's foreign policy agenda will be packed with issues like terrorism, food, energy and water security issues and visa regimes. At present, regional integration in South Asia is limited. The situation will most likely change in the next 20 years. Borders will become softer and connect rather than divide. This will present both challenges and opportunities.

India, being the pre-eminent country, will have to take the lead in forging closer links with its neighbours and forging a sense of South Asian identity. Many of the instability scenarios predicted in this volume can be altered if India takes the initiative in crafting polices which put premium on connectivity rather than separation. India will need not only a different policy outlook but also human, diplomatic and financial resources to put in place policies which secure India by forging closer links with her neighbours at different levels. India's delivery mechanism must be improved significantly if it has to earn the respect of its neighbours.

The next 20 years will see a rapid change in the neighbourhood and will therefore be years of uncertainty. If nothing is done now to prepare the country for these uncertain years, India will suffer massively. At the same, time through proactive policies India can look for opportunities that will surely arise as the region changes. That is the larger message of this volume.

Note

1. See Arvind Gupta, 'South Asia in the Next Decade: A Futuristic Perspective' and Nirupama Rao, 'South Asia 2020: Moving Towards Cooperation or Conflict?' in Smruti S. Pattanaik (Ed.), *South Asia: Envisioning a Regional Future*, Pentagon Security International, New Delhi 2011.

Chapter 1

AFGHANISTAN
LIKELY SCENARIOS AND INDIA'S OPTIONS

Vishal Chandra

THE EMERGING SITUATION

With every passing year, one wonders where Afghanistan is headed. Violence is at an all-time high, calling into question all elements of the Western approach and strategy towards the Afghan war since 2001. A discerning sense of pessimism and uncertainty has come to characterise the Western thinking on the Afghan situation. The Western discourse today is more about the way out of what is perceived as an un-winnable war rather than the way forward in what the US President Barack H. Obama had once described as the 'war of necessity'. The withdrawal of Western forces at a time when Afghanistan is far more destabilised and insecure since 2001 inevitably raises several issues of concern. After a decade long direct intervention and engagement, the Western strategy and approach today is one of growing apathy and indifference towards the future of Afghanistan.

The persistent politico-military stalemate, effectively manoeuvred by the Pakistan-backed Taliban and their allies, has made the war increasingly unviable and unsustainable for the West. The Taliban guerrillas along with the Haqqani network have quietly succeeded in raising the rate of attrition among the Western forces, who may have been winning the battles but not the war. The Taliban and their allies despite not winning the battles appear to be gaining an upper-hand in the war. While the Western coalition constantly suffered from differing rules of engagement and perceptions about the War on Terror, the Taliban and their allies have instead consolidated their influence and made common cause against a vastly superior Western military. The weaknesses inherent in the post-Taliban process have also invariably worked to the advantage of the Taliban and their Pakistani sponsors.

Whether the US would withdraw its forces from the Afghanistan-Pakistan region by 2014 is not a matter of conjecture anymore. The US would like to maintain some form of military presence in Afghanistan for years, beyond 2014. However, it is doubtful whether it can stabilise the country. Meanwhile, the three critical components of the current US strategy—Afghanisation of the reconciliation process aimed at the top insurgent leadership operating from Pakistan; rebuilding of the Afghan National Security Forces (ANSF); and security transition to the the ANSF by 2014—are least likely to yield the expected results. Presently, Afghanistan appears to be on the verge of entering into a prolonged phase of anarchy and violence.

The whole idea of negotiating 'peace' with the Taliban leadership has emerged out of the increasing limitations of both Kabul and the ISAF against the Taliban. The peace and reconciliation process led by Kabul and backed by the international community seems to be dividing the country. The non-Pashtuns are opposed to the reconciliation process and regional strong-men in areas dominated by the minority ethnic groups have started preparing for the eventuality of a protracted civil war after the withdrawal of foreign troops from Afghanistan. They perceive the reconciliation process as capitulation to the Taliban and feel threatened by the prospect of the Taliban returning to power in Kabul. It is in fact opening up yet another opportunity for the Pakistani establishment to re-engineer the politics of Afghanistan. Whether the US would be able to temper the geopolitical aspirations of the Pakistani establishment remains to be seen. However, it is certain that Kabul does not have the institutional strength to withstand the impact, foreseen and/or unforeseen, of any power-sharing arrangement with the hard-core Taliban leadership. Of particular concern is the plan to hand over security responsibilities to the Afghan army and police, both of which are far from being in a position to take on the Taliban onslaught (Haqqani group included) on their own.

For now, the year 2014 could be regarded as another watershed in the making. By then President Obama's first and President Karzai's second (and final, as per the Afghan Constitution) presidential term would have come to an end, and NATO is expected to have withdrawn bulk of its troops. If the West decides to remain engaged and somehow manages to retain a limited force level in Afghanistan beyond 2014, it is not clear as to how it would help in improving the situation on the ground. The Taliban and their Pakistani allies feel they have an upper-hand and that they can wait out the West. Even if in years to come the US/ISAF registers big operational successes, maintains bases in parts of the country and sections of Taliban defect from the core group, the Af-Pak situation will continue to pose ideological and physical challenges to both regional and international security.

India's Position and Challenges

India has always regarded political upheavals in Afghanistan as its internal affair, and has worked with the successive internationally-recognised governments in Kabul. Even during the Taliban regime (1996-2001), India continued to support and work with the UN-recognised government of Burhanuddin Rabbani. After the overthrow of the Taliban regime, India supported the Bonn Process and has since fully supported the Hamid Karzai-led administration in Kabul. The policy conundrum now is what is going to happen after 2014, when Karzai's second term as president and ISAF's extended deadline to withdraw come to an end. It is not clear as to what kind of leadership or political arrangement will emerge in Afghanistan after Karzai.

With the resurgence of the Taliban factor, growing differences between the West and President Karzai, draw-down in Western troop levels, and Pakistan's continuing struggle to retain its influence within Afghanistan and clout in the Obama Administration's strategy towards Af-Pak, India is apparently in a fix as to how to deal with the Afghan challenge. India has so far not been a major player or a transforming factor in the Afghan conflict. However, given its long-term security concerns, it is important for India to constantly evaluate its responses and policy towards the rapidly changing scenario in Afghanistan. At the same time, India also needs to understand as to where it figures in the varied Afghan perception.

India has its genuine concerns about the return of the Taliban to power. India wants Afghanistan to be a strong, independent and a relatively moderate Islamic state, capable of thwarting Pakistani designs and a bulwark against the expanding Wahabi-Deobandi form of extremist Islam. But what if the Taliban as part of a coalition comes to power? How should India engage the new leadership? Is it possible to identify forces and constituencies within Pakistan and Afghanistan to evolve an effective counter-discourse and a counter-force to the extremist ideologies as part of a patient well-engineered long-term approach to the Af-Pak challenge? Presently, there is a huge gap in what India wants and the means (leverages) available to achieve its objectives in Pakistan and Afghanistan.

Despite India committing reconstruction assistance worth US $2 billion, it stands increasingly marginalised in the Western strategy as well as in regional mechanisms. At the regional level, it is also important to gauge the perception of regional countries (apart from Pakistan) about India's current and potential role and vice-versa in the Af-Pak region. How are other regional countries likely to respond to the Af-Pak challenge in years beyond 2014? As of now, responses of regional countries to the Afghan situation is determined by the nature of their individual relationship with the US and perceptions about its presence in the region.

The current debate in India on the Afghan issue varies from working towards an internationally-guaranteed neutral Afghanistan, to exercising the military option in terms of deploying troops. The questions being asked are: should it continue to support the Western strategy or should India have a relatively independent approach and deepen its engagement with various Afghan factions and actors, including the Taliban? There is a perception that India's cautious and restrained approach may not suffice given the magnitude of long-term ideological and tangible security challenges likely to emerge from the Af-Pak region after the withdrawal of Western forces and given the Pakistani intransigence in de-Talibanising its Afghan policy.

It is generally believed that the Pakistani establishment will continue to strive to deny space to India in Afghanistan. In such a scenario, should India reach out to the Pakistani establishment or identify and work closely with certain anti-Pakistan Afghan elements to keep up the pressure on Pakistan, as was the case in the late 1990s? Will this work to India's advantage in the longer run? Given the demographic profile and the ground realities of the Af-Pak frontier, both historical and contemporary, India may have to factor in the Pashtun/Pakhtun indifference to India's strategic concerns in the region. It is worth exploring on what terms and conditions should India be engaging the US as well as Kabul to protect and secure its interests in Afghanistan in times to come. There is also the perception that India, while continuing with its reconstruction and humanitarian assistance, should keep out of the factional politics given the highly externalised nature and politics of the Afghan War.

As a neighbouring country, India certainly needs to take a long-term view of its interests and policy approaches towards Afghanistan. India does not have the option of disengaging from Afghanistan for that will further marginalise it within the country and the region. India needs to assess the extent to which the Afghans are willing to go with its objectives and interests. India may need to explore policy alternatives keeping in view the post-Karzai, the post-West, and scenarios beyond both, in the next 20 years. Prospects of collapsing states, shifting borders, big power cooperation/rivalries, mega transnational projects like Turkmenistan-Afghanistan-Pakistan-India (TAPI) gas pipeline leading to new geopolitics in Eurasia, or regional organisations, such as the Shanghai Cooperation Organisation (SCO), or regional countries other than Pakistan getting engaged in Afghanistan, cannot be summarily ruled out.

ISSUES LIKELY TO SHAPE FUTURE EVENTS

This section explores three alternative scenarios for Afghanistan and suggests some policy alternatives for India. In the next two to three years, the following issues are likely to shape the future course of Afghan conflict:

i. **Status of Force Agreement/Strategic Partnership:** The US and Afghanistan finally signed a strategic partnership agreement on May 2, 2012. The agreement clearly reveals the inability of the two countries to conclude any security agreement like the Status of Force Agreement (SoFA), the US had signed earlier with Iraq, to retain its forces there. The May agreement says that the two countries would 'initiate negotiation on a Bilateral Security Agreement' soon after the signing of the strategic partnership agreement. Differences over certain operational and authority issues, and the possible fallout of the prolonged American presence both at the national and the larger regional level, seems to be holding parts of the Agreement back for now. Much would, therefore, depend on how effective the limited US presence would be after 2014, and how the West would deal with the Pakistani establishment which seems to be positioning itself for a post-2014 scenario. The US *aid-and-raid* approach, in its present form, has thus far failed in enlisting effective cooperation from Pakistan's military establishment. However, the Agreement is deemed necessary for the survival of the government in Kabul and the strengthening of the Afghan army and police.

ii. **What after Karzai?** The leadership question is important here. It is still not clear if both presidential and parliamentary elections could be held in 2014-15, and how credible the electoral exercise will be if the ISAF pulls out/draws down from southern and eastern parts of the country which would inevitably fall under direct Taliban control. Finally, if elections could not be held then what are the possible alternatives available in terms of political arrangement to ensure that there is no political vacuum in Kabul. This could also be an opportunity to temporarily bring US-

Pakistan together if both reach a consensus on post-Karzai leadership. This may subsequently lead to defection from the Taliban, with the so-called 'moderate' Taliban joining the government. However, a Pakistan-brokered deal with the Taliban or an alternate political arrangement is not likely to gain acceptance among vast sections of Afghan population.

In case of failed political transition in 2014, there is a possibility of greater tension between the US and Afghanistan, on one hand, and between the US and Pakistan, on the other. This may lead to greater anarchy or even a new round of civil war in parts of the country. There could also be a special operation by the US commandos against top Haqqani and Taliban leadership based inside Pakistan (like Operation Geronimo on May 2, 2011 to kill Osama Bin Laden). NATO's supply lines are likely to remain disrupted leading to greater pressure by the US on Pakistan and further reliance on the Northern Distribution Network (NDN).

Wild Cards: Targeting and assassination of senior members of the Afghan government, including the president and the vice-presidents, or a leading opposition figure from the north; elimination of senior Taliban leadership based inside Pakistan; or a high profile attack by al Qaeda on the US interests anywhere in the world. Military escalation in standoff between Iran and the West, or instability in West Asia, could also have a serious bearing on future Western commitment in Afghanistan.

FUTURE SCENARIOS

Key Drivers

A modest attempt has been made here to prospect the Afghan war's likely future, based on a set of key driving factors. However, given the rapid pace of developments in the Afghan war and the known unpredictability of Afghan politics, building future scenarios is a challenging exercise. Prior to drawing the probable future scenarios, it would be useful to identify and ponder over some of the key drivers of the Afghan conflict and war based on high impact-high uncertainty model. The key domestic and external drivers are often too interlocked to be elaborated here as separate categories.

1. US Objectives and Future Strategy

The US objectives and strategy will remain a critical driver in shaping the future of Afghanistan. The US has a strategic presence in the West Asian region and wants to expand its influence in the Southern and Central

Asian region as well. Therefore, the US considers maintaining its presence in Afghanistan as a huge strategic advantage, but only to the extent that it is manageable. The cost of retaining military foothold in Afghanistan will have to be weighed against the advantages that would accrue to the US. Against this backdrop, the US has difficult choices to make, i.e., whether to stay engaged or opt for total withdrawal. However, each of these choices will have their impact on Afghan and regional politics. Wholesale withdrawal will amount to abandoning Afghanistan. This is likely to embolden the Taliban and make the process of rebuilding Afghan state structures and reconciliation difficult. In case of the Taliban coming back to power in Kabul, there may be a hardening of position amongst the ethnic minorities and the situation in Afghanistan may return to the 1990s. However, if the US decides to stay on for a longer period, helps the ANSF to evolve into a regular force which can take on the Taliban and provides critical support to the process of democratisation, it may be possible to transform the socio-economic and political situation in Afghanistan.

2. Peace and Reconciliation with Insurgents

The process of peace and reconciliation is another high-impact driver in the Afghan case. The reconciliation process as it stands today has not managed to reach out to the top Taliban leadership. However, the process has managed to reconcile some of the lower rung Taliban operatives. If the reconciliation process succeeds, it may open a limited opportunity for different warring groups to try and evolve a reasonably effective consensus on rebuilding Afghanistan. If the process fails, it will lead to chaos and civil war and destabilise Afghanistan further. In case there is an opportunistic decision from the Taliban side to join the process to facilitate the process of troop withdrawal, it may still lead to a period of uncertainty in Afghanistan. Reconciliation process, as it stands today, is noted for its ambiguity and competing interests of diverse actors involved in this multi-track process. It is not clear as to what exactly reconciliation with the Taliban would mean? At the moment, it seems to be be adding to the general suspicion about the process and dividing the Afghan nation. Perhaps, what is being attempted are temporary deals and not a comprehensive nation-wide reconciliation process.

3. Afghan National Security Forces (ANSF)

One of the vital components of the Western exit strategy is phased transition of security to the ANSF by 2014. The ANSF is in a formative phase. It is dependent on external assistance and gradually assuming responsibility in some locales. If the ANSF is trained, equipped and funded until it develops into an effective deterrent to rising internal as well as external challenges to Afghanistan, Kabul would remain weak and vulnerable. If international efforts do not focus on enhancing the professional capabilities and logistical capacity of the ANSF post-withdrawal, it will lead to a situation where there will be desertions to fill in the ranks of the Taliban and various militias across the country. This will aggravate the ongoing conflict in Afghanistan.

4. Regional Responses and Politics
The role and response of regional countries, other than Pakistan, is greatly determined by the nature of their relationship with the US. However, the regional responses do play a role in the internal political dynamics of Afghanistan. Some of the regional countries have a role in destabilising Afghanistan further. If countries in the region play a constructive role in augmenting the capacity of the Afghan Government, revival of Afghan economy, and encourage a comprehensive national reconciliation process rather than focus on forcing the US to withdraw, the Afghan situation is likely to improve dramatically. However, if they stick to the present strategy of helping different factions to fight against each other and invest their resources in upturning the process of democratisation in Afghanistan, it is likely to prolong the state of instability.

Based on the above drivers the following three possible scenarios can be worked out:

Scenario I: A Highly Destabilised Afghanistan
There is a growing opposition to President Karzai continuing after 2014, pending presidential and parliamentary elections that could not be held due to insecurity over large parts of the country. Karzai is not allowed to change the Constitution in order to seek third term either. A transitional caretaker government is established. A large chunk of the US and NATO-led force have withdrawn from the country. The remaining US forces along with the Afghan army and remnants of NATO-led force are struggling to retain control over provincial capitals and key roads connecting south with Kabul, reminiscent of a similar change faced by the Soviet and Afghan troops in late 1980s. Militia commanders of the former Northern Alliance try to build up an alliance in view of growing Taliban activity in the north and threat to Kabul. However, some of the leaders from the north continue to support President Karzai. A new round of power jockeying begins. Loose political formations/coalitions emerge projecting themselves as an alternative to Karzai.

The UN/US interlocutors struggle to bring various factions together to form an interim/transitional government so that presidential elections could be held. The situation in some ways is similar to one prior to signing of the Bonn Agreement in December 2001 with various groups/factions vying for influence. Pakistan strongly demands inclusion of sections of Taliban in the post-Karzai political set up. At the same time, Pakistan continues to support elements of Afghan insurgency building up pressure around the capital city of Kabul. Both US and Pakistan try to persuade China to get engaged in Afghanistan in a proactive manner. However, China plays it safe and stays out of the internal power struggle going on in Afghanistan.

An extremely fractured interim/transitional set up emerges in Kabul well after 2014. The US plays a key role in selecting the next line of leadership but is at variance with Islamabad on the issue. The US/NATO continues to train, mentor and fund the ANSF. The ANA is still to evolve as a capable force and suffers from prospects of fragmentation due to defections to the factional militias consolidating their position. The Taliban have established full control over areas in the south-east and in regions surrounding Kabul by 2020, threatening to cut north from the Kabul region. Battle lines are drawn between Taliban and a loose alliance of groups from the north. Tension between the US and Pakistan is rising as the Afghan-US joint facilities come under frequent attack from the Pakistani Islamist groups who are fighting alongside the Taliban inside Afghanistan. The interim/transitional set up is unable to function due to constant internal pulls and pressures. Some of the leading members of the transitional government are assassinated and there is complete chaos in Kabul.

Elections could not be held even by 2018-20 and the transitional government collapses. All state structures established after 2001 have withered away. There is no single authority in Kabul. After 2020-25, the US further reduces its presence and instead strengthens its support to certain Afghan factions who soon take over large parts of the capital region. Other regional countries also pitch in and start supporting their respective proxies. This opens up a limited opportunity for cooperation between the US and some of the regional countries so far opposed to the idea of heavy US presence in the region. A full scale civil war breaks out by 2025 and a new round of diplomatic initiatives is launched to make Afghan factions reach a compromise with Islamabad again playing a lead role.

India's Likely Position

In the absence of central or an effective government in Kabul, India is likely to face a major policy dilemma as to who to deal with in Afghanistan? India makes strenuous effort to strike a balance in its effort to reach out to all groups. Initially, refrains from identifying itself with any particular group or faction but supports indigenous efforts for political reconciliation by relatively moderate groups. India and other regional countries support limited/selective inclusion of Taliban in the political process. However, India remains relatively marginalised in regional efforts. Other than Pakistan, Russia, China and Iran seek to play a larger role with US dependence growing on the Northern Distribution Network and as Iran arms its proxies. China, given its economic investments in infrastructure/energy projects in Central Asia and parts of Afghanistan, and rising threat from religious extremism and spurt in drugs production, also seeks a role in the politics of Af-Pak. As the situation further deteriorates after 2020, and Islamabad gains influence, India's presence diminishes, limited to pockets in the north, as a new wave of violence and religious radicalisation sweeps through the Af-Pak region.

Scenario II: Fragile but Relatively Stable Afghanistan

A consensual presidential candidate acceptable to the US and Pakistan emerges after 2014. Pakistan brokers limited reconciliation between the Taliban commanders and the US forces at the provincial level. Temporary ceasefire is declared in some areas. New rounds of presidential and parliamentary elections are held though people in the south and east are largely unable to cast vote and there are reports of electoral frauds from across the country. Some influential low- or mid-level Taliban commanders however win parliamentary seats. Sections of Taliban are also inducted into the new government especially at the provincial level in the south, with some even represented in the government in Kabul. Later, some of the Taliban guerrillas and low-level commanders have also been integrated into the Afghan army and police which is adding to the social tension within. Most of the south and east however remains largely under the influence or control of the Taliban.

The suspicions of the non-Pashtun groups from the north are assuaged and their political interests protected by devolving greater powers to the provinces. A minimal understanding between the Taliban elements and a council of leaders from the north is reached. The US keeps up the pressure on Rawalpindi through drone strikes and special operations against insurgent leadership inside Pakistan.

Some influential elements of Taliban leadership are eliminated. Friction between 'integrated Taliban' and those based in Pakistan, and between 'integrated Taliban' and the Haqqani network emerges. Pakistan continues its limited support for the Taliban opposed to the government. The ANA, though still weak, is gaining in strength. The West continues to mentor, train and fund the ANSF. The West maintains minimal troop levels and continues to fund institution building. Regional countries though suspicious of West's continuing presence reconcile with minimal Western presence. China and Russia increases their presence in Afghanistan and are contributing to the process of reconstruction by investing in developmental activities especially in areas where their economic interests are involved.

India's Likely Position
India remains engaged in Afghanistan through small development projects and enhanced capacity building programmes. India reaches out to the Pashtun tribes in the south and expands its small development projects even in areas under Taliban influence. However, threat to the Indian presence remains high. Though India continues to play a key role in building the capacity of the Afghan government, it is kept out of the Afghan security sector.

Scenario III: A Balkanised Afghanistan
President Karzai's term is over by 2014. Factional fights break out across the country. The political system established after the overthrow of the Taliban in late 2001 withers away. Though the US maintains a limited number of troops in Afghanistan, it has no control over the situation. The US carries out intense drone strikes and a series of special operations against the Taliban, and the Haqqani network inside Pakistan. The ongoing effort for reconciliation with the Taliban leadership completely breaks down. Open hostilities break out between Taliban and a loosely aligned anti-Taliban coalition from the north. The ANA withers away. The country is in a state of total anarchy. Pakistan completely disrupts the NATO supply lines. The US-Pakistan relations are at its worst. The UN makes prolonged efforts to build consensus among Afghan factions, but fails. After 2020-25, decision is taken by the leadership in the north to cede from south. Pashtuns by and large oppose the move and fully support the Taliban. Pakistan too is opposed but fearing revival of demand for Pashtunistan tries to keep Taliban under check. Top Taliban leadership however tries to make a comeback to Kandahar. While the Pashtun South witnesses a rise in fundamentalism, old Pashtun nationalism emerges

simultaneously. An 'independent Pashtunistan' including Pakistan's Khyber-Pakhtunkhwa region is announced. Pakistan sees rise in ethno-nationalism with Baloch and other ethnicities demanding greater autonomy.

Meanwhile, infighting breaks out in the north among various ethnic factions. North and south are competing for control over Kabul. Both north and south plunge into violence and anarchy. As Afghanistan unravels, Iran and the Central Asian Republics grapple with huge influx of refugees. Pakistan is in a state of complete disarray. Regional countries interfere in internal politics through their proxies in Afghanistan. China plays a very cautious role and prepares to disengage itself from economic activities inside Afghanistan because of the prevailing uncertainty.

India's Likely Position

India engages the leadership in both north and south. India looks at the north as a bulwark against Pakistan's support for militant Islamists. India builds a strong strategic partnership with the north and explores strong ties with Pashtun groups in the south, though it is not easy to distinguish between nationalists and Islamists.

THE MOST LIKELY SCENARIO

The above three scenarios cannot be seen as completely independent of each other. The situation in Afghanistan is currently so uncertain that it is difficult to state as to which one of the above scenarios could be regarded as the most plausible. However, based on some broad historical determinants and contemporary political trends, an attempt can be made to build the most likely future scenario as the Afghan conflict and war enters the fourth decade.

Afghanistan with virtually all state institutions destroyed, with no single authority enjoying national legitimacy; and with people's perception severely polarised along social and ideological lines, is likely to remain in a state of socio-political ferment for decades to come. Since the overthrow of the monarchy in 1973 and subsequent destruction of the old political order, no alternative political system or effective national institutions of governance could evolve in the country. The Western attempt to create a new political system after the overthrow of the Taliban regime in December 2001 too has failed for various reasons. The perceptions about state, its orientation and authority, distribution of power, and forms of governance are often too divergent and vary from region to region and one ethnic group to another. If the predominantly

Pashtun south with relatively stronger tribal system generally stands for a centralised political structure, the more heterogeneous north remains supportive of the idea of a more decentralised or a federal system. As the Western engagement draws down, one is likely to see further fragmentation of government authority with multiple centres of power jostling for political space and influence in anticipation of security and political vacuum in years beyond 2014.

As 2014 approaches and most of the American troops withdraw, the authority of the Afghan Government is further fragmented and diluted. Kabul and Washington, having agreed on a Strategic Partnership Agreement whereby thousands of American and some troops from NATO countries would be stationed at joint Afghan-US military facilities across the country beyond 2014, continue to have persisting differences on various issues. The West-sponsored reconciliation initiative continues to be rebuffed by the Taliban and Haqqani leadership operating from Pakistan. America however continues to rely on drone strikes and conducts special operations against insurgent leadership operating from Pakistan. The relationship between Washington and Islamabad remains tense. President Karzai is unable to continue beyond his term and presidential and parliamentary elections are delayed. Hectic diplomatic efforts are on to build consensus on the composition of a caretaker transitional government. As the Taliban continue to gain in strength especially in areas around Kabul, groups from the north build alliances to deal with growing security vacuum. The rising drug production and revival of poppy cultivation in additional areas further adds to the power of factional commanders and the insurgents.

Despite differences between the US and Pakistan on the post-Karzai arrangement, a caretaker transitional government which is recognised by the UN is appointed in Kabul pending presidential and parliamentary elections. As elections could not be held even after a prolonged delay due to lack of security and resources, the caretaker transitional government collapses and the parliament is dysfunctional. By 2020, the joint Afghan-US military facilities are constantly under attack from the Taliban and the Haqqani network with large number of Pakistani Islamist militants now fighting along with them inside Afghanistan. Defections from the Afghan army and police are frequent. However, the West continues to fund the Afghan army which now has a strong air corps. The Afghan army is solely responsible for the protection of Kabul and some of the urban centres jointly with the American units. The US carries out special operations against the top Taliban leadership inside Pakistan and at the same time tries to build and support a coalition comprising mainly factions from the north and some Pashtun militia from the south and east, including few low or mid-level former Taliban commanders.

Attempts are made at the provincial level to strike deals with the Taliban commanders controlling parts of south and east but without much success as there is no strong central authority in Kabul. There are instances of Taliban infighting as well. Some of the regional countries hitherto opposed to the Western presence are supporting the American efforts to keep the Taliban at bay. NATO and Russia are working closely to ensure supplies for the remaining American-led force fighting in Afghanistan. Groups from the north are asking for *de facto* partition of the country. The international community is engaged in a new round of diplomatic initiatives to bring various Afghan factions together. Political uncertainty and violence continues.

INDIA'S POLICY OPTIONS

It is difficult at this point in time to assess as to what extent the Afghans share India's concerns or are willing to go with India's interests in the long-run. India's interests are pretty much well defined. As per official statements: 'India considers extremist ideologies to be very dangerous and a national security threat. To that extent, India wants to utilise its development programme in Afghanistan to (deny such ideologies space to grow) help Afghanistan stabilise and emerge as an economic hub linking South and Central Asia through a network of trade and transit linkages that would benefit the people of the entire region'.[1]

However, India has limited leverages in Afghanistan. It has not nurtured different sections of the erstwhile Northern Alliance well and does not have much influence over them at the moment. The Pashtuns remain largely indifferent towards India. Though India fully supported the leadership of Hamid Karzai, a Pashtun, it is not a neutral country in the perception of the Pashtuns in general given India's perceived proximity to the Tajiks from the north. For the non-Pashtun groups, India is a possible counter-force to the Pakistan-sponsored Pashtun insurgent groups, especially the Taliban.

Also, India hardly figures in the Western strategy towards Afghanistan and Pakistan. India's presence and relatively huge contribution to Afghan reconstruction has often invited Western scepticism and criticism in view of her historically adversarial relations with Pakistan. In the Western perception, much of the instability in Afghanistan is due to the India-Pakistan rivalry. It is generally believed that the Afghan problem cannot be resolved until India and Pakistan resolve the Kashmir issue. Often historical facts pertaining to the problematic relationship between Pakistan and Afghanistan since 1947 and especially after 1970s are missing in the current Western discourse loaded with Pakistan's India-centric constructs and threat perceptions. Despite all goodwill that India enjoys among sections of the Afghan people, its influence and leverage remains extremely limited. In fact, India cannot be regarded as a major force neither in the Western strategy nor in the regional initiatives pertaining to Afghanistan. Nevertheless, India cannot afford to take its eyes off the developments in its immediate Western neighbourhood as Pakistan-sponsored networks of religious extremism and terrorism continue to pose ideological as well as physical threats for both India and Afghanistan.

RECOMMENDATIONS

- Being a close neighbour, India must take a long-term view of its Afghan engagement as Afghanistan is not likely to stabilise for decades to come. It may be increasingly difficult for India to sustain its presence and maintain the momentum of its relationship with the Afghan people in years beyond 2014. In the absence of an effective central government in Kabul, a major challenge before India would be whom to talk to or engage in Afghanistan. The training and capacity building programmes that India has been conducting for Afghans too may get disrupted. This, all the more, makes it important for India to expand its engagement with various Afghan factions, including the Taliban elements willing to work with India.

- It would be in the long-term interest of India to evenly develop its relations with diverse ethnic groups in Afghanistan. This would require varying approaches as relations with various Afghan groups have its own dynamics. This is all the more important when dealing with the Pashtun groups. Any over-identification with a particular Afghan group/faction is not a feasible idea in a country as multi-ethnic and as factionalised as Afghanistan. It would be politically expedient for India to be always prepared to deal with the Afghan government of the day, whether it includes or excludes the Taliban. India's Afghan policy needs constant evaluation in the light of the rapidly changing environment in both Afghanistan and Pakistan and politics beyond the Amu Darya.

- India must engage the next generation of Afghan leadership and should remain a key development partner of the Afghan people. While reaching out to the new political formations that might emerge in the years to come, India must find innovative ways to invest more on tapping the Afghan youth. Training Afghan youths and professionals in Indian institutions will keep India connected to diverse sections of the Afghan population even in the worst of times.

- India must support indigenous initiatives for national unity. India's backing for the supposedly Kabul-led reconciliation process despite concerns over the rising influence of both Taliban and Pakistan is an exercise in public diplomacy. With the US-backed government in Kabul trying to reach out to the Taliban, the idea of India completely denouncing the Taliban does not hold much ground. Taliban as an organisation has acquired a dynamic of its own. Today, it is a much more decentralised entity and prospects of defections cannot be ruled out. Political reconciliation between Kabul and the top Taliban leadership is a tricky issue. Whether Kabul and the US are able to use reconciliation as a mechanism to avert full comeback of the Taliban or not remains to be seen.

- Though the Taliban leadership continues to be patronised by the Pakistani establishment, that is no affirmation of their absolute control over the Taliban. In fact, it may be argued that whether Pakistan will ever be able to have a strategic depth within Afghanistan or not, the Taliban have certainly secured a reverse strategic depth within Pakistan. The possible pulls and pressures between Taliban assuming a more autonomous character and Pakistan trying to keep them under control is worth taking into account. It is the extremist ideology of the Taliban that needs to be countered and neutralised in the region, and not gullible Pashtun youths joining the Taliban guerrilla units out of a sense of frustration over lack of employment opportunities and developmental work in the region.

- India needs to better its understanding of the historical, political, ethnic, tribal and religious dynamics of Afghanistan and north-western Pakistan. A conscious effort must be made to reconnect with the Pashtun communities. India must explore possibilities of reaching out to the local Pashtun media. Conscious efforts can also be made to enrol Pashtun students and professionals especially, from the border areas for scholarship programmes in

Indian institutions. An Afghan Cultural Centre in India can also go a long way in communicating ideas.

- Given the fractious nature of Afghan politics and the prevalent regional dynamics, India should firmly avoid any temptation for a direct military involvement in Afghanistan. However, as a follow-up to the Strategic Partnership Agreement India signed with Afghanistan in October 2011, institutionalising its engagement with the Afghan army, police and the Afghan intelligence should be a constant endeavour. India must also avoid looking at its role in Afghanistan only through the prism of its relations with Pakistan. Otherwise, India may end up being manipulated by other forces, including Afghan factions. It will also work to the advantage of religious radicals and the Pakistan army in the domestic politics of Pakistan. It is sure to draw into competition a host of other regional forces as well.

- Since the Pakistani establishment will continue to try and deny space to India in Afghanistan, it is important that India develops or builds its leverages within Pakistan and Afghanistan. India must also reinforce the security of its embassy, consulates and personnel engaged in reconstruction projects even if it calls for additional deployment of paramilitary forces. The prospects of a highly destabilised Pakistan in the decades to come cannot be completely ruled out. Pakistan may emerge as a bigger challenge for both India and the West.

- The emerging partnership with the US, at one level, and with regional countries and forums, at another, must be fully utilised by India to build an effective consensus on the need to confront the key sources of religious extremism and terrorism in the region. However, the tendency of most of the regional countries and forums to shy away from recognising these sources in the Pakistan-Afghanistan region, and working towards a regional strategy to deal with them, is further complicating the issue. The US decision to shift its focus towards the Asia Pacific region may lead to an altogether new geo-political competition in Asia. India will have to closely watch the shift in US' Asia policy and regional reactions to it as it seeks to take a long-term view of the multiple challenges it is likely to face from its turbulent north-western neighbourhood.

- Though regional groupings/mechanisms are not likely to play any effective or a direct military role in the stabilisation of Afghanistan in the near-term, India must continue to try and engage other regional countries like Iran, Russia, and the Central Asian Republics, both bilaterally and also through multilateral forums. Meanwhile, it is also pertinent that India keeps track of the thinking on the Afghan issue in these countries, and also their perception about India's presence and role in Afghanistan.

NOTE

'India in Afghanistan: A Development Partnership', Ministry of External Affairs, Government of India, available at: http://www.mea.gov.in/mystart.php?id=8400, accessed on January 12, 2012.

Chapter 2

BANGLADESH
ILLEGAL MIGRATION AND CHALLENGES FOR INDIA

Sreeradha Datta

INTRODUCTION

The issue of illegal migration is highly emotive and sensitive in Bangladesh and all governments have regularly denied the existence of the phenomenon. Although this has often been flagged in the meetings between border officials, Bangladesh finds it difficult to accept the fact that its citizens are illegally crossing over into India in search of livelihood. Academic communities in both countries have viewed the problem in the light of sociological and historical factors, but Bangladeshi politicians have been very defensive and unwilling to examine the issue through a rational prism. Rather ironically while Bangladesh push-sells its 'hard working, disciplined, multi-skilled, easily trainable human resources [which] remain [Bangladesh's] greatest asset',[1] and has been discussing the issue of legalising migration of its working population to different parts of the world (including Malaysia and Brunei), this subject remains a taboo as far as India is concerned.[2]

The steady flow of Bangladeshis into India in search of livelihood had initially resulted in demographic changes in the bordering states of West Bengal and the Northeastern states of Assam, Tripura and Meghalaya. But gradually, this phenomenon transformed into a much larger social problem in the far corners of India, as Delhi, Mumbai, and Hyderabad, etc. Climate change, lack of new agricultural techniques leading to low levels of food production, and inability to use water resources efficiently will mean that larger numbers will seek employment opportunities outside, mainly in India.

Much of the insurgency in the Northeast region, especially in Assam, revolves around the issue of Bangladeshi migrants. The question of illegal migration is also being viewed within the overall context of radicalisation of the Bangladeshi society. Cadres of the *Jama'at-e-Islami* of Bangladesh have been active in Northeast India, with reports of Pakistani support to radical groups in Bangladesh adding another dimension to the problem.

Unless the issue of illegal migration is resolved comprehensively, it will have implications for our foreign and security policy besides being highly sensitive politically.

DEMOGRAPHIC CHANGES, SECTARIAN DISCORDS, AND SECURITY CONCERNS

Statistics of Illegal Migrants

There is no consensus about the exact numbers of Bangladeshis who have entered India illegally and have stayed back. There is no exact data as the numbers are as varied as the agencies and stakeholders that are involved in collating it. However, it is possible to arrive at rough estimates.

Although most of the illegal migrants enter through West Bengal and other states of Northeast India, they are scattered over different parts of India. In 2004, the Congress-led UPA Government came up with a figure of 1,20,53,950 illegal Bangladeshi immigrants living in various parts of India (as per the data provided by Minister of State for Home Affairs on July 14, 2004 in response to an unstarred question in the Rajya Sabha).[3] However, it was clarified by the Ministry 9 days later in the same House that the figures were not reliable.[4] Previously, the BJP-led NDA Government had estimated that there were '15 million Bangladeshi migrants living in India illegally'.[5] In October 2008, former Deputy Prime Minister L.K. Advani put the number of Bangladeshi migrants in the country at around 35 million.[6] Taking these estimates into account, there is a possibility that between 10-35 million Bangladeshis are illegally residing in India. Substantial numbers of Bangladeshis cross over without legal documents while some come with visas and do not return.[7]

THE CAUSES OF MIGRANT FLOW

The Pull Factor

Bangladeshis migrate to India because of both political and economic reasons. The first wave of migration was prompted by political reasons.

During the early years after the formation of Bangladesh (this was also true in the aftermath of the Babri mosque demolition in 1992) the changed political situation led to considerable forced migration of Hindus into India, who took advantage of the economic and social support extended by their relatives across the border or even by those who had migrated earlier. In the next phase, the flow of both Hindu and Muslim migrants increased due to economic reasons, especially during the 1980s through the 1990s, however, the numbers of Muslims were substantially more than the Hindus. Some political parties in the bordering provinces of West Bengal, Assam and Tripura do not oppose migration from Bangladesh, because the migrant population acts as vote banks for them. That apart, some commentators have suggested that Bangladesh is propagating the idea of *lebensraum* (expanded living space or habitat) which has led to such large presence of Bangladeshis especially in the border region. Inevitably, despite attempts by the Indian Government to resolve the problem, the solution has remained elusive. Indeed most of these illegal migrants continue to provide cheap labour in the Indian metros, while a sizeable number of them, especially in the Northeast, who entered illegally in the past 40 years, are now landowners and businessmen.[8]

There are several studies that have documented this problem. Apart from the security considerations that this issue involves, the humanitarian concerns are overwhelming for both India and Bangladesh. Human trafficking is flourishing and has its network across the borders in Bangladesh, India and Pakistan. Families pay thousands of rupees to middlemen to get into India from Bangladesh, and few of them move towards the border with Pakistan. This flow of undocumented population also involves thousands of children and women being trafficked across the border. There is a deeply entrenched network on both sides of the border that manufactures illegal documents for the migrants and facilitates the entry of (as well as provision of residential access to) these undocumented migrants in India. According to one study, earlier, each immigrant had to pay Rs 1,000 to Rs 2,000, now they are being charged between Rs 5,000 to Rs10,000 per document per person.[9]

The Push Factors Emanating from Bangladesh

Population Pressure

The population growth rate in Bangladesh is tabulated in Table 2.1.

Table 2.1: Population Growth Rate in Bangladesh

2000	2001	2002	2003	2004	2005	2006	2007	2008	2009	2010	2011
1.59	1.59	1.59	2.06	2.08	2.09	2.09	2.06	2.02	1.29	1.55	1.45

According to the latest World Population Data Sheet brought out by the Population Research Bureau (PRB) in 2011, Bangladesh's population is likely to reach 226 million by the mid-2050s—a 37 per cent rise from present levels.[10] Bangladesh is one of the most densely populated countries in the world, with a total area of 55,598 sq miles (143,999 sq km), a population density of 966 per sq km and total cultivable land of 8.29 million hectares.[11] The population of Bangladesh which was 118 million in 1991 increased to 162.2 million in 2010, as per United Nations estimates, and the population density will increase to about 1350 per sq km in 2030.[12] All indications suggest that, despite aggressive measures to control the birth rate, the population will double in less than 40 years, with about 90 per cent of the growth occurring in rural areas. The density will undoubtedly keep on increasing, outstripping the state's ability to provide for the bare necessities.[13]

Presently a little more than one quarter of the population lives in urban areas, where population density is 200 times greater than the national figure and population growth is twice the national average. It is estimated that the population of urban areas will increase to 50 per cent by 2040. Dhaka city, now inhabited by 12 million people, will be the fourth most densely populated city of the world by 2025.[14] By 2030, half the population (nearly 100 million people) will be living in urban areas, most of them below the poverty line.[15] At present there is no specific organisation in Bangladesh dedicated to studying this issue. The Bangladeshi Supreme Court expressed its deep concern about over-population in the country in August 2010. It issued a ruling, asking the Government to explain within four weeks why it (the Government) should not be asked to take steps to control over-population, create an independent ministry and make separate allocation for population control.[16]

This rapid population growth puts severe pressures on the limited land resources, leading to land degradation in some areas. Bangladesh is characterised by high agricultural density which coupled with high population growth puts 'tremendous pressure on the existing land and resources'. Because of the growing number of the poor, the access to development programmes is limited to only a few.[17] This creates incentives for the population to cross the border into India, which offers greater economic opportunities.

The Bangladesh Economy
According to the current governor of Bangladesh Bank, the economy is

now on the threshold of a higher growth path; on course for a 6.7 per cent real GDP growth in 2011, and is likely to be well above 7 per cent in 2012.[18] The Bank's overall assessment of the economic activity indicates that the economy will perform reasonably well in the coming years. As per the prediction of the official Economic Review Bangladeshi economy (for the year 2011) is poised to attain a growth rate of above 8 per cent by 2014. Although more moderate estimates project the economy's likely growth at 6.3 per cent, as against Bangladesh Bureau of Statistics' projection of 6.7 per cent, according to the IMF's latest *World Economic Outlook*, Bangladeshi economy grew by 5.7 per cent in 2009-2010, while the forecast was for 6 per cent growth, despite the fact that the overall investment scenario remained depressed.[19]

Notwithstanding the above, experts feel, population must be regulated through capital formation, which can ensure a higher rate of productivity at the existing standard of living, to increase economic growth. As per the latest government figures put out by the 2011 *Economic Survey of Bangladesh*, about 40 per cent of the population lived below the poverty line.

The Government, exporters and policy makers, who had been seemingly complacent about being immune to the global economic crisis fallout, even in the last half of 2008, are now waking up to the problems associated with the demand-drop in the US and Europe. The Bangladeshi economy, largely dependent on remittances, has also begun to face the effect of the global downturn. Bangladesh Bank data showed in 2009 that 63 per cent of Bangladesh's $7.9 billion remittance, during 2008-09, came from the Gulf, a region where economies are now contracting because of the falling oil prices and global downturn. Remittance from more than 6 million expatriate Bangladeshis in the 2009-10 fiscal year totalled $10.97 billion dollars, around 13.20 per cent higher than the previous year. In 2010-11, it touched $11.65 billion and by May 2012, it reached $11.77 billion.[20]

According to government estimates, the number of legal migrants from Bangladesh exceeded 6 million in 2009, or about 4 per cent of the population. In recent years, the annual outflow of migrants dropped appreciably, a trend that exhibited a sharp increase in 2007 and 2008, when the number of migrants had crossed the 8 million mark.[21]

Around 80 per cent of all Bangladeshi migrants are located in oil-exporting countries, of which the Kingdom of Saudi Arabia alone accounts for 41 per cent. Other major destinations outside the Middle East include Malaysia, which accounts for a hefty 11 per cent, but in terms of remittances its contribution is only about 3 per cent. However, Bangladesh's labour export, the country's second biggest source of foreign exchange, has fallen by 21 per cent in 2010. Due to political turmoil in the region, there has been a drop in labour migration from Bangladesh and only 385,000 Bangladesh workers went abroad in 2010 as against 475,000 in 2009. Kuwait, that had 40,000 Bangladeshi workers some years ago, accepted only 21 persons in 2010. Kuwait reflects the declining trend observed in Saudi Arabia and the United Arab Emirates. The Gulf region absorbed over a half of the Bangladeshi workers abroad who sent home $10 billion in 2008-09.[22]

Bangladesh is a huge labour surplus country. According to the government statistics brought out in the *Labour Force Survey 2005-06*, the country had an economically active population of about 56.7 million, out of which 54.1 million were employed in different professions. The study revealed that there were about 2.6 million unemployed people in Bangladesh, which would put continuous pressure on the government to create more jobs to bring down the current rate of unemployment of about 4.5 per cent.[23]

Diminishing Land Availability

Agriculture is the backbone of the economy accounting for 20.60 per cent of GDP and 48.40 per cent of employment. More than 90 per cent of the population derives its basic calories from rice. Rice alone accounts for 18 per cent of the GDP and 55 per cent of the people are employed in its production, processing and marketing sectors.[24]

The problem is aggravated by the cropping intensity in Bangladesh that has already reached 180 per cent, one of the highest in the world. Furthermore, agricultural land is increasingly being diverted to other uses such as housing, roads and industrial development. To be sustainable, future production must be achieved with less land, less labour and less water with no harm to the natural environment.[25]

By the year 2030, the population will be requiring 39.8 million tonnes of rice and keeping the area more or less constant and the required total yield would have to be 3.8 t/ha (tonnes/hectare) against the present yield of 2.58 t/ha (with average farm size of less than 1.0 acre).[26] It is a herculean task to say the least.

Given the large number of people dependent on food subsidies, regularly occurring natural disasters have compounded Bangladesh's problems. Floods and cyclones followed one another during a period when there was global food crisis, causing a severe food crisis in

Bangladesh. In 2009, Bangladesh Government had ordered the purchase of 400,000 tons of rice from India at TK 30.10 per kg or $430 per metric tonne.

Climate Change Affects Land Holdings

Drought and flood-prone Bangladesh is also vulnerable to climate change. Given the higher population density, more people are exposed to the risk since opportunities for migration within the country are limited. According to the *National Geographic* issue of May 2011, in an average year, 40 per cent of the total land area is flooded and annually river erosion washes away one per cent of arable land. Bangladesh would be faced with extraordinary policy challenges due to relentless population pressure, deforestation, and long time-lag inherent in even successful programmes to control global warming. Bangladeshi scientists estimate that up to 20 per cent of the country's land may be lost to flooding by 2030, creating as many as 20 million 'climate refugees'.

The new Climate Change Vulnerability Index by Maplecroft rates 'Bangladesh as the country most at risk due to extreme levels of poverty and a high dependency on agriculture, whilst its government has the lowest capacity of all countries to adapt to predicted changes in the climate.' Bangladesh has a high risk of drought and the highest risk of flooding. This was illustrated during October 2010, when 500,000 people were driven from their homes by flood waters created by storms.[27] A study carried out under the BDCLIM (Bangladesh Climate) project indicates that the average annual runoff in the Brahmaputra basin would decline by 14 per cent by the year 2050 as a result of climate change. This will affect agriculture production. The combined effects of a rising population and falling cultivable area will generate a huge surplus pool of labour.

Thus, given the present indicators, Bangladesh will be unable to provide sufficient land, food or employment to its people. While the skilled and semi-skilled workers will continue to seek employment in different parts of the world, India will continue to be the natural choice for several thousands of Bangladeshis every year who cannot find any occupation in Bangladesh and elsewhere.

INDIA'S RESPONSE

The issue of detection and deportation of foreigners in the Northeast and West Bengal has been mired in legal battles. Given the volatility of the issue of illegal Bangladeshi migrants in India, over the years, the Indian state has initiated a few legal measures to address the problem.

Responding to a Public Interest Litigation (PIL) in 1999, the Supreme Court of India asked the centre and the state governments of West Bengal, Assam, Meghalaya, Mizoram and Tripura to file affidavits on the repatriation of illegal Bangladeshi migrants. The PIL filed by the All India Lawyers Forum for Civil Liberties had alleged that over 10 million Bangladeshi migrants had illegally crossed over into India and were causing severe strain on the resources of the poor Northeastern states as well as West Bengal. It had sought a direction from the court to the centre to identify these Bangladeshi nationals and repatriate them with the help of National Human Rights Commission (NHRC) and other agencies. However, only a limited number of illegal settlers have been identified and deported so far.

Legal Mechanisms

Some steps to identify these illegal migrants were taken under the Foreigners Act, 1946 and under the Illegal Migrants Determination by Tribunal (IMDT) Act, 1983 of Assam. The failure of the IMDT Act led to its being struck down as unconstitutional in July 2005 by the Indian Supreme Court. The poor implementation of the IMDT Act was reflected in the 16 tribunals that were finally approved compared to 30 tribunals provided for in the original Act. Also, between 1983 and 2000, the 16 tribunals in Assam identified about 10,000 illegal migrants and deported just 1400. That the IMDT tribunals did little to tackle large-scale illegal traffic from Bangladesh is clear from the fact that as against 300,000 Bangladeshi's deported between 1962 and 1984 under the Foreigners Act, 1946, the new IMDT Act saw fewer detection/detentions.[28] For instance, only 7,854 Bangladeshis faced prosecution under the Act in 2001, 5,652 in 2002 and 26,796 in 2003. The incorporation of some provisions of the IMDT Act, through the backdoor, in the Foreigners' Act, only in respect of the Northeastern states has not been of much help. In order to check illegal migration India must ensure that the Foreigners' Act is made applicable to the whole country in its full rigour.

Regarding the central issue of their repatriation, the union government has expressed its inability to do anything about it. In its view, due to ethnic, linguistic, cultural, physical and social similarities, Bangladeshi nationals tend to merge easily with the local population making it difficult to identify them.

Fencing

Continuous illegal migration prompted India to fence its international borders with Bangladesh. Initially this project was meant to be completed by 1997 but the work has not moved along as planned. Out of the total length of 3,436.59 km to be fenced, so far fencing of 2,735.12 km has been completed (which include 695 km of Tripura's total 856 km long border with Bangladesh). In Meghalaya, Muktapur and Pyrdiwah areas in East Khasi Hills district have remained a bone of contention. There are nine disputed areas in the Meghalaya sector which are regarded as vulnerable areas by India and claimed by Bangladesh. This issue is under review at present. It is estimated that the entire fencing will be completed by the end of 2012.[29]

There are indications that the fence has brought down the numbers of people crossing over illegally into India. In 2007, a total of 4,206 infiltrators were arrested as against 5,130 a year before.[31] As an additional measure, in 2006 the Cabinet Committee on Security decided to install floodlights along 2,840 km of the border at a cost of Rs.13.28 billion and this is likely to be accomplished by end 2012.[30]

SCENARIOS

Irrespective of the levels of economic development and population control measures adopted by Bangladesh government, illegal migration to India is likely to continue. Although the levels of illegal migration may be controlled to some extent with various measures undertaken by India and Bangladesh jointly, it is a problem that India will be facing for several years to come.

Given the complexities inherent in the issue, the problem requires a multi-pronged approach. At the unilateral level, India will have to evolve a more effective mechanism to address the gaps in the present methods. This would range from ensuring that local political parties resist the urge to use the migrants as vote banks and to ensure that the border control mechanisms are effective. The difficult part, however, will be to deal with the Bangladeshis who continue to remain in India. At the bilateral level several measures are required to ensure that two sides are able to discuss the issue and arrive at mutually acceptable solutions. Measures to build a positive image of India will ensure continued positive bilateral atmospherics. Domestic opinion plays an important role in shaping Bangladesh's policy towards its larger neighbour, India. Given the sharp political polarisation at the domestic level and continued association of India with the Awami League, the attempts to reach out to the opposition parties need to be buttressed and strengthened through inter-actions at various levels.

The difficulty also lies in making Bangladesh accept illegal migration as a problem and an issue that needs to be addressed. For this, the subject needs to be raised and discussed at the official and societal levels. First and foremost the Government of Bangladesh has to be made to accept the existence of the phenomenon. The *modus operandi* for the next step will have to be worked out with their support and through joint efforts. The engagement has to be broad based involving various sectors ranging from government to think tanks, NGOs, parliamentarians and students. From the analysis above, it is obvious that the main drivers of change on the issue of illegal migration from Bangladesh will be: successful population control measures in Bangladesh; sustained economic growth in Bangladesh; and the overall state of India-Bangladesh relations. Based on these drivers, three scenarios can be envisioned by 2030.

Scenario I: Friendly Neighbours

Bangladesh controls its population growth only marginally as predicted and despite its sound economic growth, there is very little that Bangladesh can do to stop migration to India. Despite this situation, the relationship between India and Bangladesh is friendly. Bangladesh is more sensitive to Indian concerns especially on the migrants' issue. The bilateral ties are stable. Indian companies invest in Bangladesh thus creating employment opportunities for people. Therefore, India and Bangladesh are able to fully appreciate and utilise the new trade and connectivity routes that have been established. Bilateral discussions for introduction of work permits for Bangladeshis are taken up. The two sides have also been able to tap the labour market that Bangladesh offers through work permits issued for specific projects and jobs and effective monitoring mechanisms. With high rate of growth and development, several Bangladeshis illegally residing in India choose to return to their homeland. India liberalises trade allowing entry of ready-made garments and textiles from Bangladesh which generates further good will for Indians and with India now able to meet some of the energy deficit in Bangladesh from its Northeastern states through a energy grid built with Indian assistance ensures Bangladesh's continued support for similar projects. Joint border control mechanisms are in place and illegal migration from Bangladesh is reduced considerably. Bangladesh and the Eastern and Northeastern states of India are closely interconnected through railways roads and ports. Transit rights through Chittagong and Mongla ports (for which Indian has sought approval from Bangladesh) prove beneficial to both sides. India undertakes several infrastructure projects within Bangladesh that improve Bangladeshi economic performance create strong stakeholders within that country who support continued interaction with India. Moreover, river-water sharing issues are resolved and India and Bangladesh take a common stand vis-à-vis China on the Brahmaputra issue.

Scenario II: Normal Neighbours

Bilateral relations between India and Bangladesh improve but negative perceptions about India remain. The Bangladesh Government is less cooperative on issues like migration and cross border movement. Border *haats* and border trade improve substantially. The legal mechanisms for cattle/buffalo trade ensure reduction of tensions at the border. Relations are good but Bangladesh does not cooperate in stemming the flow of migrants and refuses to take back those identified as illegal migrants. Population control measures are not being emphasised as much as required. Lack of industrialisation means low absorption of labour within Bangladesh so pressure to migrate to India continues, given India's higher growth levels. The two main political parties come to power alternately and the fluctuation in the relations between the two countries is accepted as normal. However, India's private sector is not willing to commit huge investment in Bangladesh. The net outcome is that illegal migration to India continues with the covert support of Bangladeshi authorities. India continues to raise this issue with Bangladesh but does not take tough measures against it fearing that Bangladesh will lean more towards China. Illegal migrants who enter India in the past manage to merge with Indian society and work with transnational criminal groups creating periodic political and security concerns.

Scenario III: Difficult Neighbours

In an unstable political situation, India becomes a factor in the domestic political situation in Bangladesh and public perception turns against India. China offers military and economic packages to position itself as an alternative to India. Also the theory of *lebensraum* is promoted with covert support from the Government of Bangladesh. As a result, there is a serious danger of a change in the demographic profile of the border areas. Despite India's economic growth and greater influence in the international community it is still unable to find a way to deal with the illegal Bangladeshis who are residing in India. This population gives rise to security concerns and works with anti-India elements both in India and in Bangladesh. Bangladesh border forces also back the actions of the political actors and border skirmishes once again become a regular feature.

The thin majority of the coalition government has given the opposition more manoeuvring space. Religious elements gain strength in the polity because of growing sympathy and feeling of perceived persecution. Bangladesh witnesses serious political instability during 2014-2019. Anti-India sentiments rise and become more pervasive. Hindus and minorities feel threatened and move to India in larger numbers. With India adopting strict border control measures, violence at the border breaks out frequently. There is a diplomatic standoff at the borders and political instability in Bangladesh heightens with worsening economic conditions aggravated by periodic cyclones and floods and droughts. Indian companies are no longer interested in making investments in Bangladesh. Multilateral institutions provide some temporary relief but not enough to sustain the economy on a long-term basis. Population continues to grow and all these cumulatively lead to larger numbers migrating to India.

RECOMMENDATIONS

Below are a few policy recommendations.

Economic Measures

In the positive bilateral atmospherics today India will need to initiate a bilateral dialogue with Bangladesh over the issue. Both the question of the millions that are already residing in India, and the issue of unceasing flow of Bangladeshis into India, need to be addressed. The issue of work permits for Bangladeshi labourers may be considered.

- Initially, India can invite Bangladeshi workers to work on bilateral projects like railway infrastructure, road development, ICP development and other works undertaken by India in the Northeast region.
- Growth of the Bangladesh economy will have a positive impact on flow of illegal migrants to India. At present there are very few large infrastructural projects undertaken in Bangladesh which could generate large-scale employment. Greater investment by India would be useful towards that end. Creation of employment opportunities in the migration-prone poor districts of Bangladesh could significantly reduce the flow of economic migrants.
- India, without compromising on its economic gains, can address Bangladeshi demands on trade issues. The lowering of the negative list, especially those 46 items that form components of its ready-made garment industry, will give a greater fillip to its core industry. Bangladesh being a Least Developed Country

(LDC), India can make those economic concessions without any significant impact on its own industries. There are several other economic opportunities that India could seize upon at the present moment including helping Bangladesh establish quality engineering and management colleges.

- As a larger economy, the removal of the negative list by India may be considered. The political dividends will outweigh the economic losses thus incurred.
- Energy trade with Bangladesh would also entrench India to a great extent in Bangladesh economy. Bangladesh is in dire need of meeting its energy demand and Indian presence in this sector will enable India to increase its influence. All this will increase India's negotiating strength on issues—especially that of illegal migrants.

Border Control Measures

On the one hand India has to build impregnable borders, while on other hand allow easy cross-border movement, which will ensure people that people take the legal route. Fence should be fitted with sensor lights and rely on technology rather than manual monitoring. There is low level of communication about what is expected from population living close to the borders. Awareness levels in the border areas are abysmal. Border management needs to address these gaps. Joint campaigns which involve people from both sides would have greater impact. Based on the performance of the border *haats*, this scope of this experiment should be widened to establish border schools, technical institutes, etc. In addition:

- Implement the no-firing policy fully. Ensure accountability to ensure that the image of India as an enemy ceases to exist.
- Fencing needs to be completed speedily and monitored effectively. This would create misgivings but also ensure that Bangladesh knows that India means business. The state governments and the Indian border forces seem receptive to such an idea.
- The vegetation cover along the international border (at a distance of about 150 metres on either side) needs to be cleared regularly to ensure all-weather visibility.
- India and Bangladesh need to strengthen their military ties. They are being revived after a long gap but much more can be done in terms of increasing visits, contacts at various level as well as by selling military hardware. Apart from initiating joint exercises, India should consider the China model of gifting hardware in the initial instance, and offer technical expertise that Bangladeshi

military is in need of. They have to be weaned away from Pakistan and China. There can be no overnight successes but sustained efforts are essential.

- Implementation of decisions and agreements should be accorded serious attention. Promises to build villages after the Sidr cyclone in 2007 are yet to be fulfilled. This is amongst many other unfulfilled promises. Prompt action on the promises made would go a long way in reducing the anti-India constituency that exists in Bangladesh.

- Insecurity of life and property among religious and ethnic minorities is one of the push factors for Bangladeshi nationals to cross over to India for shelter. The Bangladesh Government has not been particularly mindful of the need to create conditions in which the minorities can live in their native land in peace and dignity like members of the majority community. The rise of radical Islam and related problems in Bangladesh has to be contained by both bilateral and regional efforts With bilateral trade and commerce interdependence deepening India will be able to get its concerns addressed more effectively.

Long-term Measures

- India has to tactfully encourage the Bangladesh Government to ensure that population control measures and campaigns reach out to the rural areas, In the last few years UNDP, DFID, etc., funding for population control campaigns has been reduced. The NGO sector that had initiated such programmes have to be given more support and funding by India.

- To promote close India-Bangladesh ties, innovative measures like the joint management of rivers, common electricity grid, transport connectivity, Free Trade Areas, etc., may be designed to lead to a symbiotic intermeshing of the long-term interests of the two countries. India as a global power will have to evolve a regional labour market in which all South Asian countries are participating. But this predicates upon India managing its differences with Pakistan in the foreseeable future.

- Migration needs not to be viewed only in negative terms. The migrants support economic activities in several regions of India as a labour workforce. This necessitates the development of a mechanism for regulating labour movement from one state with surplus labour to another with a labour deficit.

NOTES

1. Bangladeshi High Commissioner to Brunei, M Shameem Ahsan, argued out the benefits of employing Bangladeshi workforce as reported by *The Brunei Times*, March 27, 2011, available at http://www.bt.com.bn/news-national/2011/03/27/bangladesh-thankful-job-opportunities, last accessed on December 14, 2011.
2. 'Bangladeshi Prime Minister Arrives in UAE', Suryatapa Bhattacharya, *The National*, January 16, 2011 available at http://www.thenational.ae/news/bangladeshi-prime-minister-arrives-in-uae, last accessed on December 14, 2011.
3. Minister of State for Home Affairs Sri Prakash Jaiswal's statement in the Parliament on July 14, 2004, cited in Chandan Nandy, 'Illegal Immigration From Bangladesh To India: The Emerging Conflicts', Slifka Program in Inter-Communal Coexistence Brandeis University, Mellon-MIT Foundation on NGOs and Forced Migration, November 30, 2005, available at http://web.mit.edu/cis/www/migration/pubs/rrwp/chandan_nandy_immigrants.pdf, last accessed on November 18, 2011.
4. Statement by the Minister of State in the Ministry of Home Affairs (Shri Manikrao Gavit) on July 23, 2004, available at http://164.100.47.5/newdebate/deb_ndx/202/23072004/11to12.htm, last accessed on December 14, 2011.
5. LK Advani, Deputy Prime Minister and Union Home Minister, Government of India, in his statement before the Parliamentary Consultative Committee on Home Affairs, New Delhi, December 16, 2003, p. 10.
6. 'Terrorism Compounded by Illegal Migration: Advani', Zee News, October 31, 2008 available at http://www.zeenews.com/Nation/2008-10-31/479991news.html, last accessed on November 18, 2011.
7. As per the reply to a query under RTI, Act MHA has stated that as on December 31, 2009, there are 73,000 persons from various countries who have stayed back after expiry of their visa period of whom nearly 50 per cent were Bangladeshis. Source: RTI information dated January 8, 2010.
8. Josy Joseph, 'Securitization of Illegal Migration of Bangladeshis To India,' Working Paper 100, January 2006, Institute of Defence and Strategic Studies, Singapore available at http://www.rsis.edu.sg/publications/WorkingPapers/WP100.pdf, last accessed on November 18, 2011, last accessed on December 14, 2011.
9. Shutapa Paul, 'Illegal immigration: East Bengal in West Bengal', *India Today*, January 14, 2011 available at http://indiatoday.intoday.in/site/Story/126587/The%20Big%20Story/east+bengal+in+west+bengal.html, last accessed on November 18, 2011.
10. See Population Reference Bureau, *2011 World Population Datasheet*, 2011, available at http://www.prb.org/pdf11/2011population-data-sheet_eng.pdf, last accessed on December 20, 2011
11. Aloysius Milon Khan, *DFID Bangladesh Country Fact Sheet*, February 2008, available at http://www.iptu.co.uk/content/trade_cluster_info/bangladesh/factsheet_feb08.pdf, last accessed on November 18. According to this study population may be 200 million by 2035, and 240 million by 2050.
12. 'World Population Prospects: The 2010 Revision', United Nations Population Division available at http://esa.un.org/unpd/wpp/Excel-Data/population.htm, last accessed on November 18, 2011.
13. 'The population bomb is ticking', *Daily Star*, July 17, 2010 available at http://www.thedailystar.net/newDesign/news-details.php?nid=147050, last accessed on December 14, 2011.

14. Ibid.
15. 'Sanitation, Hygiene and Water Supply in Urban Slums', Fact-sheet updated July 2008, available at http://www.unicef.org/bangladesh/URBAN_Water_Sanitation_and_Hygiene.pdf, last accessed on December 14, 2011.
16. 'Court concern about population boom', *Daily Star*, August 18, 2010, available at http://www.thedailystar.net/newDesign/news-details.php?nid=151121, last accessed on December 14, 2011.
17. Mohammad Mohiuddin Abdullah, 'Impact of population on National Economy', *The Daily Star*, January 11, 2011, available at http://www.thedailystar.net/newDesign/news-details.php?nid=169510 , last accessed on December 14, 2011.
18. Atiur Rahman , Monetary Challenges for Bangladesh in FY2011, CPD Dialogue on Growth, Inflation, at Centre for Policy Dialogue (CPD), February 13, 2011, available at http://www.bangladesh-bank.org/mediaroom/speech/feb132011gs1.pdf, last accessed on December 14, 2011.
19. See 'Bangladesh Bank Economic Review 2010', Ministry of Finance, Bangladesh at http://www.mof.gov.bd/en/; also, Sajjadur Rahman, 'Economic Review 2010', *The Daily Star*, December 31, 2010, available at http://www.thedailystar.net/suppliments/2010/12/HNY2011/13.htm, last accessed on December 14, 2011.
20. See data on Bangladesh Bank website available at http://www.bangladesh-bank.org/econdata/wageremitance.php, last accessed on December 14, 2011.
21. Report prepared by Maxell Stamp Ltd, 'Study on the International Demand for Semi-skilled and Skilled Bangladeshi Workers' April 201, International Labour Organization, p.IV, available at http://www.ilo.org/wcmsp5/groups/public/@asia/@ro-bangkok/@ilo-dhaka/documents/publication/wcms_140660.pdf, last accessed on December 14, 2011.
22. 'Arab Uprisings and Their Impact on Bangladesh', *The Financial Express*, Dhaka, January 04, 2011, available at http://www.thefinancialexpress-bd.com/more.php?news_id=482&date=2011-04-01, last accessed on December 14, 2011.
23. See data provided in 'Key Findings of Labour Force Report 2010', available at http://www.bbs.gov.bd/WebTestApplication/userfiles/Image/keyfinding/Labour%20Force%20Survey%202010.pdf, last accessed on December 14, 2011.
24. Md. Nasiruddin, Dr. Mian Sayeed Hassan, 'Agricultural Research Priority : Vision-2030 and beyond', December 2009, available at http://www.barc.gov.bd/documents/Final-%20Dr.%20Nasir.pdf, last accessed on December 14, 2011.
25. Ibid.
26 Ibid.
27. *Climate Change Vulnerability Index 2011*, May 2011, available at http://maplecroft.com/about/news/ccvi.html, last accessed on December 14, 2011.
28. 'SC Strikes Down IMDT Act as Unconstitutional,' *Economic Times*, 13 July, 2005, available at http://economictimes.indiatimes.com/articleshow/1168803.cms, last accessed on December 14, 2011.
29. *Annual Report 2010-11*, Ministry of Home Affairs, pp. 38-39.
30. Ibid., p. 40.

Chapter 3

BHUTAN
INDIA-BHUTAN RELATIONS IN THE NEXT TWO DECADES

Medha Bisht

INTRODUCTION

With land area of roughly 38,394 sq km, Bhutan is a small Himalayan kingdom with a total population of 6,95,819. Bhutan's population can be conveniently categorised into three groups: the Sharchops, Lhotshampas and the Ngalungs (often called Drukpas). While the Sharchops and the Ngalungs live in the Eastern and Western Bhutan respectively, Lhotshampas reside in the Southern region. The Ngalungs are the ruling group who control the monarchy and the National Assembly, with a prominent place in the economy. The Ngalungs migrated from Tibet and are also called Drukpas. They follow the Drukpa Kagyu school of Mahayana Buddhism.

Located between India and China, Bhutan is of strategic consequence for India's neighbourhood policy. These concerns pose a potential challenge in the coming years, with China's efforts to improve connectivity and enhance trade with South Asian countries. Even as internal pressures from the National Assembly of Bhutan are pacing up to resolve the disputed area, so far the boundary in Northwestern and Central Bhutan has not been demarcated, thus making the strategic Chumbi Valley—a vital tri-junction between Bhutan, India and China, which is 5 km from the Siliguri corridor—a space of contested aspirations. The Siliguri corridor, also known as the 'chicken's neck' connects India to Northeastern

India and Nepal to Bhutan. Bhutan and China last met on January 13, 2010, and completed their 19th round of boundary talks. Both sides decided on a joint field survey, in order to harmonise the reference points and names of the disputed areas. The focus of the stated joint-field survey was on the disputed areas in the Western sector which constitute the pastoral lands of Doklam, Charithang, Sinchulumpa and Dramana. This exclusive focus on the Northwestern sector is important due to its close proximity with the Chumbi Valley, which is of geostrategic importance for both India and China, because of its shared borders with Tibet and Indian state of Sikkim. Surrounded by China and India, two rising economies, the final decision on boundary between Bhutan and China can have unintended strategic consequences for the landlocked Himalayan kingdom.

Urgent and sensitive as this issue is, the historical equation between India and Bhutan has acted as a safety-valve and averted any strategic uncertainty in this regard. Over the last 60 years, Indian diplomacy has enabled deep political and economic ties with Bhutan and successfully tackled the challenges emanating from both internal (the political flux in Bhutan during the 1970s) and external factors (primarily China's claiming tactics and intrusion of non-state armed groups in to Bhutan from India's North East). The root of this bonhomie shared by both countries goes back to 1958, when Jawaharlal Nehru visited Bhutan on horse-back. During the visit, Nehru discussed prospects of Indo-Bhutan bilateral ties including controlled modernisation of Bhutan. According to Indian diplomat, Jagat Mehta, both Nehru and the King expressed their concerns about expansionist trends in Chinese foreign policy. Nehru reportedly prodded the King to take a break from Bhutan's traditional policy of isolation[1] and establish ties with its southern neighbour. The conscious decision of Bhutan to go South, was expedited by China's aggressive posturing on territorial issues particularly during the 1950s (1954, 1958 and 1961) when China published maps showing Bhutan's territory as part of China. While Bhutan, so far has followed the 'middle path' approach by taking equally cautious measures of not offending the Chinese, some potential challenges remain. These challenges may be triggered by the internal contradictions between Bhutan's efforts to liberalise at one level (politically and economically), and its penchant for preserving its conservative religious and cultural ethos at another.

The pointers to Bhutan's desire for opening up can be gauged from development in the economic and political front. With its first parliamentary elections held in 2008, Druk Phuensum Tshogpa (DPT) won by landslide victory as against the People's Democratic Party (PDP), bagging 45 out of 47 seats in the National Assembly (the lower house of the Parliament). Though democracy has not been firmly established in Bhutan, the country has a burgeoning civil society with 16 NGOs covering a wide range of issue areas. Presently, there are a total of nine newspapers and magazines in circulation and 37 publishing houses, supplemented by several radio stations and a public television system.

As per the Press Freedom Index 2010, published by Reporters without Borders, Bhutan's media freedom ratings have improved remarkably and Bhutan is ranked 64th among 178 countries—up from a lowly 157th in 2003. However, an important development is the domestic debate on the state funding for political parties. While one group primarily led by DPT, the ruling party, has argued for state funding of political parties, others, primarily Tsering Tobgay, the opposition leader who leads the PDP, has staunchly opposed it. The main point of contention has been that the established parties will always have an upper hand over the new or non-established ones as the ruling dispensation can divert state money for propaganda purposes to win the next elections. It is argued that the practice of state funding will favour incumbency factor, discouraging the growth of democratic politics. The proponents, however, argue that in the absence of state funding, business houses in Bhutan would play out their respective agendas and interests. Given that the societal fabric of Bhutan is dominated by a few business houses and there is a sharp urban-rural divide, there is great possibility, as is being argued for advancing the agendas that cater to personal and not national interests.

Economically, Bhutan has maintained rapid growth rate, exceeding 6.5 per cent since 2005. Its economic policy is encapsulated through the Economic Development Policy 2010, Fiscal Incentives 2010, and Foreign Direct Investment Policy 2010. Through these policies Bhutan hopes to boost private sector growth, attract foreign investment and create employment opportunities for national economic reliance. Eighty per cent of Bhutan's total trade is with India, which accounts for 92 per cent its exports and 72 per cent of its imports. Hydropower accounts for 45 per cent of total exports. As per the latest figures available, Bhutan's current account deficit expanded from 1.7 per cent of GDP to 14.3 per cent of GDP in 2009-2010. Its balance of payments flows continue to be dominated by developments in the hydropower sector and flows of official aid in grants and loans. With the Memorandum of Understanding (MoU) signed on December 2009, India decided to import 10,000 MW of power by 2020. While some projects are in progress, on others Detailed Project Reports (DPRs) are being prepared. The 2009 MoUs which encompassed issues such as health, prevention of illicit trafficking of narcotic drugs, civil aviation, information technology, agricultural research, cooperation on search and rescue operations and technical cooperation on environment related issues, illustrate that Bhutan-India relations is becoming even more comprehensive and broad based.

Robust and comprehensive as the bilateral relationship is, the strategic location of Bhutan nevertheless, as stated above, could pose some challenge. A key concern in the coming years will be China and how India and Bhutan cope with this externality. There are already concerns on the Indian side over increasing Chinese forays into Bhutanese territory and efforts to engage Bhutan at various fora in the past years. China has so far built six roads close to Bhutan's border towns in the north and northwest.[2] Since 2007, Chinese forces have also dismantled several unmanned posts in Bhutanese territory and according to a statement by the Secretary of International Boundaries of Bhutan, Dasho Pema Wangchuk, 'in 2009 Chinese soldiers had come seventeen times to the army posts of Bhutan'.[3] While such incursions may be regarded as typical Chinese pressure to keep Bhutan on the tenterhooks, it has deprived the locals of their forest resources and medicinal herbs. This has been repeatedly raised in the National Assembly of Bhutan and there is a great deal of pressure on the government to contain the intrusions. While on the one hand, China is playing hard ball on boundary issue with Bhutan; on the other they are trying to entice the Kingdom into its fold. Not surprisingly, a Chinese company has been given a contract to construct the world's tallest Buddha statue in Thimpu. Cultural exchanges between the two have taken ascendancy. In 2005, for the first time, Chinese cultural troupe visited Bhutan with an aim to build stronger ties between Bhutan and China. As a counter to India's strong relations with Bhutan, China has also been contributing to Bhutan's modernisation process by exporting farming and telecommunication equipment. The fifth session of the National Assembly debate, in May 2010, noted that China had already offered to invest in Bhutan on projects relating to health and education services.

INDIA-BHUTAN DIPLOMATIC ENGAGEMENT: AN OVERVIEW

Bhutan and India entered a new phase of partnership in 2007 when, at the insistence of Bhutan, the 1949 India-Bhutan Friendship Treaty was revised. This was a significant symbolic development as Article-II, which obliged Bhutan to be guided by the advice of India, was dropped. The revised Article-II states that 'both countries shall cooperate closely with each other on issues relating to their national interest. Neither Government shall allow the use of its territory for activities harmful to the national security and interest of the other'. The revised treaty recognises Bhutan's and 'sovereignty and territorial integrity'—elements, which were absent in the earlier version. The Treaty can also be called the framework for future interaction, highlighting cooperative partnership rather than a relationship built on financial dependence.

India-Bhutan relationship is perhaps the only bilateral engagement in South Asia which has stood the test of time. While Bhutan, all through these years, appreciated India for its economic assistance and cooperated actively on the security front, India for its part has been sensitive to Bhutan's developmental needs. At the official level, Bhutan has explicitly conveyed that India's interests will be safeguarded. The relationship has helped Bhutan shape a unique developmental trajectory based on Gross National Happiness (GNH). Bhutan's economy has grown substantially over the past years. The development cooperation between the two can be effectively divided into three significant phases. The first phase (1960-1980) focused on building the social and physical infrastructure. The second phase (1980-2000) saw substantive efforts towards democratisation and decentralisation. The third phase of the relationship is focussed on developing hydel projects, which has expanded into other areas such as information technology, disaster risk management, education, security and research cooperation.

Over the last few years, India-Bhutan cooperation covered a number of issue areas. On the educational front, India provides 50 scholarships annually to Bhutanese students to study in the institutes of higher learning in India. Another 50 scholarships are provided under the Colombo Plan. In the field of Defence, Indian Military Training Team (IMTRAT) trains and equips the Royal Bhutan Army and prepares its members for attending a number of training courses at the Indian military training establishments. The Royal Bhutan Army is Bhutan's military service and includes Royal Body Guards. Membership is voluntary and the minimum age for recruitment is 18. The standing army numbers about 8,000. Annual budget is about US$ 13.7 million, which accounts for 1.8 per cent of GDP.

India and Bhutan bilateral relations are characterized by the regular high level political interactions which are instrumental in strengthening bilateral ties. In the last three years there have been four visits by the fifth King of Bhutan, Khesar Namgyal Wangchuk including the latest one, when the King and HM Ashi Jetsun Pema, the Queen visited India in October 2011. The Indian External Affairs Minister also visited Bhutan on February 2011. A grant of Rs 15 crore was made and was directed towards areas related to education development and towards preservation of environmental and cultural heritage. The Prime Minister of Bhutan has paid four visits to India after 2008.

Interaction between the democratic institutions of the two countries such as the Parliament and Election Commission has also increased. The Bhutanese Speaker visited India from July 9-12, 2011, for the South Asian Association for Regional Cooperation (SAARC) Speaker's Conference. An MoU between the National Assembly and the Lok Sabha was signed by Smt. Meira Kumar, Speaker of the Lok Sabha and Lyonpo Jigme Tshultim, Speaker of the National Assembly of Bhutan on November 24, 2011. The purpose of the MoU is to provide a framework for enhanced partnership, cooperation and continuous interaction between the National Assembly of Bhutan and Lok Sabha of India. The Prime Minister of Bhutan was also invited to deliver Hiren Mukherjee Memorial Lecture at the Indian Parliament on 20 December 2011.

To strengthen people-to-people interaction both countries have paced up cross-cultural interaction. The second series of the Literary Festival 'Mountain Echoes' were held in Bhutan in May 2011. Events such as these have generated tremendous interest among the people of Bhutan including academia, journalists and students. These have widened the canvas of our bilateral cooperation.

India and Bhutan were also part to a sub-regional initiative on 'Climate Summit for Living Himalayas', which was held at Thimpu in November 2011. A framework on cooperation was signed by Bhutan, India, Bangladesh and Nepal to undertake regional cooperative actions on climate change.

Economically, India is the leading trade partner of Bhutan and a free trade regime exists between the two countries. The Agreement on Trade and Commerce signed between two countries in 2006 established the right of duty-free transit for Bhutanese merchandise for trade with a third country. Sixteen exit/entry points in India have been identified in the Agreement for Bhutan's country trade. The two countries have been meeting regularly at the secretary level, where issues related to border management are discussed. The seventh border meet was held in September 2011.

The internal security dimension has resurfaced in recent past. According to some reports, United Liberation Front of Assam, (ULFA) and National Democratic Front of Bodoland (NDFB) have been training the Communist Party of Bhutan (MLM) and its two wings, Bhutan Tiger Force and United Revolutionary Youth of Bhutan. According to some reports, the Communist Party of Bhutan-MLM was formed in the United Nations

(UN) Refugee Camps in Eastern Nepal and comprises of Bhutanese refugees of Nepali origin.[4] CPB-MLM aims to overthrow the regime in Bhutan, and has opposed the democratic elections in Bhutan. Moreover, the militant groups are reportedly using the Southern jungles of Bhutan as a transit route to enter Arunachal Pradesh. However, information and intelligence sharing along with hot pursuit of Northeast militant groups trying to establish bases in Southern Bhutan has raised the security bar to discourage such activities across the border.

Nevertheless, there have been some incidents of IED blasts in Bhutan in the last few years, such as the blasts at Phuentsholing on the eve of Royal wedding on October 10, 2011. These attacks have raised fears of a resurgence of militant activity in Bhutan, which is a concern for India as well. The United Revolutionary Front of Bhutan has taken the responsibility of the twin blasts in Southern Bhutan which took place in October 2011. The statement issued by URFB states: 'On the eve of Royal wedding, to draw the attention of the King Jigme Keshar Wangchuk towards the gross national sufferings of the Bhutanese people, the URFB ignited two explosives at Phuentsholing.'[5]

The NDFB (anti-talk faction) in the past two years has also raised the frequency of attacks on the Bhutanese security personnel. As per some inputs given by Indian intelligence, cited in an Indian media report, 'There are a number of mobile camps of anti-talk NDFB inside Bhutan. These camps are located close to the international border, and are very convenient for sneaking in and out for the militants.'[6]

The non-violent movement, Gorkha Janamukti Morcha (GJM), had also been linked to the Communist Party of Bhutan and some media reports allege that the movement is being supported by the Bhutan's Maoists.[7] Though GJM General Secretary, Roshan Giri, has negated such claims, the issue was a subject of discussion in the district border parleys held by both countries on periodic basis. With the signing of Gorkha Territorial Administration accord on July 2011 between GJM, the West Bengal government and the Central Government, the demand of statehood by ethnic minorities has been mollified; however, Bhutan would be cautiously watching the developments as demographic concentration of the (Gorkhas) Nepalese would increase the prospects of illegal migration across the porous border and the possible intrusion of anti-monarchy groups.

BHUTAN'S FOREIGN POLICY ENGAGEMENT

Bhutan has upscaled its sub-regional diplomacy with neighbouring countries. In 2010, Bhutan hosted the Sixteenth SAARC Summit in Thimpu. Not only did Bhutan successfully showcase itself to the outside world but also made special efforts to forge some consensus on the issue of climate change. The SAARC Development Fund (SDF) was officially launched on April 29, 2010 at Thimpu, which is also the Permanent Secretariat of SDF. Climate change mitigation and adaptation measures will be an area of growing concern for Bhutan in the years to come as melting glaciers, changing weather patterns, earthquakes and flood outbursts would pose a challenge to Bhutan's national development. According to recent findings, published in three reports by International Centre for Integrated Mountain Development, based in Kathmandu, Nepal's glaciers have shrunk by 21 per cent and those of Bhutan's by 22 per cent over the last 30 years.[8] At the Sixteenth SAARC Summit, the South Asian countries decided to formulate a common SAARC position on climate change, and contentious issues such as separate financing for adaptation and mitigation, and technology transfer were also discussed.

Bangladesh is Bhutan's second largest trading partner and both countries have shared a progressive relationship in the past. Trade, culture and environment have been identified as three nodal points for future cooperation. Transit has been an issue of some interest between both countries, where Bhutan has expressed interest for using the Mongla Port for trade with third countries. Presently Bhutan relies on Kolkata port for its trade with third countries. On the issue of transit, it has been deliberated that Banglabandha land port will be used as an entry and exit point for Bhutanese transit goods and the Teesta River could be used as the potential water way transit, particularly through the Doikhawa border in Lalmonirhat district. Bangladesh, on its part, has expressed keen interest in importing power from Bhutan. However, developments on these fronts are fluid and contingent on India's political gesture to facilitate sub-regional trade between both countries.

A visible trend between both countries is the absorption of Bangladeshi labourers in the growing construction industry in Bhutan. At present, officially, there are 500 Bangladeshi labourers in Bhutan and more workers can be brought in, in response to the demand of the construction industry. The exact number of illegal Bangladeshi workers in Bhutan may be more than this estimate.

Bhutan-Nepal relations have been frozen over the issue of refugees in the last few decades. Bhutan's policy on the issue of ethnic Nepalese can be gauged from the state ideology mentioned in the Sixth Five Year Plan of Bhutan (1987-1992). The Sixth Five Year Plan enunciates the 'One

Nation, One People' policy, which was aimed at creating a unified code of conduct for Bhutanese citizens. It could be said that this policy was considered necessary given the devolution process being initiated by the fourth King. The fact that ethnicity is intertwined with cultural identity is illustrated in Bhutan's Eighth Development Plan (1997-2002) which explicitly states, 'for Bhutan lacking military might or economic strength, cultural identity is the means to give security.'

In July 1993, the fourth King of Bhutan, Jigme Singye Wangchuk, and the then Nepalese Prime Minister, Girija Prasad Koirala, exchanged views on the refugee issue during the SAARC meeting in Dhaka. Both leaders decided to establish a Ministerial Joint Committee whose mandate revolved around three objectives: frst, to identify the different categories of people claiming to have come from Bhutan to the refugee camps in Eastern Nepal; second, to specify the positions of the two governments on each of these categories; and third, to arrive at a mutually acceptable agreement on each of these categories, which would provide the basis for the resolution of the problem.

In the subsequent talks between Nepal and Bhutan, a categorisation and verification scheme was devised, according to which the camp population was categorized into four groups. These consisted of: (i) bonafide Bhutanese refugees who were forcibly evicted; (ii) Bhutanese who had voluntarily migrated; (iii) non-Bhutanese; and (iv) Bhutanese who had committed crimes. In 2000, a Joint Verification Team was established, which accorded the 'Category One' refugees the right to repatriate. Certain conditions were placed on the other three categories of refugees and since then, the 'identity' of a bonafide Bhutanese citizen, has become a contentious issue. Though till date there have been 17 rounds of ministerial talks between Bhutan and Nepal, all of them have been unsuccessful in reaching an amicable solution. Prime Minister Thinley's statement in April 2011, that there was no place for third party intervention on the issue of refugees and that the repatriation will be limited to only a select category of people defined as 'bonafide', is indicative of the fact that there is little resilience in Bhutan's stated position on refugees. Also, with cultural assimilation having taken roots in Bhutan and with no open opposition or dissent within its territorial boundaries, Bhutan has decided to further its economic engagement with Nepal. Informal trade already exists between both countries. In fact, during 2008-2009, exports to Nepal stood around Nu 300 billion and import from Nepal stood at Nu 200 million.

Meanwhile, as part of the third country resettlement programme, which was initiated as a solution to manage refugees settled in the seven districts of Eastern Nepal, diaspora of ethnic Nepalese is now spread over eight countries (United States, Canada, Norway, Australia, New Zealand, Denmark, Netherland, and United Kingdom), with the largest numbers (42,000) in the United States. As per the latest figures, 50,000 refugees have been settled in Western countries. Out of the total 63,000 left in the camps, around 47,000 have expressed their desire for resettlement. This has, however, created some disquiet amongst the refugee leaders, who complain that the resettlement efforts might weaken or marginalise any future efforts towards repatriation of ethnic Nepalese to Bhutan. How the Bhutanese diaspora grows and organises itself at the international/transnational level is going to be an area of some interest in the coming years.

POTENTIAL CHALLENGES

As Bhutan is opening up at both political and economic levels, it would be pertinent to identify some potential challenges and their impact on Bhutan's foreign policy engagement.

Economic Model: A major challenge for Bhutan would be to mitigate the consequences of opening up its economy, i.e., providing liberal conditions for sustaining foreign investors, while at the same time encouraging indigenous private sector participation. The broad goals identified for economic development are self-reliance and full employment by 2020. A way through which Bhutan can respond to the changing economic environment is by putting performance requirements on investors to upgrade domestic skills and add value through internalisation of technical knowledge. However, a potential challenge could be an increase in cross-border population movement leading to undesirable social and political complications. Given that democracy is taking root and domestic political agendas in Bhutan can be influenced and manipulated by external powers, Bhutan will also have to be cautious of prioritising foreign investors as they often come along with political leanings.

Export-Import Imbalance in Hydel Trade: While India-Bhutan power cooperation has been perceived as an exemplary model in South Asia, challenges can emerge in the coming years. Bhutan's hydro generation capacity is seasonal and goes down to one-sixth of its total capacity during the lean season, which means that Bhutan has to import power from India during the winter months to meet its domestic demand. As per some estimates, the domestic winter demand has reached 237 MW and is expected to rise further to 308 MW by 2011.[9] Bhutan already imports power from India for domestic consumption for Eastern Bhutan during the winter months. However, according to the Royal Government of Bhutan's projection, by 2016, given the domestic needs, the import of electricity could cost Bhutan Nu 407.3 million. It has been argued that this would put excessive financial pressure on Bhutan. As a panacea to this challenge, in the last Eastern Regional Power Committee Meeting on June 20, 2011, Bhutan proposed to supply peaking power from its existing hydro-power plants to coincide with India's peaking hours in return for importing power in the off-peak period. Apart from this proposition, Bhutan has also emphasised that such an arrangement should have no financial implications for the net energy imported by Bhutan to meet its shortages. Some alternative proposals under deliberation are: (a) the netting off module, under which power would be imported at the same tariff as that which it is exported; (b) diversions of streams in Bhutan to Chukha and Tala, with an added addition of 30-40 MW; (c) power banking, where power can be exported tariff-free in summer to an energy bank, which can be later used in winter; and (d) construction of thermal plants based on gas and coal in Eastern Bhutan. While the first phase of power cooperation between both countries had been progressive, there is no certainty that a similar pattern will be replicated in the second phase.

Nature of Democratisation: The process of democratisation in Bhutan has been unique, as it was not demanded by the people but was initiated gradually by the fourth King himself. As there has been more continuity than change in Bhutan, it is too early to gauge any shifts in Bhutan's foreign policy engagements. While at present the fourth King himself determines the broad contours of Bhutan's foreign policy, this might not be the case in the coming years when democratic institutions take roots. It would be appropriate to state that in the coming 5-10 years, the process of democratisation in Bhutan will largely be associated with the issue of good governance. As development partnership is an important area in Indo-Bhutan relations, India's role and impact as a development facilitator would take centre-stage in national debates. The national media in Bhutan has been expressing concern over the domination of Indian construction companies in the Bhutanese market. There are also concerns being raised over the absence of Bhutanese contractors and the benefits that accrue from joint agreements on hydel power development.

Meanwhile, unlike the past, technical and quality problems associated with Indian projects are being played out by the national media. Recently, the Tala hydel project had some technical problems with four runners worth Nu 280 million showing cracks. Also, a 500 MW High Voltage cable worth Nu 40 million failed after being installed in the Tala power house. On the quality of construction, there are issues pertaining to increased sedimentation and design flaws. In comparison to the other hydel projects, Tala was also the worst hit by the floods caused by cyclone Aila in 2009. Thus, as is evident, with a strong media which substantively focuses on such issues, Indian development assistance will come under the radar of public debate and opinion.

Bilateral Relations with SAARC Countries: A potential shift in Bhutan's foreign policy in the coming years would be the way in which Bhutan manages its bilateral relations with the SAARC countries. Till now Bhutan has refrained from engaging with Pakistan, but this might change as both countries have been expressing their interest to cooperate closely. Issues of sharing information and good practices on hydel power generation, preservation of environment and disaster management amongst others, have been identified by both countries as potential areas of mutual cooperation. Bhutan is also keen on expanding trade and energy cooperation with Nepal and Bangladesh and as these sentiments are reciprocated from Bangladesh and Nepal too, these issues could become an important point for further cooperation in the years ahead. Though Bhutan has not had to countenance Indian intervention on the refugee issue, because India distanced itself from the issue, given the broad gamut of issues and actors, the latter should be equipped with an adequate response to the deal with the issue in response to the changing realities.

Bilateral Relations with non-SAARC Countries: Whether Bhutan has accepted India's security concerns as its own especially in relation to its approaches towards China, needs to be addressed in the broad context of Indo-Bhutan relations. The internal debate in Bhutan reveals that the National Assembly representatives have been pushing for a quick settlement of the border issue with China and normalise their bilateral relationship, as they consider non-resolution of the issue as being detrimental to their national security interests. According to the Bhutanese Ministry of Finance (*Annual Report 2009-10*), China is the already the fourth largest importer from Bhutan. With China's rail link stretching right up to Yatung, economic relations between the two countries could be formalised in future. With Japan and India as important economic players in Bhutan, growing Chinese investments in Bhutan could change the economic equation in the coming years.

Non-Traditional Challenges: Bhutan is most vulnerable to climate change as it the abode of Himalayan glaciers. There are challenges of glacial and dam bursts, which can flood downstream areas in Assam and Bangladesh. There are 677 glaciers and 2,674 glacial lakes in Bhutan out of which a total of 25 glacial lakes have been identified as potentially dangerous. Thorthomi glacier is a high risk glacier jeopardizing the valleys of Central Bhutan, particularly Punakha and Wangdiphodrang. The Basochu hydropower project and upcoming Punachangchu hydroprojects (both I and II) are located in the Punakha-Wangdiphodrang valley. In 2010, the former Environment and Forest Minister of India, Jairam Ramesh, had raised the issue of downstream impact of these projects, particularly on Assam, where there has been a lot of opposition to the dams being constructed upstream in Bhutan. The environmental impact of hydel projects in the near future could become a challenge for India-Bhutan relations in the coming years.

DRIVERS AND SCENARIOS 2030

Given the broad background outlined above a few scenarios for 2030 have been identified. The primary drivers for India-Bhutan relationship are: state of the economy, boundary dispute between China and Bhutan, and, democracy.

Drivers

State of the Economy: The economy of Bhutan has been identified as a critical driver as Bhutan is dependent, to a great extent, on external aid. Domestic endowment is highly dependent on hydel-power generation, which determines its natural proclivity towards India. While revenues from power exports have so far proved promising and made India-Bhutan power cooperation rewarding, the impact of climate change and hydel projects questions the sustainability of revenue inflow. Reduction of power exports will not only impact socio-economic development in Bhutan but also make it vulnerable to external aid, which can be motivated by vested political interests. Economic security of Bhutan is thus in Indian interest. The leverage which India exercises in monitoring this aspect perhaps becomes significant. Being a landlocked nation Bhutan is dependent on India for transit facilities to expand trade relations with third parties. India as a transit country thus has potential policy space for facilitating Bhutan's economic security. Along with power trade, Bhutan's integration with the regional neighbourhood and beyond will be rewarding in the long term. An economically strong Bhutan, which has integrated its economy with India, Bangladesh and Southeast Asian countries can, therefore, be a safety net for India-Bhutan relations by 2030.

Boundary dispute between China and Bhutan: Territorial security has been a core determinant of Bhutan's foreign policy. In the past, China's assertive claims have not only made the Himalayan kingdom insecure, they have also pushed it towards India—a move that has benefited Bhutan both economically and politically. Given the mutual trust embedded in India-Bhutan bilateral relation, Bhutan has refrained from playing the China card. However, once the boundary dispute is settled, China and Bhutan would establish formal diplomatic relations. Border trade would pick up. Also, tourism and cultural exchanges will be areas for further cooperation. China's influence on Bhutan's northwestern constituencies (Haa, Paro, Samste) would not only increase, but with a settled boundary China's offensive capabilities would make India's Siliguri corridor strategically vulnerable. In the absence of Bhutan-China boundary settlement, China would adopt claiming tactics on Bhutan's territory. India's security umbrella to Bhutan in this situation would play a decisive role on whether Bhutan chooses to go North.

Given the mutual trust embedded in India-Bhutan bilateral relation, Bhutan has refrained from playing the China card.

Democracy: The degree of democratisation is an important indicator in Bhutan as it can redefine and perpetuate certain perceptions at the domestic level. The democratisation drive would be triggered by a vociferous media, responsive democratic institutions in Bhutan and impact of Indian aid. If Indian aid benefits the people of Bhutan, its soft power can be rewarding in the long term; on the contrary, if Indian aid squeezes up the policy space for domestic stakeholders, perceptions inimical to India-Bhutan relationship can thwart the process of official engagement built on decades of trust and political goodwill. While there is little possibility that the monarch will take a backseat on foreign policy issues, consensus and debate on certain issue areas (related to development) will sharpen up and collective decision making will be strengthened. It is quite possible that the divide between rich and poor will widen, with wealth concentration in the hands of a few. The iniquitous distribution of wealth could create dissatisfaction, which will make certain pockets in Bhutan soft targets for anti-state mobilisation. Mobilisation could take place across ethnic lines, and spread across Southern and Eastern Bhutan. With open borders between India and Bhutan activity of insurgent groups could pace up, thus making the region highly conflict prone. Proximity of Eastern Bhutan to Tawang is an additional issue of concern for India. The threat to Indian security would be high if militant groups which are anti-India and Bhutan manage to consolidate bases in this area.

Based on these drivers, three scenarios for 2030 have been identified.

Scenario I: Bhutan Moves Further South

By 2030, Bhutan expands trade relations with Bangladesh and South East Asian countries. Bangladesh becomes the hub for facilitating trans-regional trade and connectivity enabling Bhutan to move beyond India. Border *haats*, cultural exchanges, trade and tourism between Southern and Eastern districts of Bhutan and India's Northeastern states and Bangladesh periodically take place. Bhutan's sub-regional diplomacy has become multi-layered encompassing official as well as people to people contacts. To manage threats from insurgent groups along the shared border, security cooperation between Bangladesh-India-Bhutan gets further strengthened.

India as a transit country remains vital for Bhutan's economic survival, and trade with Bangladesh and other third countries via the ports in either Kolkata or Bangladesh becomes a common feature. Water transit for goods is operationalised via the Teesta which flows through Sikkim and West Bengal.

A power grid between the three countries is established, which is beneficial to both Bangladesh and Bhutan. Observing the success of power grid, Nepal expresses its interest in exporting power, which further strengthens the idea of a South Asian regional grid. India, meanwhile, gets the wheeling charges for facilitating power exports to Bangladesh. However, the constituencies in Northwest Bhutan want equal regional development and, therefore, emphasize trade connectivity with Tibet. Due to the geographical location of Bhutan and the consequential benefits, integration further South is preferred.

However, limited amount of trade does exist between Bhutan and China, which is not of political concern for India. As some groups emphasise the need to establish trade and connectivity with China too, due to availability of infrastructure, the South seems to be natural choice for augmenting economic security. The political importance of India in Bhutan's foreign policy calculations makes the boundary dispute between China and Bhutan a subject of protracted discussion and Bhutan refuses to compromise on strategic disputed areas located in the Northwest of the country.

Bhutan's regional engagement with Bangladesh and Southeast Asian countries gives rise to exemplary sub-regional cooperation, with Bay of Bengal Initiative for Multi-Sectoral Technical and Economic Cooperation (BIMSTEC) playing an important role in trans-boundary connectivity.

Scenario II: Bhutan 'Balances' India with China

China and Bhutan by 2030 establish formal diplomatic ties. Bhutan adheres to 'One China' policy and supports China on the issue of Tibet at international fora. Economic relations between the two countries are growing, and China is facilitating infrastructural connectivity between Northwest Bhutan and Southern Tibet. China-Bhutan interaction has increased due to the settlement of boundary dispute. Given the boundary demarcation, there are pressures from Northwestern constituencies in Samste, Haa and Paro to increase trade and investment activities with China.

As construction of roads and other infrastructure requires investments, Chinese companies are invited for financial support. With pressures already inside Bhutan to diversify investment and trade partners, China with its economic might is a natural choice. With informal trade already existing between both countries, there are proposals floating for formalising the same. As India-China relations are strained, the Indian Army is deployed on important passes and regular patrols have been increased to deter any PLA intrusions.

While this complicates issues for Bhutan, Bhutanese media and civil society argue that they must not antagonise China and rather invite it to fill up the economic space left by India. Given the pace of democratisation, the views of National Assembly members are important. The fifth King believes in collective leadership and has decided to augment ties with China keeping balanced regional development in mind. India, for its part, has started covertly supporting certain parties from Southern and Eastern Bhutan. The level of mutual suspicion increases.

Scenario III: Limits of Democracy

Democracy has taken roots in Bhutan by 2030, with strong institutions and monitoring mechanisms in place. With the opening of democratic spaces and constitutional institutions building up, accountability of elected representatives has increased. While the role and place of the monarch, who continues to control the reins of foreign policy, remains strong, the national debate centres on domestic issues, primarily good governance. Bhutan is still a guided democracy. As India is the largest development financier of Bhutan, it has some presence in local debates and national discussions. Thus, by 2020, the role of Indian aid, and its unintended consequences, find a controversial place in election manifestoes and national politics of Bhutan.

By 2030, as India-Bhutan partnership on construction of hydro dam builds up, opposition in Assam grows stronger. The opposition primarily stems from Bhutan's upper riparian activities such as mining and dam construction. Meanwhile, in Bhutan there is a concern regarding Bangladeshi and Indian migrants which has become a topic for debate and discussion in the National Assembly. The Bhutan Communist Party manages to consolidate its base in Southern Bhutan. Though the Bhutanese Government does not change its policies towards ethnic groups, vote bank politics elevates local fears and perceptions from being marginal to central. Meanwhile pressures to resolve boundary dispute with China increase, as it impedes the development of Northwest Bhutan. While Bhutan-India bilateral relations are strong, there is some disquiet in domestic circles to diversify trade beyond India and invite foreign direct investments (FDI) from other countries. Export of power to Bangladesh becomes an important issue as there are voices criticising India for adopting a bilateral approach. This, they argue, has stymied the growth of private sector in Bhutan, as there is little incentive for private players to invest in hydel projects.

RECOMMENDATIONS

The scenarios above are a product of various factors interacting with each other. In 2011, Bhutan is on the threshold of change. While it wants to open up to foreign direct investment, give fillip to its own private sector, it also wants to keep its cultural identity intact. The role and place of the King is sacrosanct and any opposition on this ground is unacceptable. Bhutan, so far, has employed a policy of middle-path—it has been cautious about not antagonising China and, at the same time, strengthened cooperative ties with India. India's Bhutan policy has been generous and restrained. While India has facilitated economic growth in Bhutan, it has also followed a cautious policy of not rubbing Bhutan on the wrong side by remaining silent on the issue of ethnic Nepalese (Lhotshampas). In a nutshell, Bhutan-India relationship can be defined as beneficial bilateralism.

However, domestic realities are changing—new voices, new institutions, new perspectives, and new policies are coming up. In this scenario, the best policy path for India is to strengthen Bhutan's look-South policy and integrate Bhutan's economy with its own economy as well as that of Bangladesh. BIMSTEC can be an appropriate platform and should be utilised for the purpose. Policy overtures should be filtered with local perceptions and Bhutan-India energy cooperation should be expanded to Bangladesh. India has so far made inroads into Bhutan through economic security; facilitating a regional approach is perhaps the best way to sustain and generate further political good will. An absence of such an approach could change political equations in the long term and might give rise to scenarios (II and III) as identified above. Based on the scenarios, some recommendations are listed below.

- Trade and transit ties between Bhutan and Bangladesh should be encouraged by India. An energy grid between the three countries (Bhutan, Bangladesh and India) should be facilitated. India's consent on energy transit would provide a fillip to joint venture projects between Bhutan and Bangladesh, an issue which could facilitate sub-regional cooperation and trans-border connectivity.

- A combined impact assessment of hydel dams and potential possibilities of glacial lake outburst floods (GLOF) and landslide dam outburst floods (LDOF) should be undertaken by the Indo-Bhutan Joint Technical Team. Seismic and ecological concerns need to be addressed in a comprehensive way and made available for public scrutiny. Also, there is an absence of basin-wide studies to assess the cumulative impact of hydro power projects along the same river basin. This can be particularly alarming given the intensive construction of hydro-power projects by 2020. Thus, a basin-wide study, which includes the socio-environmental impact on Bhutan's extended neighbourhood, is imperative to alleviate local anxieties. Also, the National Environmental Commission in Bhutan, which has the primary responsibility of monitoring and enforcing mitigation measures to manage adverse environmental impact of hydel projects, lacks institutional capacity. Institutional capacity building on this front could be a prospective area of cooperation between both countries.

- India should be cautious of the growing public sentiment in North-West Bhutan, particularly the discontent amongst some National Assembly representatives regarding the location of IMTRAT headquarters in Haa district. Most of the forts in the district headquarters in Bhutan serve as administrative headquarter and house the monastic body. However, in Haa district, the fort is occupied by the IMTRAT. This issue has bred some discontent amongst the local people, who have been unhappy that the symbolic structure is being used by IMTRAT. Cultural sensitivities of small countries need to be handled seriously.

- Indian development aid should factor in local perceptions. Choice and selection of projects and their location has an important consequence for bilateral diplomacy. More emphasis should be laid on indirect costs, i.e., its impact on local environment, employment generation for local people and its impact on socio-economic upliftment. Bhutan is strategically important for India. Overlooking local sensitivities can create diplomatic baggage in the long run.

- India and Bhutan should continue with their policy of periodic political coordination and interaction at multiple levels. While both countries have strong institutional mechanisms at place (border, flood management, energy, etc.), people-to-people interaction through local border *haats* should be encouraged. Bhutan should also be encouraged to develop a paramilitary force along its border areas so that security cooperation with India can be further strengthened.

- Given that there are anxieties in India regarding the package deal—the land-for-land exchange proposition of the Chinese—the present development partnership between Bhutan and India should be directed towards meeting India's strategic concerns. The fact that the Northwestern sector is particularly important for India's security concerns should be conveyed to the Bhutanese establishment. However, Indian companies should be discouraged from investing in areas which have high diplomatic cost.

- It is in the long-term interest of Bhutan and India to factor in local perceptions and opinion and encourage people-to-people diplomacy. Cross-border interaction (economic and cultural) should be encouraged and Indian policy should be cautious of not squeezing the domestic space for Bhutanese stakeholders. Likewise, any local grievances should be factored in India-Bhutan economic engagement. Selecting/choosing projects for development aid should also be carefully prioritised by India.

- Sikkim should be a high priority area for the government. A mechanism should be set up by the Ministry of External Affairs and the Ministry of Defence where coordination and briefing on issues related to Chinese intrusions into Bhutanese territory and posturing by PLA forces along the border areas should be discussed. Inputs by 33 Corps, which is responsible for the security of Sikkim as well as Bhutan, should be particularly factored in.

- While Government of India's economic assistance has been a key area of the bilateral cooperation, both countries should also encourage cooperation through the private sector. Bhutan is on the threshold of new economic expansion in areas of tourism, IT, education and other services, where it is keen to set up institutions of international excellence and has invited FDI. A lot of Indian companies have expressed interest in the hydro-power sector in Bhutan. It will be in India's long term interest if there is a close partnership in the form of joint venture projects or FDI between the private sectors of our two countries. Since the Bhutanese market, as such, may be small for large or medium Indian corporates, business cooperation could focus on the companies from border states such as West Bengal and the Northeastern states where the joint venture companies could have a larger market, which would include Bhutan as well as neighbouring Indian states to enable them to be cost-effective and competitive.

Notes

1. Jagat Mehta, *Negotiating for India: Resolving Problems through Diplomacy*, New Delhi: Manohar, 2006, p. 46.
2. 'Bhutan-China Boundary Must be Finalised', *The Kuensel*, June 24, 2006, available at http://kuenselonline.com/2010/modules.php?name=News&file= article&sid=7125, accessed on January 11, 2012.
3. 'Border Talks Proposed for January 2010', *The Kuensel*, December 7, 2009, available at http://www.kuenselonline.com/modules.php?name=News&file=article &sid=14160, accessed on January 11, 2012.
4. See country report on Bhutan for the year 2008 at http:// http://www.satp.org/satporgtp/countries/bhutan/index.html, accessed on January 11, 2012.
5. Report on the official website of the Druk National Congress (DNC) available at http://www.bhutandnc.com/Sep-Nov,11.htm, accessed on January 11, 2012.
6. 'NDFB Militants Strike in Bhutan', *Times of India*, February 20, 2011, available at http://timesofindia.indiatimes.com/city/guwahati/NDFB-militants-strike-in-Bhutan/iplarticleshow/7535965.cms, accessed on January 11, 2012.
7. Pinak Priya Bhattacharya, 'Bhutan Maoists Aiding Gorkha stir?', January 25, 2009, available at http://articles.timesofindia.indiatimes.com/2009-01-25/kolkata/28001487_1_bhutanese-refugees-gorkhaland-gjm-leaders, accessed on January 11, 2012.
8. 'Where are the Snows of Yesterday?', Kuensel Online, November 26, 2011, available at http://www.kuenselonline.com/2011/?p=21760, and 'Scientists Say Himalayan Glaciers Melting', December 05, 2011, Sunday Mail, Adelaide, available at http://www.adelaidenow.com.au/scientists-say-himalayan-glacial-melting/story-e6frea6u-1226214607126, both accessed on January 23, 2012.
9. *Annual Report 2011*, Royal Monetary Authority of Bhutan, available at http://www.rma.org.bt/RMA%20Publication/Annual%20Report/annual%20report%202009-2010.pdf, accessed on January 23, 2012.

Chapter 4

CHINA
MANAGING INDIA-CHINA RELATIONS

Prashant Kumar Singh and Rumel Dahiya

INTRODUCTION

At broader level questions that confront India are: what does a strong China mean for India; and will Sino-Indian relations will be largely co-operative, confrontationist or a mixture of the two? The intentions behind China's military modernisation are unclear. China is also expanding its presence and influence in South Asia and the Indian Ocean Region. Chinese and Indian interests are beginning to overlap in a number of areas extending from the Pacific to Africa. Going forward, Indian policy-makers will need to develop an overarching framework which deals with elements of cooperation and competition in Sino-Indian relations. In the last few years, Sino-Indian relations have expanded considerably in all areas. Institutional framework for mutual cooperation has also been developed. However, from time to time, misunderstanding and lack of mutual trust manifest despite the massive increase in Sino-Indian trade and economic relationship. The challenges for India in the next few years will be to manage the complex relationship with China while protecting its national interests.

The answers to the research questions are based on research of available literature, interviews with around three dozen Indian and Chinese scholars[1] and detailed discussions within the IDSA. The nature of the questions is such that their answers cannot produce any definitive conclusions. The answers are an attempt to produce an analysis based on cogent argumentation by taking into account the political nature of questions. The issues of military modernisation and economic relations have been addressed in a political context rather than in technical terms.

INDIA-CHINA ECONOMIC RELATIONS

India's economic relations with China so far have primarily been guided by the logic of economics. However, in years to come, issues like continued trade imbalance and competition for depleting resources are likely to create friction in economic relationship. Geopolitical and geostrategic considerations are also likely to start impacting this relationship. In the next 5-10 years, China will continue to be India's single largest trading partner and there is unlikely to be any major change in the pattern of trade with India exporting raw materials and importing capital goods, machinery and components from China. India's own manufacturing sector may not take off so remarkably in next few years, such that all available minerals will be used indigenously. However, going forward, exportable surplus of raw materials is bound to come down with growing domestic demand and policies discouraging raw material exports.

It is difficult to visualise a scenario in which the bilateral trade will be more equitable any time soon. On the contrary, there is a likelihood that the trade imbalance will grow as the export of minerals from India declines and China makes a push for increasing exports of its plant, machinery and manufactured goods to compensate for impending slowdown in exports to Western markets. There is already a concern in India about growing trade imbalance favouring China, estimated to be about $20 billion which, if not corrected urgently, may be detrimental to sustain healthy bilateral trade relations. There is an increasing demand from India on China to facilitate larger imports from the former to address the issue of trade imbalance. India would be focusing on exporting precision engineering goods, IT services and pharmaceutical products to China.

Although there is great potential for bilateral trade between the two countries to grow further, this potential can only be realised if China permits imports from India without imposing non-tariff barriers, and trade imbalance is reduced. Trade imbalance is an issue that India and China need to address urgently because it is bound to become a serious issue in the domestic politics in India. In the face of growing disquiet against China dumping cheap and, at times, poor quality equipment and goods thus harming the interests of domestic industry, India may have to take unilateral measures to curb imports from China. This will create friction unless China acts swiftly to increase imports from India. The current pattern of India-China trade is clearly unsustainable.

Although China is apparently more open and receptive to addressing economic rather than political issues, there has not been much progress on resolving the issue of galloping trade deficit. China accepts that the trade deficit is a valid issue which needs to be taken care of. There seems to be a readiness to address the complaints that there is a pro-Western market bias in China and the Indian companies are disfavoured by government departments and agencies.

Under the free trade regime of the World Trade Organisation (WTO), there is little scope for using trade as a political weapon. It is unlikely that India can get China to address its political and security concerns more seriously by manipulating bilateral trade and by inserting some occasional conditionality. In fact, resolving trade related issues themselves will take a lot of energy and time.

It is logical to suggest that if the two countries work towards increasing their economic interdependence, the cost of conflict will also increase. For example, the US-China economic interdependence is so great that there is a compulsion to keep their political tensions under check. So is the case with the China-Japan relationship. Bilateral trade between China and Japan was about $339 billion in 2010. However, this has not refrained China from raising the ante with Japan on the sovereignty issue. In the case of economic relationship between India and China, it has moved away from a state of mutual indifference (during pre-1990s) to a stage where both countries are actively bargaining with each other.[2] However, despite impressive trade figures between the two countries, they can never reach the US-China level of interdependence. The nature of the two economies makes them competitive rather than complimentary. The political issues and mistrust between the two countries will continue to figure in their interaction.

So far, the political and the economic relations between the two countries seem to have been managed by different political and economic entities so far. It is likely that business and politics will cross each other's path in India-China relations at some stage. To take their mutual interdependence to a higher level, the two countries have to graduate from purely export-import based trade relations to investment-based relations in which they invest in each other's infrastructural projects and in projects where long-term investment is required. This will take care of the long-term scenario bring projected now, in which India's own manufacturing sector grows to absorb much of the raw material available in India and their bilateral trade volumes go down. At the same time, there is likely to be a greater political resistance to permitting Chinese companies' entry into critical areas. Poor performance of Chinese equipment may also be limiting imports and investments from China, if the experience of frequent breakdown at power plants at Yamunanagar and Khedar (near Hissar, Haryana) is any indication. Even issues related to acquisition of land for projects in which Chinese companies are involved may be opposed by people thus hampering smooth investment by Chinese companies.

Besides, if industrialisation in Tibet creates mass disaffection, as evoking 'loot-of-national-wealth' is a running theme in Tibetan nationalist discourse, then the security situation in Tibet may worsen and migration of Tibetans to India may accelerate, which may impact India-China relations. The Government needs to be watchful of the development process in Tibet and popular reactions to it.

It is imperative for both countries that deepening of mutual interdependence be based on equality of benefits. A high level of mutually beneficial economic interdependence between them can help in managing inevitable competition for securing resources, markets and trade with other countries. But even economic interdependence will not be sufficient to overcome fundamental differences arising out of imminent clash of national aspirations within the same geographical space. A rising China is not likely to accept a peer competitor in its neighbourhood. Geopolitical aspirations of the two countries and differences in value systems may always weigh upon bilateral relations.

No doubt, India-China relations have moved beyond the bilateral context of border dispute and the Tibet issue, arming and supporting Pakistan, and the expanding Chinese footprint in India's immediate neighbourhood. Now, the global context is also shaping the perceived competition between them. Rising trade volumes have not stopped China from creating additional friction points like stapled visas for residents of Jammu & Kashmir and damming of Brahmaputra. There is a view that prosperity has made China arrogant and more assertive, which is evident in during the recent global economic meltdown. The commentators have linked its recent assertion in South China Sea with its increased confidence in the wake of its successful handling of the meltdown. It may, however, be forced to moderate its behaviour in the face of combined push back by a number of its neighbours. There is also a possibility that China's leadership might be sensitive to any such unfavourable external environment and resort to enhanced coercive diplomacy against some of its neighbours to arrest this trend. In the Indian context, the concern is that the power differential that grows with continued faster growth in its economy may make China even more assertive and insensitive towards India, especially on the territorial and other issues. Unsavoury comments by the Chinese media regarding the news report about ONGC Videsh's foray into South China Sea reveals China's adversarial attitude towards India.

It is imperative, therefore, that while the economic component of the relationship should be given due importance, the larger issues of geopolitics and geostrategy should not be lost sight of. If China can take an overtly hostile position vis-à-vis Japan despite strong trade and investment relations, one can safely deduce that India-China economic relations, which are not as strong, will hardly prevent China from taking tough line against India where and when it feels necessary. These issues will become more pronounced if China's economic growth falters due to global economic factors resulting in reduced demand and structural deficiencies within its economic system. In such a scenario, China's leadership may find it necessary to externalise the resultant internal difficulties and pin the blame on its adversaries. The economic and security competition with India will become fierce and potential for conflict will rise in case India's rate of growth overtakes that of China on a sustained basis. Initially, China may leverage its huge reserves to outbid India externally for resources and friendship and stimulate demand internally but would hardly continue to play a losing game. That would generate strong impulse to show India its place.

In fact, even India's continued economic growth is not a given. India's growth can also falter in the face of governance deficit and political instability. But that would not be a cause of conflict since India's strategic culture does not support externalising its domestic problems. Therefore, economic interdependence will not be a major factor in shaping bilateral relations, rather the weakness of China's economy and higher growth of India's economy that may create deep frictions.

THE BORDER DISPUTE

So far there have been around 37 rounds of talks at various levels. In the 1980s, the two countries held eight rounds of vice-minister level talks; the Joint Working Group (JWG), instituted after Prime Minister Rajiv Gandhi's visit to China in 1988, has met 15 times; and the special representative mechanism, an outcome of Prime Minister Atal Bihari Vajpayee's visit in 2003, has held 14 rounds of talks. The last round of special representatives' talks took place in October 2010. All that these talks have managed to achieve are two CBM agreements signed in 1993 and 1996; the exchange of maps in the Central Sector in 2000; and the setting of political parameters for resolving the boundary dispute in 2005.

There is a perception that progress is too little and too slow. Some Indian analysts have argued that China has become less interested in resolving the boundary dispute and has recently become more assertive about its claims on Arunachal Pradesh, and particularly Tawang. They argue that China is uncomfortable with a rising India. They see a connection between the cementing of India-US relationship in 2005 and the hardening of China's position on Tawang and Arunachal Pradesh. In support of their argument, they cite China's hyper-reaction to Prime Minister Manmohan Singh's visit to Tawang and India giving the Dalai Lama permission to visit Tawang; China's objection to an Asian Development Bank loan for a project in Arunachal Pradesh; and the Chinese Ambassador's statement that Arunachal Pradesh is part of China, on the eve of the Chinese President Hu Jintao's visit to India in 2006.

They also cite the Chinese Foreign Minister's statement at a conference in Germany in 2007 that China's interpretation of the 'settled-principle-not-to-be-disturbed' clause in the agreement on political parameters for resolving the boundary dispute was different from that of India and characterise it as China's back-pedalling on the agreement. All this happened after India-US defence deal in 2005. They also argue that China's stance with regard to the status of Sikkim continues to be ambiguous even after having recognised it as part of India in 2003.[3] Thus, in a nutshell, they suggest that China seems disinclined to resolve the boundary dispute in order to keep India under constant strategic pressure. As Mohan Malik argues, 'An unsettled border provides China the strategic leverage to keep India uncertain about its intentions and nervous about its capabilities, while exposing India's vulnerabilities and weaknesses and ensuring New Delhi's 'good behaviour' on issues of vital concern to China. More importantly, unless and until Beijing succeeds in totally pacifying and Sinicizing Tibet as it has Inner Mongolia, China is unlikely to give up the 'bargaining chip' that an unsettled boundary vis-à-vis India provides it with.'[4]

In this context, a legitimate question arises: what is in India's interest—early resolution of the boundary dispute or resolution sometime in the future? There is no doubt that the dispute should be resolved at the earliest because the lingering boundary dispute puts pressure on the assessment of our security needs and affects India's self-perception. It perpetuates a mistrust which can flare up at any time in the future. Moreover, the perpetuation of the boundary dispute allows motivated external and internal stakeholders to interfere in the dispute. What needs to be determined is whether it is China's policy not to resolve the dispute except on its own terms; whether the lingering boundary dispute really harms us in strategic and defence terms; and whether we can live with this unresolved issue, and for how long? The bottom line is that it is not politically feasible for India to make any territorial concession and a rising China will not settle the issue unless clear disadvantages emerge for it due to its non-resolution.

There is also a view that the Indian side has been relatively keener on resolving the boundary dispute whereas the Chinese side has always argued for increasing cooperation between the two countries and putting the dispute on the backburner.[5] China's confidence in its power, the very low threat perception from India, and its willingness to wait till India is willing to accept the Chinese point of view, probably explain its somewhat stoic attitude towards the border problem. On the other hand, India has its own reasons for wanting to resolve the issue early. The deep-seated cartographic anxiety in national psyche, the psychological scars of the 1962 war, a hostile external and internal security environment, and the negative anti-India fallout of China-Pakistan relations make India treat the resolution of the boundary dispute as a priority issue, but 'not at any cost'. At the surface level, China's repeated insistence on leaving the boundary dispute for the future generations to resolve seems to be a deliberate Chinese move to keep India off balance. However, discussions with Chinese scholars reveal that China's insistence on not putting too much pressure on the resolution of the boundary dispute has to do with the Chinese realisation of complexities involved in this issue.

Regarding the 2005 agreement, Chinese scholars say that what the two countries have achieved on the boundary dispute after a long-drawn process of negotiation are only the political parameters. If this agreement is not honoured, the two countries will have nothing concrete in their hands regarding the resolution of the border dispute. The Chinese scholars argue that the Indian side should understand that principles cannot be very specific, and the settled-population-not-to-be-disturbed clause of the agreement is not as specific as the Indian side tends to believe. Moreover, they argue, it is the success of the special representative mechanism that, within two years of its institution, it could agree on the political parameters for the resolution of the boundary dispute.

Chinese scholars also argue that India should know that the second phase of the boundary talks in which the actual areas are to be identified is going to be a long drawn out and painstaking process and that the latter needs to have patience. They refute the charge that China does not want to resolve the boundary dispute so that it can keep India under strategic pressure. They counter it by saying that, firstly, this argument is an extension of China-containing-India theory; secondly, the unresolved boundary issue puts pressure on China also as it has its own area of insecurity in Tibet. If the boundary question is resolved successfully, China will be able to ask India to curb the activities of the Tibetan-Government-in-Exile and Tibetan Youth Congress (TYC) more firmly. Thirdly, they argue, it is not only in India that there is growing concern over the unresolved boundary dispute. Prime Minister Manmohan Singh's Tawang visit and India's permission for the Dalai Lama to visit Tawang is an issue that concerns the Chinese people and the Chinese government has had to continuously placate public opinion on the issue of Tawang. They further argue that the Government of India should be fully conscious of the fact that there are constituencies within Tibet which do not accept India's authority over Tawang and India's control over Tawang is an issue of concern for them. Fourthly, Tawang and Arunachal Pradesh are under Indian possession. Why will China not be desirous to resolve this issue? They claim that there is no ambiguity in Chinese understanding about the status of Sikkim. Fifthly, they say that China's position on Arunachal Pradesh and Tawang has been consistent all along. Recent Chinese assertions on Tawang and Arunachal Pradesh after 2005 have nothing to do with the improvement in Indo-US relations.

This argument is, of course, not valid. The Chinese claim that their position on Arunachal Pradesh and Tawang has always been the same is not correct. Many Chinese scholars are now arguing that Zhou Enlai and Deng Xiaoping never offered a package deal, never accepted India's claim in the Eastern sector, or the validity of the McMahon Line. But there is enough literature available to suggest that Arunachal Pradesh, and particularly Tawang, have gained prominence only recently in the Tibetan context. The literature on the border talks in the 1980s does not give any hint that China had any thoughts on Tawang.[6] It must be noted that Tawang has become a point of reference for the Chinese government to prove its pro-Tibetan credentials and score points over the Dalai Lama who has accepted India's authority over Tawang. Further, whether China's claims on Tawang and Arunachal Pradesh are a reaction to the Indo-US relationship is a tricky question. Although there may not be any direct link between the two developments (because the Indo-US relationship does not pose any threat to China)[7], the recent Chinese assertion on Tawang and Arunachal does have an indirect link with growing Indo-US cooperation.

India's augmentation of its military strength in the Northeast and its growing proximity to the US during the same period is being perceived as India's 'new forward policy' in China. Many Chinese experts claim that the military balance in the border areas favours India, and the present situation is somewhat akin to the developments in late 1950 when India was making forward deployments in the border areas and cooperating with the US on Tibet. Therefore, India needs to be pre-empted upfront by asserting territorial claims on Tawang and Arunachal Pradesh so that there is no misconception regarding Chinese weakness. In reality, however, there is a major asymmetry in China's favour, in deployable force levels, due to the differences in the state of infrastructure and resources available for inter-theatre strategic mobility of formations.

Although some Chinese scholars perceive that the resolution of the boundary dispute will definitely lead to a better security environment in Tibet and that the identification of the areas for actual give-and-take is not an easy task, this is a purely hypothetical position. There are many other drivers that determine the contours and contents of the complex Sino-Indian relations. The border dispute is just one factor. It is doubtful if the Chinese government, the People's Liberation Army (PLA) and the Communist Party of China (CPC) are really keen for an early border settlement. In fact, none of the major stakeholders within China appears to differ much from the others in its approach towards India, although PLA may be more hard-line than the others. All of them would like the issue to be resolved when overall power differential turns even more favourable for China so that it can drive a better bargain.

One could argue that a strong and powerful public opinion, perceptions of a weak leadership in China that lacks the courage for bold initiatives, and Tawang's politically motivated and hyped-up Tibet connection constrains China from according high priority to the resolution of the border dispute. Although the media in China is still substantially under state control, it has got some autonomy of late. The bloggers' community has become very influential in China and multiple voices are being raised on foreign policy issues. However, there is a common sentiment that when China is powerful again after a century of humiliation, why it should concede anything to India. Although the authority of the CPC remains unquestioned, it has its own insecurities. It is scared that concessions on boundary issues with India, Japan, Vietnam and other countries may provide a powerful pretext to dissenters to mobilise the people behind them. Besides, the present leadership lacks charisma and does not command the same respect and awe as the first and second generation leaders. Furthermore, the Chinese Government does not have a clear policy on any package deal. Ideally, it wants to keep Aksai Chin and wants India to recognise it as such. In addition, it seeks concessions from India on Tawang area of Arunachal Pradesh. Its argument is that India will still retain more than 50 per cent of total disputed territory. It may offer some concessions to India in the Western region (but not Aksai Chin), if India agrees to cede Tawang to China. But there is no consensus in China as to what to concede and how much to concede in any likely resolution of the boundary dispute. Claim on Tawang is justified by China on religious grounds but a possible claim on Kailash-Mansarovar by India on similar grounds figures nowhere in Chinese discourse. Obviously, claims on Tawang and Arunachal are linked to the larger question of relative position of the two countries in the global hierarchy of power.

As a Chinese scholar put it: 'It is difficult to concede anything when you are powerful and strong.' This is also true for India. The reality is that at present both the countries are strong and powerful enough to have this feeling of holding on firmly to what they have and strive to get back what they think was theirs and they have lost. The question is whether India can secure substantial concession in the Western sector without conceding to China what it considers important for itself in the Eastern sector. It is good that the two countries have decided to conduct the border talks in secrecy—learning lessons from the failure of border talks in 1950s. The Indian Government will have to settle the border dispute with China keeping in mind the sentiments of the people, the political parties and the Parliament.

All said and done, the CPC still has the capability of selling any such agreement to its public. Whether the future leadership will have the capacity to reverse the tide of nationalism and carry the public with it on this issue is an open question. There is also a question whether the Government of India will be able to generate the required national consensus on any concession to China. As an Indian respondent put it: what would be the Indian public's reaction to a new map of a 'beheaded India', which is what it will be if Aksai Chin is conceded to China in the North, or a 'bandaged arm India' if Tawang is conceded in the East? Will any government of the day be able to face a no-confidence motion on the issue of boundary settlement with China by making concessions?

Dealing with the public, the opposition parties and internal factional politics on this issue is more difficult for any ruling party in India than for the Chinese Government or the CPC as China's national obsession is presently with the US, Japan and Taiwan, and not with India, whereas in India people are very sensitive about China (and, of course, Pakistan). This is not to deny that the Chinese public perception about India is likely to change as India grows economically and militarily. The public reaction in the times of 24×7 media coverage and a hyperactive civil society, lack of political consensus, and the absence of clarity on acceptable parameters of the deal are the questions that India has to grapple with as much as China. It seems that the Chinese side is more aware of the gravity of these factors than the Indian side.

There is yet another weighty consideration which may be defining China's attitude on resolution of the boundary issue. Should India's security concerns vis-à-vis China ebb, it will be in a position to divert its resources towards internal development and shift sizable forces from the India-China border to the India-Pakistan border. That would strengthen India's position vis-a-vis Pakistan and reduce Pakistan's salience as a military balancer against India; developments which China cannot countenance.

Therefore, the question is not whether we should strive for the early resolution of the boundary dispute or not; rather, how well we can handle this issue. It will hardly serve any purpose to push for early resolution of the boundary issue under the present circumstances. The boundary issue, therefore, is likely to defy solution anytime soon. A solution that would be satisfactory from India's point of view ought to involve retention of areas occupied by China before the 1962 war and return of territory captured during war, with the status quo in the Central and the Eastern sectors. This does not seem likely now. But unsettled boundary dispute has the potential to provide China an excuse for initiating a conflict whose real motive will be to settle the issue of regional leadership.

TIBET

Whether India should have a fresh look at its Tibet policy is very closely related to the question of whether India should strive to resolve the boundary dispute with China at the earliest or should it be left to be addressed in the future. This question arises because of the growing Indian dissatisfaction over the slow pace of the boundary talks, China's close strategic relationship with Pakistan, and China's ambiguous stance on Jammu & Kashmir. The Indian disappointment is that India has made two unilateral concessions by extending its support to the 'One China policy' and accepting China's sovereignty over Tibet, but it has not received any concession from China in return on the border issue. In this context, some Indian analysts have argued that India should take a fresh look at its Tibet policy. They say that the Chinese non-compliance with 1954 agreement between the two countries and the continued presence of Tibetan refugees in India can become the pretext for reviewing India's Tibet policy. The thrust of their argument is that by revising its policy on Tibet, contesting the Chinese authority over Tibet and making China feel insecure in Tibet, India can pressurise China for the early resolution of the boundary dispute.

Against this backdrop, this chapter explores whether any such policy revision will serve any purpose and what would be the repercussions.

No country has ever recognised Tibet as an independent country. Britain had invented the principle of Chinese suzerainty and Tibetan autonomy. The basic motivation for this principle was to secure trade rights in Tibet and make Tibet a buffer. But after its withdrawal from India in 1947, Britain changed its position on Tibet. More recently, in 2008, David Miliband's statement on Tibet described Shimla Conference (1914), McMahon Line and suzerainty/autonomy differentiation as an anachronism, thus completely toeing the Chinese line on Tibet. The US has never recognised Tibet as an independent state, and it never considered Tibet as impacting its core national interests even at the height of the Cold War.[8] In the post-Cold War period, the European Parliament and some European governments have extended their moral support to the Tibetans. But again, there is a limit to this support as China is a strategic partner of the European Union. In short, Tibetans have had no effective international backing except on the human rights issue, which is receding in the background in the face of economic compulsions of the West. It is also unlikely that they will get any backing in the near future.

India's own position on Tibet has progressively favoured Chinese authority over Tibet since the 1954 agreement between the two countries in which India surrendered its extra-territorial rights in Tibet. Whatever little ambiguity regarding India's Tibet policy existed was removed by the India's declaration during Prime Minister A.B. Vajpayee's 2003 visit to China that the Tibetan Autonomous Region is part of Chinese territory. Therefore, if India wants to revise its Tibet policy and begin colouring Tibet differently on maps or issuing stapled visas to Tibetans from Tibet, then it will be the first country to challenge Chinese sovereignty over Tibet.

What would be the purpose of doing this? Should India take up the cause of Tibetan independence? Or, should it use its revised Tibet policy to force China's to address the boundary dispute more seriously, or for that matter reciprocate China's practice of issuing stapled visa to some of India's citizens? Firstly, there is no convincing political reason for India to bring about a drastic change in its six-decade old policy on Tibet. Taking up the Tibetan cause is meaningless when the Dalai Lama and the Tibetan-Government-in-Exile have themselves given up the demand for independence. Furthermore, there should be no illusion that the US and the countries of the European Union are waiting for India's revision of policy on Tibet to change their approach towards Tibet and support Tibetan independence. India should not underestimate China's economic leverages with the US and the EU and their deep mutual interdependence. The international mood is generally not in favour of separatist movements.

Secondly, can India really secure any meaningful concession on the border from China by creating a sense of insecurity in Tibet? This argument is based on the view that China would agree to resolve border problems only when it feels insecure. This argument is flawed. The demarcation of the border between Russia and China started after an agreement in 2004 and was completed in 2009. Likewise, China and Vietnam also completed demarcation of their land border in 2009. China resolved these issues when it was passing through the most confident phase of its national life, at least in modern times. On the other hand, China did not hesitate to go to war in the 1950s against the US in Korea and against India in 1962 when it was not that strong.

To assume that by revising its policy on Tibet, India can get China to address the boundary dispute on India's terms is far removed from the reality. If India modifies its policy on Tibet in anti-China terms, China will definitely retaliate and further harden its position on the territorial dispute. Any such move by India will justifiably reinforce the Chinese view that India is a following a 'new forward policy'. This situation may or may not bring the two countries to war, but it will certainly wreck whatever has been achieved by the two countries in their bilateral relations. This will create complications for India in Jammu and Kashmir. China is already shifting its position subtly. It is probably true that the shift in China's policy on J&K is linked to its worries about stability in Tibet. Any policy revision on Tibet by India will provoke China to formally drop its policy of neutrality over Kashmir further politicising and internationalising the Kashmir issue. Furthermore, India should expect China increasing its resistance and objections to India in various international forums like the United Nations Security Council (UNSC).

India can, however, take a more nuanced position by articulating the need for peaceful resolution of Tibetan issue by China domestically so that Tibetan refugees in India can return home with honour. China does not buy the argument presently that it is in its own interest to cut a deal with Dalai Lama. But India can articulate the need for protecting and preserving the cultural and religious autonomy of the Tibetan people and their ethnic identity for the sake of preventing Tibetans from agitating from its soil. It can also be argued that India's acceptance of Tibet as an integral part of China is predicated upon its being treated as an autonomous region. This position should, however, be taken only if China continues with its present position on J&K, or if it starts blocking flow of river waters; otherwise, it could be construed by China as an unnecessary and serious provocation. Judging from China's recent behaviour, including its assertiveness on border dispute, it would be safe to deduce that shadow of Tibet looms large on China's relationship with India. For the present, it is perhaps enough to stop reiterating our position on Tibet on every occasion. That would be sufficient to cause uncertainty in China about India's likely motives but without causing strong enough provocation. Non-iteration of Tibet being an integral part of China in the joint statement following the visit of China's Premier to New Delhi in December 2010 was the right thing to do. China would definitely not have liked it but would have got the not-so-subtle message of the need for reciprocity.

CHINA'S RESPONSE TO THE POST-DALAI LAMA SCENARIO

Since 1979, there have been two phases of Sino-Tibetan talks: the first in the 1980s till 1986-87, and the second from 2002 onwards. In these talks, China has not conceded an inch whereas the Dalai Lama has come around to accepting the Chinese position on a variety of issues: autonomy, the borders of Tibet, the withdrawal of the Chinese troops from Tibet, and adoption of the Hong Kong model. During the talks in the 1980s, Dalai Lama's representatives were pitching for autonomy in which only defence and foreign affairs were to be vested with the central authority. Now, the Dalai Lama has lowered his expectations and indicated that he will be satisfied with cultural and religious autonomy and some degree of political space.[9] However, the Chinese communist regime is extremely distrustful and disrespectful of Dalai Lama. The maximum the Dalai Lama can expect to get is permission to live in Beijing, the post of the Vice-president in National Peoples' Congress (the post he had before fleeing to India), and some degree of religious-cultural autonomy.

China does not bother much about the Tibetan community in exile. In fact, it has been insinuated that whenever China has entered into talks with the Dalai Lama, it has done so just to divert the international attention from some internal situation.[10] With time, the security concerns about threats to Tibet have waned in China's security perceptions. The mainstream Chinese argument is that the Tibet movement will have no future after the death of the present Dalai Lama. The exiled Tibetan community can, from time to time, cause embarrassment to China but it does not pose any serious threat to it. China's claims about ushering in growth and development in Tibet can be debated. The relative difference between the prosperity of Tibetans and the Han Chinese settled in Tibet can also be debated. But it is undeniable that Tibet is passing through a phase of unprecedented prosperity compared to the past. This has given rise to a Tibetan middle class that identifies with Chinese rule.[11] Over last 60 years, a section of young Tibetan communists has also emerged who occupy the lower and middle rungs of the CPC in Tibet. This section is dead against the Dalai Lama and his return.

Therefore, the post-Dalai Lama scenario may not be unfavourable for China. The reincarnation (the new Dalai Lama who will be a child) will take around 20 years to assume full charge. It is not sure whether he will become as adorable a face of the Tibetan movement as the present Dalai Lama. China seems quite assured that the Tibetan movement in exile will drastically weaken in the post-Dalai Lama period. Handover of political authority to Mr Sangay does not seem to have caused disquiet in China. Meanwhile, there should be no doubt that China will come up with its own Dalai Lama despite the fact that the legitimacy of successor chosen by China will always be questioned by majority of the Tibetans. But the presence of the two Dalai Lamas is likely to create a schism in the Tibetan spiritual universe in the long run.[12] It would not be an exaggeration, therefore, to say that China is optimistic about the post-Dalai Lama period. At the same time, continued unrest in Tibet—sometimes violent and other times expressed through self immolations—embarrasses Beijing. China may also find it to its dismay that in the absence of a revered figure to guide and control them, the young Tibetans may become more vocal and militant. Should that situation arise, China is likely to deal with the agitators sternly and demand tough action against them on Indian soil as well. The issue of the incarnation, if the successor is found in India, will also create friction between India and China, which may also result in conflict. The post-Dalai Lama period will, therefore, be full of uncertainties. The TYC, with a strong presence in Switzerland, USA and India is unlikely to give up the path of agitation from time to time even if its effectiveness cannot be predicted at this stage.

INDIA-CHINA RELATIONS IN SOUTH ASIAN, SOUTHEAST ASIAN AND EAST ASIAN CONTEXTS

As far as South Asia is concerned, China recognises that India enjoys a natural social, cultural, political and geographical advantage over it. China is not in a position to erase Indian influence in the region, although it has not stopped trying to do so. According to a Chinese scholar, China divides South Asian countries into two categories: Afghanistan, Pakistan and Nepal in one category, and Bhutan, Bangladesh, Sri Lanka and Maldives in the other. China has got strong security and political motives in Pakistan and Nepal, whereas mainly economic considerations prevail in Bangladesh and Sri Lanka. In fact, all the Chinese scholars and policy makers the author met and interacted with (during the preparation of this chapter) hardly had anything to say about Bhutan, Bangladesh, Sri Lanka and Maldives. They said that Bangladesh and Sri Lanka wanted a Chinese presence in their countries to boost their confidence, but China does not have any interest other than economic in these countries. In fact, China has a general appreciation for India's handling of its relationships with South Asian countries other than Pakistan. However, some articles in Chinese press often ridicule India for not being able to have friendly relations with any of its neighbours. Some India watchers in China remark that India has shed its old behavioural and attitudinal problems—characteristic of the much touted 'Indira doctrine'. Now the security scenario is generally favourable for India, and China does not want to disturb this. However, they argue that Nepal and Pakistan are critically important for the security and territorial integrity of China in Xinjiang and Tibet.

A friendly Pakistan is necessary for security and stability in Xinjiang since China is genuinely convinced about the important role that Pakistan can play in controlling terrorist activities in Xinjiang. The arrest and killing of some separatist leaders from Xinjiang in Pakistan are cited in this regard. But China understands that the Pakistan Government has limited capacity to control terrorists. At the same time, it is fearful that a disintegrated Pakistan or a Pakistan where the writ of the federal government does not run will become a safe haven for Uighur terrorists. Besides, China does not want to be identified as an anti-Islamist force in the world. Therefore, analysts in China argue that it maintains a distance from the American or Indian stance on terrorism in Pakistan and the non-state actors operating from Pakistani territory.

There is a view in China that the resolution of the boundary dispute or its becoming irrelevant will reduce Chinese temptation to support/use Pakistan against India. China has less economic incentives in Pakistan than in India. In this scenario, Pakistan will remain important for China only because of Xinjiang but lose its geo-strategic importance in the Indian context. Of course, US withdrawal from Afghanistan and strategic engagement between India and Afghanistan may impel China to engage more deeply in Afghanistan, which may, in turn, create an impulse for greater strategic cooperation between China and Pakistan to counter India's growing influence in Afghanistan.

Chinese policy makers and scholars are extremely sympathetic towards Pakistan and extremely concerned about the internal situation in Pakistan. They insist that the international community should not allow Pakistan to collapse because that would be disastrous for regional security.[13] However, they rule out sending troops into Pakistan to support the Pakistani regime in any scenario except under a UN-led mission. They say that China would extend economic and political assistance to Pakistan. However, it would not want to be trapped in the quagmire of Islamic Jihad. China realises its social, cultural, political and military limitations which will not allow it to replace the US in Af-Pak region or in South Asia at large. Nevertheless, China wants to stay engaged with Pakistan, and it has indicated its strong support for Pakistan and promised never to desert it, during one of the worst periods of political instability, economic hardship and diplomatic isolation that Pakistan has faced for a long time. China also deputed one of its most senior leaders, Vice Premier State Councillor Dai Bingguo to Islamabad in December 2011 to convey China's unshakable support to Islamabad.

Chinese South Asia experts claim that China has scaled down its military cooperation with Pakistan and unlike in the past, the China-Pakistan relationship is primarily guided by economic considerations today. This is, however, not borne out by facts. India continues to be a factor in China's Pakistan policy. Chinese South Asia experts do not mince words in saying that 'too weak a Pakistan' and 'too strong an India' are not good for the region. They also say that India should help in stabilising Pakistan. They basically imply that India should offer Pakistan a favourable deal on Kashmir. It is clear from their talk and views that China's relationship with Pakistan continues to have an anti-India 'balance of power' mindset. China is aware of India's sensitivities about its involvement in developing infrastructure projects in Pakistan occupied Kashmir (PoK), Gilgit Baltistan, Punjab and Sindh. Yet, it goes ahead unmindful of India's concerns. It also continues to provide military assistance, both conventional weapon platforms and components for strategic weapons. It can be safely deduced that China is unlikely to give up its support for Pakistan to balance India within South Asia.

The PLA has been influencing China's India Policy in the Pakistani context, its approach towards terrorism in South Asia and, above all, China's Tibet policy. China's transfer of missile and nuclear technology to Pakistan is an uncontested fact. Besides, it has been recorded that whenever India and Pakistan have come close to confrontation in the last 20 years, the Pakistani political and military leadership have paid visits to China and extracted positive political statements from the Chinese leadership about China-Pakistan friendship, seeking to put indirect pressure on India. Besides, it has also been noted that China has, in some cases, supplied military assistance to Pakistan in the immediate backdrop of the latter's crises with India.[14] In fact, contrary to some of the Chinese claims, no notable let-up has been observed in China's military cooperation with Pakistan. It continues and finds newer areas like supply of unmanned aircraft to Pakistan. Now, there are indications that the PLA might be taking interest in China's Nepal policy too. Geostrategic and security considerations continue to be the most important drivers of close Sino-Pakistan relations. This relationship presents India a potential two-front war threat. If Pakistan stops being a threat India's relative position vis-à-vis China would improve considerably.

Sino-Pakistan relationship serves as a model for other South Asian countries to emulate. There is an opinion in some states in India's neighbourhood that by following this model they could stand up to India and follow a more independent policy. They could also benefit economically and diplomatically by associating more closely with Beijing. China definitely wants a friendly regime or government in Nepal that curbs the activities of Tibetan refugees there. However, its expanding footprint in Nepal through cultural centres and a broadening engagement with political parties, military, media and academia suggests that its interests go beyond that. China, it seems, is positioning itself as an alternative to India in Nepal thereby reducing the salience of Indo-Nepal ties. Similar attempts continue to be made to lure Bangladesh, Sri Lanka and Maldives into China's sphere of influence. The obvious deduction is that China is not willing any more to accept India's undisputed influence in the region, which allows it enough confidence and freedom to intrude into India's 'legitimate' area of influence. Pakistan will continue to remain the most important tool in China's armour to checkmate India. It is, therefore, unlikely to encourage Pakistan to normalise its relations with India even as India-China relations remain constrained by the Sino-Pak nexus.

China considers the Asia-Pacific as its home-turf where it does not want to lose out to any other power, including the USA. Chinese scholars and the policy makers make very cautious and benign remarks about India-China relations in the Southeast Asian and East Asian contexts. They distrust US intentions and its agenda in the region. Much of the Chinese energy is spent (building partnerships) in the region aimed at countering the perceived anti-China strategies of the US. They argue that the US has an agenda to woo India into its fold and use it as a counterweight to China in the region, and that some Indian think tanks and media commentators are also endorsing the anti-China line peddled by the Americans. However, according to them, China is not worried because it knows that it is against Indian character to act as a pawn in the hands of any country. As an aspiring great power, it would not like to surrender its independent foreign policy to any other power. India has its own very legitimate reasons to improve its relations with Asia-Pacific countries. There may be some business competition in some sectors, but India's presence in the region does not threaten China in any way. This assessment might undergo a change if India is seen to be an active player in US policy of containing China. It is, therefore, essential that India builds good relations both with USA and China simultaneously. In fact, it will serve India's interests if India-US and India-China relations are better than US-China relations.

If we compare such benign interpretation of Indian presence in the region with India's actual capabilities, the Chinese experts seem to be adopting a very measured and academic stance. In reality, the Indian business and political presence in the region is no match for China's. India is unlikely to overtake China in economic terms in the region in foreseeable future as China is at least 25-30 years ahead of India in this respect. China has very deep political and social penetration in the region. India's cultural relationship with the region, which could have become a very useful tool of soft power, remains unexplored. The pace of India's economic integration with the region is very slow. There is no proper connectivity with the region. Furthermore, the countries of Southeast Asia are not so confident that India will either have the will or capability to be a counterweight to China in the region anytime soon. Vietnam and Singapore are perhaps exceptions in this regard. India's relations with East Asian countries like Japan, Korea and Taiwan are still evolving. Thus, at the moment, India is neither in a position to engage in a game of balance of power in the region, nor it is being treated at par with China by the regional countries. It is hoped that the situation may change by 2030, when India is likely to be more effectively engaged in the region.

Japan and Vietnam are distinctly uncomfortable with the growing Chinese assertiveness and have displayed a strong desire to forge a common front with India. The alignment is a work in progress and is likely to be looked at favourably by other countries of the region from Myanmar to Philippines and South Korea. India should take Japan's threat perceptions from China seriously despite strong economic engagement between the two. Recently, an Indian ship's presence closer to the South China Sea sparked off expression of displeasure from China, which was pretty much unwarranted given India's sovereign right of engagement with Vietnam for exploration activities in Vietnamese waters. This is well in line with the Chinese argument of benign engagement with countries in India's neighbourhood. China's assertion can be seen to be emanating from its growing military might and its intolerance of the presence of any outside force in its immediate neighbourhood. However, the situation may change if India develops robust defence ties with Japan, Vietnam, Singapore and Myanmar. This may either force China to rethink its policy of ignoring India's sensitivities in South Asia and the Indian Ocean Region or help India gain strategic counter-leverages in a region which China considers its sphere of influence. The idea of a regional military alliance to contain China may seem absurd at this point of time but it is not improbable. In fact, unless China moderates its ambitions and becomes more accommodative of the concerns of powers like India and Japan, formation of a military alliance might become necessary in the long run.

The fact remains, however, that China will do all it can diplomatically or by coercion to prevent India from developing strong defence ties with any of these countries. But the strategic trends in the region favour India at the moment. For example, Myanmar has already shown an inclination to engage with countries other than China more meaningfully. It has opened talks with Aung San Suu Kyi, declared amnesty for political prisoners and cancelled the Chinese-funded Myitsone Dam project. The USA is slowly warming up to Myanmar. Top leaders from Vietnam and Myanmar have recently made successful visits to India. Japan and India are seriously engaged in improving their bilateral strategic and economic relations. Hopefully, these developments will help dissuade China from adopting a policy of open confrontation with India, lest India should get into a tighter embrace with USA and Japan.

THE LIMITS OF COOPERATION ON GLOBAL ISSUES

The future of India-China cooperation at global and international forums on international issues is another valid area of enquiry. This enquiry is occasioned by China's open expression of irritation over the India-specific waiver by the NSG, its ambiguous position on India's claim for the permanent seat in the UNSC and its failed bid to block the ADB loan to India (in Arunachal Pradesh). Moreover, there is mutual resistance to each other's membership of the East Asia Summit (EAS), Shanghai Cooperation

Organisation (SCO) and SAARC. This kind of antipathy towards each other gives rise to speculations about how much the two countries can cooperate with each other. However, these examples have limited utility in explaining the dynamics of India-China relations. These examples only prove that there are political issues that divide them and prevent them from acknowledging each other's position at the regional and global levels. Beyond this, their behaviour towards each other has so far done no harm to either of them. Thus, these issues are too minor to upset the overall trajectory of India-China relations, unless of course this trend persists and leads to a complete disruption in bilateral relationship.

India received the NSG waiver and was finally admitted to the EAS too, despite China's reservations. China and India are observer states in SAARC and the SCO, respectively. There are indications that India may soon get full membership of the SCO with Russian backing and China has also started softening its attitude towards India's full membership of the SCO. As for India's claim to the UNSC seat, China does send ambiguous signals. But it is not that it is only China's approval that is needed for India's permanent membership of the UNSC, although India cannot get it unless China also supports it or at least abstains from voting. The overall state of cooperation between the two countries on international issues of common concern has been fairly good. They have cooperated and given voice to the Third World countries' concerns in the WTO talks on trade, and UN summits on climate. Some people opine that China does not always cooperate with India and the other developing countries on all issues and it cooperates either when its interests converge with those of the others, or if such cooperation saves it from obligations or opprobrium. This is perhaps true of all countries.

Importantly, engagement and cooperation on global or international issues are often carried out in multilateral institutional frameworks, which have their own dynamics and diplomatic instruments to deal with situations like China's last minute knee-jerk reaction to the NSG waiver for India or its attempt to block India's entry to the EAS or the ADB loan to India. India's record in handling issues with China in such forums has been impressive. As of now, China does not have ability to manipulate these bodies against India all by itself. It has succeeded only when it also had support from the USA, like on the issue of expansion of UNSC. However, if the power differential between the two countries grows further and the US makes common cause with it then China may be more successful in obstructing India's path. It is assessed, however, that the two countries will cooperate on global issues where their interests converge and will disagree where their interests diverge. There is a scope for cooperation in the process of Doha Round of trade talks, climate change dialogue, currency, labour rights and in recasting of international financial institutions like International Monetary Fund (IMF) and World Bank.

China is likely to prevent India's entry into UNSC as long as it can under one pretext or the other. It is likely to coax other nay-sayers to resist India's entry into the UNSC and utilise the differences over Japan's entry to delay reconstitution of UNSC. Degree of cooperation on global issues is unlikely to be a determining factor in bilateral relations. As of now, India appears to enjoy a better standing than China in global fora as indicated by election of the Indian representative as a member of the UN's Joint Inspection Unit in a direct contest against China's candidate. This outcome may have a sobering effect on China's behaviour since it is conscious of the need to develop its soft power.

IMPLICATIONS OF CHINESE MILITARY MODERNISATION FOR INDIA

China is expanding its military capabilities at a rapid pace. Modernisation of PLA Navy, Air Force, strategic weapons and development of asymmetric capabilities are a cause for concern. India must take cognizance of China's infrastructure development in the Tibet Autonomous Region (TAR) and also take note of reference to local war and limited war in the China's Defence White Paper of 2010. More recently, in the wake of ONGC Videsh's foray into the South China Sea for oil exploration, the Chinese media has also used threatening language. For last couple of years, reference to '1962' is increasingly being made in the Chinese media. Such assertion and articulation could not have been possible without the approval of the Chinese Government. Stability and cooperation with their neighbours is a strategic choice for both India and China. For China, continuous growth and prosperity is not simply a welfare commitment, it is also a strategic requirement for the survival of its present CPC-led regime. In the post-Mao era, the Chinese regime has been drawing its legitimacy from its commitment to growth and prosperity, not from any commitment to ensuring mass participation in governance. Therefore, China is unlikely to let its growth trajectory be disturbed unless its core interests are threatened. However, considering China's past and current strategic behaviour, military coercion will remain a tool in its armoury.

China is clear that American power is waning but is still formidable. There is a growing realisation both in China and the US that the latter will be less willing to get directly involved in a conflict between China and any other country. Even Japan, the US's closest military ally in the Asia-Pacific region, is conscious of this fact and is, therefore, keen to increase defence cooperation with Australia, India and Vietnam to check China. It is perhaps for this reason that the US is attempting to create a broad coalition to 'manage' China. Latest American moves to re-emphasise its continued interest in the Asia-Pacific, signing of a defence agreement to station troops on Australian soil, and unveiling of the air-sea battle concept are indicative of its desire to check China's geo-political and geo-strategic ambitions. There are reports to suggest that the US will position almost half of its naval assets, including aircraft carriers in Asia-Pacific in next two to three years. However, the state of US economy and its ability to prevent conflict in the Middle East/West Asia will determine the change in force redeployment.

Some Chinese scholars state: 'China has only two concerns; one is Taiwan and another is poverty'. China has not resorted to use of force to reunify Taiwan with the mainland, nor is it going to do so at least in the foreseeable future. This is despite the fact that reunification remains a national goal and a commitment of the Chinese regime to the Chinese nation. The point they make is when China is not ready to resort to force even in the straits, there is no compelling reason for China to do so against India. They argue also that the overall stable nature of India-China relations does not make for a scenario in which India might have to face any major military threat from China any time soon. This argument does not hold because China has refrained from use of force against Taiwan merely because it was not confident of handling US involvement in case of any conflict with Taiwan. It has, therefore, followed a policy of slow and incremental absorption of Taiwan.

The major challenge for India's physical security is the boundary dispute. The Chinese position has been to freeze this problem and cooperate in other fields. This position comes out very clearly in the statements of Chinese leaders and academic writings. In fact, the border dispute is kept alive through frequent intrusions. India's efforts to downplay the intrusions under the pretext of misperceptions about the LAC make it appear weak since China never uses the same excuse twice. China does not claim the boundary dispute as the single most important issue between India and China. India also does not make the resolution of the boundary dispute a pre-condition for normalising relations with China, though it accords much more seriousness to the issue than China. As per this argument, the only scenario in which a military conflict might take place is when China faces extreme insecurity and vulnerability in

Tibet and perceives a direct Indian hand in fomenting unrest in Tibet. In such a case, there could be a limited conflict on land borders.

Yet another scenario could be imminent disintegration of Pakistan as a result of a probable military confrontation with India. Considering that China's support to Pakistan and pressure on India never crossed verbal limits during 1965 and 1971 Indo-Pak wars, and it maintained neutrality during the Kargil conflict between India and Pakistan in 1999, this may be reassuring; China is, however, unlikely to countenance dismemberment of Pakistan through external involvement. The counter-argument is that India and China have overlapping spheres of influence: India is the only potential challenger to China's hegemony in Asia and it would be in China's interest to stop it from emerging as the real challenger; in China's perception India lacks both hard and soft power; there is an unresolved border issue and frequent violations are a regular feature; their political value systems are different; a degree of mutual distrust exists between them; India is reactive and not proactive; there is a power asymmetry in China's favour, and China keeps inventing new friction points on a regular basis, e.g., dams on Brahmaputra River, involvement in PoK, denial of visa to inhabitants of Arunachal Pradesh and J&K, opposition to India's membership of important institutions, possibility of physical disruption of Indian assets in South China Sea, and debilitating cyber attack on India's military or economic infrastructure, etc.

This argument leads one to think that whereas no single issue may be strong enough to cause a military conflict, a combination of two or more of these can provide a spark for an eventual military conflict even if such a conflict turns out to be limited in nature. As per this argument, possession of nuclear weapons by both sides does not guarantee peace since China intervened forcefully in the Korean conflict even when the US possessed nuclear weapons but it did not. Similarly, China did not shy away from conflict with the Soviet Union in 1969 when both states possessed nuclear weapons. Besides, it is not sure whether China views India's nuclear capability as credible.

It is true that cost of conflict in political and economic terms will be prohibitive today. However, an analysis of China's behaviour against Japan in 2010 and in South China Sea in 2011, and the fact that war is very much part of the Chinese discourse, indicate that it can either go to war when it thinks it necessary to prove a point or assert its power or when it has failed to get its way through means-other-than-war. China perceives that a collective threat from the USA, Japan and India would be dangerous for it, but that it will take time to materialise. It may end up calculating that India, being the weakest link in the emerging alliance at present, can and should be dissuaded from joining the alliance by persuasion, coercion, threat or punishment. The growing asymmetries in military balance may also embolden China to undertake a short and swift military operation to assert its power before India acquires formidable deterrence capability to make conflict a risky proposition for China. Its military strategy and doctrine have clearly defined tenets for application of force at the time of its own choosing; exploiting weakness of the enemy; when conditions are favourable, and; when there are reasonable chances of success. Moreover, in any military conflict the side that is confident of controlling the escalation ladder is more likely to initiate a conflict. China may perceive that it can control the escalation ladder, despite India having the capability to seriously disrupt China's maritime interests.

If the two countries successfully clinch an agreement on the border issue and are able to sell it to their respective people, the chances of conflict will get reduced. The Chinese economy is growing and this growth is bound to be reflected everywhere, even in its military capability. It is difficult to prove that China has aggressive intentions against India. But the degree of China's military modernisation and the level of infrastructure development in Tibet go unexplained and is much beyond the requirements of pacifying or developing Tibet. The Chinese PLA is known to be taking a tough anti-India line. It is credited with insisting on China preferring Pakistan over India and determining China's line on terrorism in South Asia. It is also a stakeholder in China's foreign policy. It is also not certain if other elements of the power structure in China see merit in developing benign and peaceful relations with India in decades ahead.

Despite scepticism in certain quarters about PLA's ability to influence CPC's India policy, the PLA remains an uncontrolled variable which could upset the apple cart defying common sense and political logic. No doubt, the political leadership of China since the ascendancy of Deng Xiaoping has tried hard to separate the PLA from political functions, and the political representation of the PLA in the Politburo and other bodies of the CPC has reduced noticeably over a period of time.[15] However, the PLA still retains its political character because the process of separation of the PLA from the Party is yet to be completed. Many scholars see the PLA as the Party's army and not so much as the country's army. Moreover, whereas the Politburo has only two members from the PLA, its membership in the Central Committee is disproportionately high, which reflects PLA's influence in the Party.

On the issue of nationalism and other issues where China's self-declared core interests are at stake, the PLA sees an independent and legitimate role for itself. The Taiwan Strait Crisis of 1996 was basically PLA's show. Recent Chinese assertions in South China Sea are again claimed to be PLA-guided. Furthermore, even at the political level, China has never shown aversion towards use of force whenever it was felt necessary, e.g., the Korean War (1953), war with India (1962), and war with Vietnam (1979). The PLA has established a Strategic Planning Division under a General Staff which shows that it will have a major say in China's strategic plans.

Furthermore, the Chinese defence White Papers have envisaged local border wars. Preparing for local wars has been defined as a defence priority in these papers. If we try to identify with whom they are envisaging local war, India is the most likely target because of the unresolved border dispute between the two countries and the problem in Tibet. The way China has transformed its military capabilities; has focused on long-range deployment military exercises; has built military infrastructure to mobilize at least half-a-million army in a short period in Tibet; and has developed high-tech acclimatisation facilities (which provide mountain acclimatisation conditions in the plains itself) make India concerned about the ultimate aim of all these preparations. The infrastructure-building in Tibet and, more importantly, focus on developing high-altitude acclimatisation facilities and deployment of more advanced missiles capable of targeting most of Indian territory directly concern India's security. It is difficult to dismiss these developments as routine capacity-building programmes and hence inconsequential for India considering the opaqueness of the PLA, China's continued military relations with Pakistan, China's objection to the Dalai Lama's presence in India, its increased assertion on Arunachal Pradesh, and the increased frequency of intrusion into Indian territory by the PLA. It is basically China's responsibility to address India's concerns about its military modernisation programme.

Although the Chinese foreign ministry is toeing a political line on India that is at variance with the generally observed PLA-inspired balance-of-power centric approach of China (in the Pakistani context), the former is yet to take full control of China's India policy. The policy continues to be influenced by the PLA. Perceived military weakness of India will incentivise the PLA to push for confrontation when the core interests of the two countries come in conflict. It continues to develop its military capabilities, and its intentions will require to be watched carefully.

While it is true that China does not articulate the boundary dispute with India as part of its core interests, the attitude of the PLA towards India warns about the possibility of China becoming insensitive towards India's concerns and interests if the present power asymmetry continues to increase unfavourably for India.[16]

KEY DRIVERS

Developments in Tibet, domestic economic and political situation in China, India's perception of China's engagement with its South Asian neighbours, and China's perception of India's own strength and relations with the powers considered hostile by China are the most important drivers in India-China relations. The future trajectory of their relations will depend on how security situation unfolds in Tibet, the trajectory of economic growth and political stability within China, and how they read each other's intentions—how India views China's relations with its South Asian neighbours and how China perceives India's relations with the US and Japan, and their mutual perceptions of comparative strengths and vulnerabilities.

Comparative economic growth of China and India will also have a bearing on bilateral relationship. As of now, China is clearly ahead of India as far as economic growth is concerned. Even if the global economic slowdown impacts China's growth it has huge capital reserves and a large unmet domestic demand. It can take mitigating measures like selective quantitative easing to support domestic industries and gradually increase domestic consumption. However, slowdown in manufacturing may result in rising unemployment, falling household consumption, unproductive overcapacity in manufacturing, rising non-performing assets of banks and financial institutions and domestic instability. Capacity of the new leadership, taking charge in 2012, to manage challenging economic, social and political environment may also be found deficient. On the other hand, a favourable international environment and better economic management may propel India's economic growth to overtake that of China. China may welcome India's growth as long as it is also grows equally robustly, since that would increase bilateral trade volumes. However, in case India overtakes China in economic growth and maintains it over a sustained period then the power differential between the two will start narrowing and China will start considering India a strong rival and a peer competitor. By present reckoning it is unlikely that the existing gap will narrow down in next two decades, in view of existing structural problems with India's economy and the governance deficit that it faces. However, such a situation cannot be ruled out altogether. Based on the interplay of these drivers, the following scenarios might unfold.

SCENARIOS IN 2030

Scenario I: The Himalayan Spring

In the post-Dalai Lama scenario, India abandons the Tibetan-Government-in-Exile. It does not permit the TYC-led resistance movement to operate in India. The Tibet issue is relegated to the margins of international politics. Tibet is stabilised by creating a large middle class which partakes of the Chinese prosperity and by granting some religious and cultural autonomy to the Tibetan monasteries. Thus, India ceases to be a strategic concern for China. Continuously increasing economic interdependence, the desire of avoiding military confrontation on part of the political leadership of the two countries, and China's sense of security in Tibet render the dispute irrelevant. This situation enables the two countries to identify a mutually agreed Line of Actual Control (LAC) in the middle sector. However, since the Tibet question still remains formally unresolved, the Tibetan community in exile and TYC remains present in India, and other constraints like strong public opinions and weak leadership persist; therefore, the two countries have been unable to clinch a full and final resolution of the problem.

Although India continues to hedge against China in Southeast Asia and East Asia, it does not set any ambitious diplomatic agenda for itself in the region and avoids entering into any US-led anti-China alliance. China also does not feel any necessity to build Pakistan-type relations with other South Asian countries. The two countries cooperate on global and international concerns. Episodes like China's objection to ADB loan to India in 2009 become a feature of the distant past. The two countries show a degree of cooperation on political issues in South Asian context like terrorism, jihadi forces/non-state actors in Pakistan and Afghanistan.

The CPC takes extra care of sustaining growth rate and reducing economic disparity among the various sections to counter the democratic dissenters who become ever more powerful; therefore China's foreign policy, increasingly dominated by the Ministry of Foreign Affairs and trade lobbies, does not want any confrontation with any neighbouring country, including India, which can derail China's growth. This realisation erodes PLA's formal position in the decision making process in general.

In this scenario, there is another more optimistic possibility. The international Tibetan movement loses its steam drastically in the post-Dalai Lama period. China's strategy to stabilise Tibet through economic development succeed. The Tibetans reconcile themselves to Chinese authority over time or they are largely resigned to their fate. India's crack down on the TYC puts to rest China's misgivings about India's hand in the Tibet problem. India accommodates China's claim on Tawang by granting a treaty-bound access to Tibetan and Chinese Buddhists to Tawang monastery. In this situation, China stops playing up the Tawang issue. Meanwhile, India's comprehensive national power and economic interdependence between India and China increase remarkably. Furthermore, although the competition between the US and China in Asia-Pacific intensifies, where Japan, Vietnam and other Asia-Pacific countries tighten their strategic relationship with the US, the South China Sea dispute does not lead to an armed conflict. India continues to follow a hedging policy vis-à-vis China and develops closer defence relations with countries of the region but it exercises a moderating influence. China is more accommodative of India's concerns to dissuade the latter from forging an alliance with the US. Meanwhile, the trade and the foreign ministry lobbies in China prevail over the PLA in China's India policy. The Party and the Government decide to extricate the PLA from India-related affairs and resolve the border dispute. India and China cooperate to stabilise Pakistan.

Scenario II: Fragile Stability

The difference between China and India in the field of economic growth and military power potential widen to the extent that China demonstrates a distinct insensitivity towards India's aspirations and claims. It is not interested in sharing Asian space with it at all. Irked by the Chinese behaviour, India continues to shelter the TYC and displays tolerance for its propaganda activities within India, though it does not fan any large-scale armed struggle in China. Despite a sustained growth trajectory and special focus on economic development of Tibet, China fails to mitigate the identity issue and intensifies persecution in Tibet. The Chinese are suspicious of Indian intentions considering India's flexibility towards the TYC. China raises its diplomatic decibel level on Tawang and Arunachal Pradesh. The two countries, particularly India, race against time to build military infrastructure on the border which brings the two militaries physically close to each other, giving rise to incidents of border intrusion as there is no legally defined boundary. The situation on the border becomes fragile. The CBMs between the two countries come under pressure.

The two countries actively play the game of balance of power and influence against each other: China in South Asia, and India in Southeast

Asia and the Asia-Pacific. In a reaction to the perceived or misperceived Indian hand in fast-deteriorating security situation in Tibet, China tightens its political and military relationship with Pakistan and sheds its neutrality on J&K. Moreover, it attempts to cultivate relations with Nepal, Bangladesh and Sri Lanka on the lines of its relations with Pakistan. India too becomes very vocal on the issues relating to Asia-Pacific and Southeast Asian countries and synchronises its policies with that of the US. It strives to increase its footprint in Central Asian countries, including Mongolia. However, China retains an upper hand in this game of balance of power and forces India to disengage from oil exploration in the South China Sea. India becomes seriously concerned about Chinese diplomatic aggression turning into a military transgression. Much of its diplomatic energy is invested in forestalling Chinese aggression.

China identifies less and less with the developing countries on the issues like climate change and world trade. Since India's economic progress remains stagnant for over a decade, India loses capability and interest in making common cause with China. Moreover, China's insensitive attitude towards the concerns of lower riparian states and its large-scale exploitation of Tibet's eco-system, which has environmental repercussions for the neighbouring countries, open up a new area of diplomatic confrontation between them in the global and regional forums.

However, as a matter of political choice, the two countries avoid direct military confrontation. In spite of enjoying relative economic and military superiority, China is not keen on military confrontation with India considering repercussions in international politics and negative implications for its growth trajectory. The leaders of the two countries rub shoulders with each other in other countries and international forums. China blocks India's entry into the UNSC and SCO. Diplomatic divergence becomes a regular feature in the interaction of the two countries in international forums. Mutual distrust grows and competition rather than cooperation defines their relationship.

Scenario III: Open Confrontation
China's strategy to stabilise Tibet through economic development fails completely. The repression of Tibetan nationalists' activities intensifies. The TYC assumes undisputed leadership of international Tibetan movement and instigates insurgency in Tibet leading China to perceive India's hand in the worsening security situation in Tibet. In this situation, the PLA takes over Tibet and asserts its views on India.

Frustration over unresolved status of the boundary, continued presence and fresh inflow of Tibetan refugees, and China's relentless military support for Pakistan define India's China policy. Political parties, military and the intelligence agencies openly accuse China of trying to undermine India. China too extends all-out support to Pakistan and anti-India non-state actors operating in the Northeast. After the American withdrawal from the Af-Pak region, China calls the shots in this region. Moreover, it forges close relations with anti-India democratic forces in other South Asian countries also. India also tries hard to prop up democratic forces in the neighbourhood.

India, which increases its overall strength admirably on the back of sustained economic growth, still lags behind China in relative terms, enters into a closer military relationship with the US, Vietnam and Japan thus increasing strategic pressure on China. The difference between China's rhetoric of peaceful rise and its action is unconvincing for its neighbours. Desperate to hold its number one position which is shifting to China, the US aggressively unites all the Asia-Pacific neighbours of China. China's economic growth slows down after it enters the middle income status and India's economic growth overtakes that of China on a sustained basis. Thus, the overall security scenario is grim for China. The overall security situation weighs heavy on economic interdependence between India and China (which in any way does not increase drastically). The cooperation between them in the international forums breaks down. China uses its position in the UNSC to punish India by blocking resolutions against Pakistani transgressions and the terrorist outfits operating from Pakistan. The strategic control of the waters of Brahmaputra River by China becomes a subject of acute concern for India. In this environment, all the CBMs collapse and the border witness periodic armed clashes between patrols.

The Chinese communist regime faces great internal political unrest and insecurity. It desperately needs some external outlets to transfer this insecurity. Meanwhile, India's patience vis-à-vis Pakistan sponsored terrorism runs out. It decides to punish Pakistan militarily, which is not tolerated by China. The PLA opens second front on the India's Northern border to save Pakistan—its all-weather friend and strategic asset—and to 'teach India a lesson' for what it perceives to be the latter's alleged hand in Tibet. The war objective of China is to snatch Tawang area from India and its political objective is to manage internal political instability.

RECOMMENDATIONS

- The above analysis brings out the fact that the Indian policy makers will need to keep a close watch on China's military modernisation and pursue cooperation in a pragmatic framework. While cooperation is undoubtedly preferable to conflict, it should also be kept in mind that the security dilemma in Sino-Indian relations has neither disappeared entirely nor is likely to. China's policy towards India for next decade or more is likely to be a mix of reasonableness, hard bargaining, no concession on relations with Pakistan or on border dispute, and occasional assertion of power. India's policy will also have to be nuanced.

- Given the turbulence in global economy and politics which is likely to continue for the foreseeable future, China's economic growth may also be affected which could lead to political and socio-economic instability over the next two decades. This may introduce some sense of uncertainty into Sino-Indian relations for which India will have to be prepared. Such uncertainty will accentuate if India's economic growth rate overtakes China's, giving rise to a sense of insecurity in the latter.

- The problems between India and China are unlikely to disappear in next two decades and India should learn to manage them and live with them. In the context of the boundary dispute, it should not be unduly worried about its resolution. Rather, it should guard its territory firmly and wait for the more favourable and opportune time. In case the international environment turns decidedly against China—chances of which seem remote at present due to extensive interdependencies that it has created with all major countries— then China may be more willing to improve relations with India. The unresolved status of the boundary should not be treated as a yardstick to measure success or prospects of cooperation with China. It is inadvisable to let too much hinge on the resolution of the boundary dispute or take any hurried decision on Tibet. Creative thinking will be required for handling the Tibetan refugees in the post-Dalai Lama period.

- India must continue with the border talks because these talks are vindication of India's position that the boundary dispute has a structural importance in India-China relations. Because of India's persistence on the resolution of the boundary dispute, China has started treating this dispute as a 'headache'. Recently, China's top foreign policy advisory body— Foreign Policy Advisory Group

(FPAG)—advocated for an early settlement of the long-running border dispute with India and argued that it should be treated as a priority issue in the Chinese Twelfth Five-Year Plan period.[17] India should increase its diplomatic interaction with the trade lobbies and the foreign ministry circles that have relatively soft attitude towards India in comparison with the PLA.

- However, it is unlikely that China will be prepared to legitimize the status quo anytime soon. It is difficult for India also to make any concession on the border issue. Therefore, the ideal situation would be to initiate new CBMs and strengthen its defences in the Northeastern region and in Ladakh and wait for the right time. After all, Russia and China resolved their border problem after 40 years of negotiation. Vietnam and China completed demarcation of their land border after 35 years of negotiation.

- India should advance its military infrastructure building without indulging in rhetoric because, going forward, this is likely to figure as an issue between the two countries. The Chinese have started arguing, albeit erroneously, that the military balance in the border regions of India is tilting in the latter's favour. It perceives the military build-up and infrastructure building by India in the border regions and the coming together of India and the US at the same time as a 'new forward policy'. They ignore the fact that China has developed much better infrastructure on its side which gives it an asymmetric advantage in terms of faster mobilisation and sustenance of forces. China displays a distinct lack of sensitivity to India's concerns in this regard. Therefore, military infrastructure building and implementing new CBMs with China should go hand in hand. India should be prepared to discuss this issue with China.

- The Government should facilitate a process of debate and discussion on the sensitive border issue and possible alternatives for dispute resolution in the think tanks, media and universities. Scholars, independent experts associated with the media, and the retired members of the diplomatic, bureaucratic and defence communities should be engaged in these debates. The purpose of this debate should be to elicit support for a negotiated settlement on the border without displaying any anxiety over the issue.

- As a next step, the Government should engage political parties and try to build a political consensus among important political players on this issue. This entire exercise will help the Government to formulate a clear policy on how to deal with China, on the basis of which it can handle its negotiations with China with much greater confidence.

- India should weigh whether there is any real strategic or political gains to be made by accepting some formulation like more open and free access to Kailash-Mansarovar in return for similar access for Tibetans to Tawang monastery. If not, forgetting the resolution of the boundary dispute and defending our actual possessions could also be a policy. This issue demands the attention and supervision of highest political leadership without which the final solution would be elusive.

- As far as India revising its Tibet policy is concerned, it will be definitely viewed as a hostile move and as India's 'new forward policy'. The fear of India revising its Tibet policy is more threatening than the actual revision. India can issue confusing and ambiguous statements on Tibet as quid pro quo for China's ambiguity over Kashmir. Posturing matters in shaping perceptions. There are lots of issues like Tibetan refugees, construction of dams in Tibet on international rivers, environmental concerns, human rights or religious persecution in Tibet, on which India can speak and can share the concerns of the other countries. India can legitimately raise the issue of the return of Tibetan refugees from India and put China in the dock on this question. However, the Tibetan refugees, the Tibetan-Government-in-Exile should not be leveraged beyond embarrassing China from time to time. India should avoid questioning the Chinese authority over Tibet unless China provokes it by revising its policy on J&K.

- Although the Government of India has handled the stapled visa issue very well and it seems that the pressure is working, this or any other similar kind of issue may come up in the future. India has to convey its red lines on any attempt by China to challenge its sovereignty and territorial integrity the moment such an attempt is made and before China establishes these as normal practice.

- On a different note, India should try to reintegrate itself with Tibet. India can propose a Himalayan economic zone which will comprise Tibet, Xinjiang, Nepal, Bhutan and the Indian Himalayan regions. It can propose to accord the TAR of China a 'Most Favoured Nation'-type status for Tibetan goods. For this, a proper mechanism will have to be devised to certify Tibetan goods. The common Buddhist heritage should be utilized for this reintegration. India could encourage religious tourism (to Buddhist sites in India) from China. The Ministry of Tourism can come up with special plans and packages in this regard. Furthermore, India can propose visa-free (or visa on arrival) access to the monastery of Tawang for the Tibetan Buddhists. The access should be limited only to the monastery in the manner the Indian pilgrims visit Kailash-Mansarovar in Tibet. All these moves will help India coming back on the Tibetan scene and alleviate Tibetan's sense of being a community under siege.

- India should follow a three-pronged policy to further consolidate its position in South Asia. It should be sensitive to the security concerns of the South Asian states, especially if such concerns are shared by majority population within the state in question. It should reintegrate the economies of its South Asian neighbours with its own. Once the economies of the South Asian countries acquire a certain level of relative parity, it should allow free movement of civilians for employment and other purposes on bilateral and multilateral basis.

- India should focus on establishing comprehensive and quality relations with regional countries (Southeast and East Asia). A stable, sound and quality relationship with these countries will automatically deliver benefits in the strategic realm. Closer defence relationship with Japan, Vietnam, Myanmar and Singapore will also be helpful. China's strategic behaviour should be constantly under watch and military ties with willing partners must be upgraded to deter any aggressive move by China in future. India should have better bilateral relations with both China and the US than they have with each other. A formal military alliance with the US or Japan should be shunned.

- India should engage China in as many regional forums as possible. Engaging China in more and more regional forums is a CBM in itself. However, India's entry into SCO should not be equated with China's entry into SAARC.

- The government should encourage high-level coordination and introduce an institutional mechanism between the Ministry of External Affairs and Ministry of Commerce and other concerned ministries to situate India-China economic relations in the right political context. Besides, it should pursue economic interdependence with China as a strategic choice. Long-term mutual investments in infrastructural projects should be encouraged.

- The issue of power asymmetry between India and China needs to be addressed at all costs. India as a big country and as an aspiring great power should not allow such asymmetry to persist which limits its options and degrades its deterrence capability. It should continuously strive to reduce its power distance with China. This approach should be adopted in a judicious manner, taking care not to upset overall macro-economic fundamentals of the country.

- Indian defence planners should beef up defences in Arunachal Pradesh, Ladakh and the joint Andaman and Nicobar command as a deterrent against Chinese moves in the Himalayas to address the worst case scenario. The Indian Navy has its advantages in the Indian Ocean and it will have this naval advantage over China at least for the next 10 years. This advantage needs to be maintained for a longer period. Asymmetries in deployable force levels, strategic weapons, surge capacity, technology application, cyber warfare, organisation and readiness of forces and jointness must be addressed forthwith to establish a credible deterrence.

- Since there is no legally recognised border or mutually agreed LAC, the incidents of intrusion and incursion will continue. Therefore, the two countries need to devise new CBMs to maintain peace and tranquillity on the border.

- In military diplomacy India needs to emulate China. Now militaries are not only meant for fighting, they are being used to build relationships among nations in other ways. China has, for example, focused on building military-to-military relations with other countries in recent years. Developing military soft power seems to be an integral part of China's military modernisation. India should realise the importance of military-to-military relations in creating an area of influence, especially in neighbouring countries. The opinion of the Defence Ministry and the armed forces should be given due weight in conducting diplomacy with China.

- It will be too much to expect that China will abandon its march to a great power status because others do not want it to. Yet, experience has shown that it can be forced to change its behaviour, at least temporarily, by a concerted response leveraging its sensitivity towards its international image. India also needs to be firm in articulating its concerns and positions vis-à-vis China in a spirit of full reciprocity and not be defensive. China must be made to understand that '1962' cannot be repeated; India has more friends than ever before and it has its red lines and core concerns which it will defend at all costs. It will judge China by its actions and not words. Simultaneously, India must also identify China's genuine fears and red lines and must not provoke China by crossing them deliberately.

NOTES

1. Those who were interviewed include Choekyang Wangchuk (Executive Director, Tibetan Parliamentary Research Centre), Mohan Guruswamy (Chairman, Centre for Policy Alternatives), Professor Madhu Bhalla (University of Delhi), Professor Alka Acharya (JNU), Professor D. Varaprasad (JNU), Professor Sujit Dutta (Jamia Millia Islamia University), Dr. Pankaj Jha (Associate Fellow, IDSA), Dr. Jabin Jacob (Senior Fellow, IPCS), Joe Thomas Karackattu (Associate Fellow, IDSA), S.S. Parmar (Research Fellow, IDSA), Dr. Hu Shisheng (CICIR, Beijing), Dr. Li Li (CICIR, Beijing), Rong Ying (Vice-President, CIIS), Professor Zhang Xiaoming (Peking University), Lora Saalman (Carnegie Foundation, Beijing), Ma Jiali (China Reform Group), Dr. Yang Xiaoping and Dr. Wu (CASS, Beijing), Professor Su Hao (Foreign Affairs University, Beijing), Li Ya (Deputy Director, Asian Affairs, Ministry of Foreign Affairs, Beijing), Professor Dingli Shen (Fudan University), Professor Du Yaokang (Fudan University), Professor Wang Dehua (Shanghai Academy of Social Sciences), Dr. Zhao Gancheng (Shanghai Institute of International Studies), Dr. Liu Zongyi (Shanghai Institute of International Studies), Dr. Shao Yuqun (Shanghai Institute of International Studies), Dr. Wang Weihua (Shanghai Institute of International Studies), Chen Lijun (Yunnan Academy of Social Sciences), Guo Suiyan (Yunnan Academy of Social Sciences), Tu Huazhong (Yunnan Academy of Social Sciences), Hu Juan (Yunnan Academy of Social Sciences), Deng Lan (Yunnan Academy of Social Sciences). The author would like to make it clear that he has preferred to provide the gist and crux of the interviews instead of the exact quotations keeping the essence of scholars' views intact. He would also like to make clear that there is overlapping of views among the scholars interviewed. Therefore, he has quoted only that scholar who emphasized the argument or point in question more prominently.

2. The author has been greatly benefited by his discussion with Joe Thomas Karackattu and his unpublished paper on this subject: 'The Salience of Interdependence in India-China Economic Relations, 1992-2008', Fellow paper presented at IDSA on 25 February 2011; manuscript under revision for publication.

3. Professor Sujit Dutta's research article 'Revisiting China's Territorial Claims on Arunachal', published in *Strategic Analysis*, Vol. 32, No. 4, 2008, covers many of these issues. In his article, Dutta presents China's positions on the eastern sector of the boundary, Arunachal Pradesh and Tawang. He makes a much nuanced academic case for India revising its Tibet policy in this article. His recent article— 'Managing and Engaging Rising China: India's Evolving Postures', *The Washington Quarterly*, Spring 2011—also covers contentious issues between India and China. In this article, he points at the hardening of China's position towards the boundary dispute. Apart from these very nuanced and academic articulations by Professor Dutta on this subject, a feeling of disappointment and frustration on the unresolved status of the

boundary dispute and on India's Tibet policy is quite visible in think tank seminars and conferences, and in the media also.

4. Mohan Malik, *China and India: Great Power Rivals*, London: First Forum Press, 2011, p. 25.

5. The tone of Indian media reports and columns, desperation expressed in the seminars and conferences and the fact that it is always Indian side which takes up this issue in any summit or dialogue with China, shape the author's conclusion. However, the Indian Government has never officially declared the resolution of the boundary dispute as a priority.

6. The reports and articles by Professor G.P. Deshpande extensively covered the border talks and issue in *Economic and Political Weekly* in 1980s. But there is no mention of Tawang in those writings as a special issue.

7. The Chinese interlocutors (mainly from the foreign ministry circles) go out of way to present a benign view of Indo-US relationship and do their level best to downplay any implications of this relationship for China. It seems that they got over from their initial knee-jerk reactions against this relationship around year 2005. They state, if at all, there is any anti-China agenda, it is more American than Indian. They are convinced that India as an aspiring great power will continue to chart its own independent course. This interpretation of Indo-US relations is coming partly from the changing political attitude towards India in the foreign ministry circles and the increasing influence of trade lobby. But the main source of such a considerate interpretation is definitely China's self-confidence and its importance for America. Moreover, on a Machiavellian note, the possibility of keeping India confused by making such kind and benevolent remarks cannot be ruled out also. This was the general and uniform expression of the Chinese scholars with whom the contributor met in China during his field trip.

8. Since the time when it first came into contact with Tibet during the Second World War, when it was supporting China's nationalist government, it has consciously avoided taking any steps that could have sent a wrong message to the nationalist government of China or offended the Communist government of China later. Although the CIA carried out some covert operations in China, they remained isolated and were not very effective. Particularly after its rapprochement with China in 1971, the US stopped mentioning Tibet in any form. Later after the Tiananmen Square episode in China in 1989 and after the disintegration of the USSR in 1991, when contradictions between China and the US started resurfacing, the Dalai Lama's international campaign—which he started in late 1980s—started receiving US congressional, media and human rights lobbies' support. But successive US presidents were very cautious not to offend China during this period. No US administration has ever questioned Tibet's status. For more details see Melvyn C. Goldstein, 'The United States, Tibet, and the Cold War', *Journal of Cold War Studies*, Vol. 8, No. 3, Summer 2006, pp. 145-164; Barry Sautman, 'The Tibet Issue in Post-Summit Sino-American Relations', *Pacific Affairs*, Vol. 72, No. 1, Spring, 1999, pp. 7-21; and Guangqiu Xu, 'The United States and the Tibet Issue', *Asian Survey*, Vol. 37, No. 11, November 1997, pp. 1062-1077.

9. Baogang He and Barry Sautman, 'The Politics of the Dalai Lama's New Initiative for Autonomy', *Pacific Affairs*, Vol. 78, No. 4, Winter 2005-2006, pp. 601-628.

10. Warren W. Smith, 'Sino-Tibetan Dialogue: Talks or Tourism?', 2004, available at www.mtac.gov.tw/pages/93/Warren%20Smith.pdf, accessed on January 20, 2012.

Meaningful talks with the Dalai Lama and his return have been a genuine concern only for the handful of liberals who think that the Tibetan movement will not collapse with the death of the Dalai Lama, and it is in the best interest of China to settle this issue once for all. But their credibility got a serious jolt after the riots in Lhasain 1987 and then in 2008.

11. Yinan Zhao and Bruce Lusignan in 'The Real Crux of Sino-Tibetan Relations', available at http//www.stanford.edu/class/e297a/The_Real_Crux_of_Sino-Tibetan_ Relations.doc&ei=GkTnT5qDGYvKrAfrr8CCCQ&usg=AFQjCNGtt4NUr5 GMNGNgxA4uT8iZw0hu4Q, accessed on October 12, 2011. The authors offer a balanced view of Chinese and Tibetan claims and counter-claims of social, economic and political claims.
12. On Tibet, India will have to grapple with two serious issues in the post 14th Dalai Lama period: the reincarnation of the Dalai Lama and the issue of the Karmapa. The question is where will the 14th Dalai Lama reincarnate as the 15th Dalai Lama—in Tibet or in some area of Arunachal Pradesh which shares Tibetan religious-cultural universe? It is very likely that there will be two Dalai Lamas after the present one: one found by the Chinese government and the other found by the Tibetan leadership in Dharamshala. If the Dharamshala leadership finds the reincarnation in Arunachal Pradesh, what would be the implications of this? One line of Chinese argument is that it would be bad for India-China relations. Their apprehension is that this reincarnation would be out of Chinese Government's reach and the Government would not be able to handle him the way it handled the Panchen Lama who was discovered in China by the Dalai Lama. The second Chinese line argues that if the reincarnation, were to be found in Arunachal Pradesh, it would further validate China's claim over Tawang and Arunachal Pradesh by re-establishing the Tawang-Tibet-China link. Furthermore, the Chinese sources claim that America would like the Karmapa to assume the leadership after the present Dalai Lama as the reincarnation will take 20-25 years to assume full charge. India has viewed the Karmapa with suspicion. It has to take a clear policy on the Karmapa.
13. Probably, this is the reason for which China has decided to establish direct relations with the influential and powerful elite families who control business, military and politics in Pakistan, as per a senior academic (Hu). He termed this 'an efficient policy'.
14. Please see, John Garver, 'China's Kashmir Policy', *India Review*, Vol. 3, No. 1, 2004, pp. 4-10.
15. Jagannath P. Panda, *China's Path to Power: Party, Military and the Politics of State Transition*, New Delhi: Pentagon Security International, 2010.
16. In recent times, China has shown a keen interest in the Indian Ocean and has expounded its vision for maintaining it as a peaceful zone. It is aware of the strategic advantage India enjoys in the Indian Ocean. Naval presence along with space and aviation technology are the areas where the Chinese concede that the Indians are in a position to compete with China. They are interested in India's Blue Water Navy plans. In fact, they realise that as of now, it is the Indian Navy that enjoys superiority in Indian Ocean. It is in this context that many in India have expressed their concerns about China's reported plans to acquire naval bases in Indian Ocean. However, there is no credible evidence that China will go the whole hog to do so or will be able to achieve this objective. There are strong and deep-seated reservations in China against acquiring foreign bases. Many Chinese take a principled position and view the acquiring of foreign bases as a kind of deviation from China's anti-imperialist policy.

Some argue that China does not have enough capacity to sustain these bases. Others argue that such moves will create complications in the South China Sea and East China Sea. These moves will force China's neighbours in Asia-Pacific into close embrace of the US (Shao). It seems that bad publicity works on China. Culturally, China's world-view is quite parochial. It defines its national interests in narrow terms and does not aspire for the UK or US-type global influence (Zakaria). All these factors constrain China against having foreign military bases. As of now, China is basically looking for its Gulf of Aden type naval access to protect its sea lanes on the high seas. There is no likelihood that China will acquire proper military bases in Indian Ocean at least in the foreseeable future. Things might change when it grows further.

17. Ananth Krishnan, 'China looks to rebalance ties with India, Pakistan', *The Hindu*, June 24, 2011, available at http://www.thehindu.com/news/international/article2132123.ece, last accessed November 24, 2011.

Chapter 5

MALDIVES
HARMONISING EFFORTS TO MITIGATE ADVERSE IMPACTS OF CLIMATE CHANGE AND ACHIEVE GROWTH

Anand Kumar

Maldives is strategically important for India because of its geographical proximity and strategic location in the Indian Ocean. It is also important because it is part of South Asia and has generally shared good relationship with India. Maldives is facing an existential threat from climate change, a fact that has been highlighted repeatedly by Maldivian leaders. Being a small country, it cannot deal with this threat alone and is looking for international cooperation. Located in close vicinity and sharing similar challenges from climate change, India is well-placed to cooperate with Maldives in this area. Climate change cooperation can thus be the basis for deepening of comprehensive and strategic partnership between the two countries.

In the Delhi High Level Conference on Climate Change and Technology Transfer in October 2009, the then President Nasheed of the Maldives smartly linked India's quest for a permanent seat in the United Nations Security Council (UNSC) with its role in addressing the issue of climate change. Nasheed described climate change to be a bigger threat than Islamic radicalism or piracy.[1] In his talks with Prime Minister Manmohan Singh in Delhi on October 9, 2009, Nasheed sought India's support for a common position on global warming.[2] The two leaders also discussed possibilities of evolving a common regional approach on climate change.

The policy makers of Maldives consider climate change as an existential threat. Thus there is a need to examine the following:

- How can India contribute towards mitigating the adverse impact of climate change on Maldives through bilateral and multi-lateral efforts?
- How can India help Maldives' economic growth without endangering its survival by harmonising its efforts with those of the Maldives?

A field visit from April 3 to April 17, 2011 was undertaken to collect first hand information on this issue by meeting top policy makers and other prominent persons from various walks of life.[3]

VULNERABILITIES OF MALDIVES TO CLIMATE CHANGE

It is believed that if sea level rise is triggered by global warming then the Maldives would be one of the first countries of the world to face submergence. In 2007, the UN's Intergovernmental Panel on Climate Change warned that a rise in sea levels of 18 to 59 centimetres by 2100 would be enough to make the country practically uninhabitable. After the Asian tsunami in 2004, up to 40 per cent of the Maldives was under water. About 100 people died, which spurred the authorities into thinking about relocating people from the lowest-lying islands. In Kandholhudhoo, about 60 per cent of residents have volunteered to evacuate within 15 years. In Maldives, 20 islands are experiencing erosion and 50 have problem of salt water contamination of fresh water supplies. (See Map 5.1 at the end of the chapter for likely impact of one meter sea level rise on various Maldivian islands.)

Maldives faces following vulnerabilities from climate change:

- Land loss and beach erosion
- Infrastructure damage
- Effect on tourism and fisheries
- Food security
- Coral reef biodiversity
- Fresh water resources
- Human health

THE DEBATE OVER CLIMATE CHANGE

The phenomenon of climate change is not universally accepted. One school of thought believes that climate change is definitely taking place.

They also predict impending doom for Maldives. According to them, if climate change continues at its present pace then the Maldivian islands would disappear from the face of the earth in some decades. The second school of thought, however, does not agree with the theory of climate change. They say that over centuries sea levels have remained more or less the same and they have not risen.[4] Hence, there is no fear of sea level rise and submergence of islands.

In Maldives, top policy makers, led by the President himself, are portraying it as a great threat to the country. The foreign ministry and environment ministry of Maldives also consider climate change a major issue. Maldivian leaders and analysts think that while the historical responsibility for environmental pollution cannot be ignored, developing countries can also not go on with business as usual. There is also a view that the over-emphasis on the climate issue is the government's strategy for getting foreign aid (in the opinion of J.J. Robinson, Editor *Minivan News*, based in Male). But the over-emphasis on climate issues has hurt the government. People are not interested in investing in a country which is going to sink. This realisation has, to some extent, mellowed the government's reactions. It now needs more foreign investment for financial stability. India has been trying to help the country by bringing in investment.

Policy/Approach of Maldives to Deal with Climate Change

As climate change is considered an existential threat for Maldives, it wants all countries to go carbon neutral. This can be achieved by cutting carbon emissions. Maldives wants a legally binding international treaty on climate change. It has itself embarked on an ambitious plan to become carbon neutral by the year 2020.[5] Now, Maldives wants to pursue the concept of 'Green Development'. On November 24, 2010, Maldives released its first ever carbon audit that calculates current and future emissions trajectories and recommends steps to reduce greenhouse gases and oil dependency.

DURBAN CLIMATE SUMMIT

The Durban Climate Summit in December 2011 was about laying the bedrock principles for future negotiations, rather than detailed plans of who will cut emissions and by how much. The 190 nations at the meet agreed to 'develop a new protocol, another legal instrument or agreed outcome with legal force'. The details are to be finalised by 2015, and all countries would have to start taking action by 2020. The Kyoto Protocol, which was to expire in 2012, was extended by another five years at the

Summit. It has also been proposed to set up a green climate fund for mitigation measures.[6]

India's Environment Minister, Jayanthi Natarajan, managed to bring in the word 'equity' into the long-term cooperation agreement. It ensured that any new deal would be subject to the provisions of the existing convention and that it would not force legally binding absolute emission cuts on India. What would be 'bound' was left open and the degree of 'binding' norms also needs to be defined.[7]

Small island states, which have a powerful moral presence in the climate talks, displayed their political inclinations towards the European Union (EU) when they tried to block India's demand that the United Nations (UN) review whether rich nations are meeting their commitments.[8] India can have one approach while participating in global climate summits. At the same time, it can also adopt a different and more understanding approach while dealing with countries like Maldives who are more susceptible to the vulnerabilities of climate change.

MITIGATING ADVERSE IMPACT THROUGH BILATERAL AND MULTI-LATERAL EFFORTS

One way of mitigating the adverse impact of climate change could be through international legal regimes. But there is little chance of harmonising the approaches of various countries. A consensus is unlikely in near future because the geography, demography and priorities of various countries are different. But the Maldivians are hopeful.

Mitigation measures taken by the Maldives alone will hardly have any impact on climate change since its carbon footprint is miniscule. Hence, it will be far more useful to focus on adaptation measures which will strengthen their ability to withstand the likely adverse impacts of climate change. While India and Maldives could face difficulty in adopting a common approach, India could help Maldives to adopt climate mitigation and adaptation measures.

Maldives is considering several projects to mitigate the effects of climate change. It is considering deploying green technologies. As part of adaptation measures, it is also considering constructing walls and dykes around inhabited islands. Parts of the capital, Male, are protected by a 3 m high wall that costs more than £30 million and took 14 years to build.[9] To raise the elevation of the islands, Maldives is considering importing river soil from Bangladesh. It is also considering deepening the Male harbour. Other options being explored are farming on the sea surface. Maldives is also poised to build a floating golf course and convention centre in what could be the first of a series of futuristic off-shore developments designed to counter the threat of global warming.

According to media reports, the Government of Maldives has signed a deal with a Dutch firm to investigate the feasibility of developing facilities that would be located among the 26 main atolls. It is likely that the company, Dutch Docklands, which has built floating islands in Dubai, will also look into the possibility of floating homes in the Maldives. The methods and procedures developed by the company for floating developments reduces the impact on underwater life and minimises the changes to coastal morphology.[10]

Following climate mitigation and adaptation measures were listed by the Maldivian Ministry of Home Affairs, Housing and Environment in 2001 in the First National Communication of the Republic of Maldives to the UNFCCC (see Table 5.1).[11]

Table 5.1: Climate Mitigation and Adaptation Measures Listed by Maldivian Government

Sl.No.	Vulnerability	Corrective Measures
1	Land loss and beach erosion	• Coastal Protection • Population Consolidation • Ban on coral mining
2	Infrastructure damage	• Protection of the International Airport • Upgrade existing domestic airports • Increase elevation in the future
3	Damage to coral reefs	• Reduction of human impacts on coral reefs • Assigning protection status for more reefs
4	Damage to Tourism Industry	• Coastal protection of resort islands • Reduce dependency on diving as a primary resort focus • Economy Diversification
5	Agriculture and Food Security	
6	Water Resources	• Protection of groundwater • Increasing the rainwater harvesting and storage capacity • Use of solar distillation • Management of storm water • Allocation of groundwater recharge areas in the islands
7	Capacity to adapt	• Human resource development • Institutional strengthening • Research and systematic observation • Public awareness and education • India can selectively participate in some of these activities

- Project for 'Strengthening National and Local Capacities for Effective Early Warning Dissemination and Response, 2008-2010'. This project aims at strengthening end-to-end early warning system for tsunami and other hazards.

- Project for 'Construction of Multi-Purpose Safe Shelter Building in Muli, 2008-2009'. It aims to provide the island community with vertical evacuation for around 1,000 residents in of natural disasters such as tsunami and flooding. The multi-purpose building will also be used for community and commercial activities during normal times.

In January 2011, the Ministry of Housing and Environment, Maldives, published the 'Survey of Climate Change Adaptation Measures in Maldives'. This report consists of a compendium of coastal adaptation options used in the Maldives based on a representative survey of 40 islands.

This assessment is divided into two broad groups of coastal adaptation measures: 'hard' and 'soft' engineering schemes. Hard engineering methods are traditional civil engineering works for reducing the impact of natural forces (e.g., sea walls). Soft engineering methods are used to enhance natural features or processes as an option for adaptation (e.g., beach replenishment).

Some of the key conclusions of the report can be summarised as follows.

a. The most widely used adaptation strategies are hard engineered solutions, particularly in inhabited islands. Soft adaptation measures are explicitly used only in resorts. Inhabited islands do not permit a number of soft adaptation measures due to cost involved. The most popular hard engineering measures are seawalls, breakwaters and groynes (strong, low sea walls). The most popular soft engineering solutions are beach replenishments and temporary seawalls or groynes.

b. Hard structures have been generally effective in serving their purpose but have unwarranted consequences for the beach system of islands.

c. The key issues with existing structures are poor design, poor construction, non-applicability of design to site conditions and over-design.

d. The main challenges for soft adaptation measures are the lack of awareness, their inability to mitigate immediate severe erosion and perception of ineffectiveness.

e. Soft measures have been highly successful in places where they have been implemented wholeheartedly, but there is a long way to before people in outer islands can be convinced to use them as explicit adaptation measures in their islands.

These coastal adaptation and other climate mitigation measures can be undertaken through multi-lateral or UN agencies. India can assist Maldives through these agencies wherever possible, or even ask its own reputed infrastructure Multi National Companies (MNCs) to do the job.

The United Nations Development Programme (UNDP) is supporting the efforts of the people of the Maldives aimed at mitigating the adverse impacts of natural disasters and climate change by focusing on enhancing their institutional and technical capacities, both at national and local levels. But this UN organisation has been mainly focusing on studies and creating guidelines for buildings, harbours, etc. They have also been engaged in awareness creation and bringing climate change adaptation in the priority of local bodies. They have two other projects that India could either consider joining or starting similar programmes.

HELPING GROWTH WITHOUT ENDANGERING SURVIVAL

India can help Maldives in its bid to deal with the problem of climate change by assisting in the adoption of green technologies. Maldives is keen to become carbon neutral. Maldives can achieve this objective by adopting green technology.

Maldives has sought the cooperation of India for accessing new technologies and data-gathering to tackle climate change. Earlier, the then Maldivian Vice-President (now President) Mohammaed Waheed Hassan had proposed that Asian countries should take a lead in seeking innovative and pragmatic solutions to complement the implementation of UNFCCC processes in dealing with challenges related to climate change.[12]

Being a nation of islands, the weather in Maldives is windy throughout the year. It also gets sufficient sunlight. But the country does not have the technology or resources to make either wind turbines or solar panels. On the other hand, several Indian corporates, such as Suzlon, are engaged in the manufacturing of wind turbines and solar panels. India can also join hands with the US in their efforts of deepening sea harbours, building walls, dykes, etc.

India can help in capacity building in Maldives. Climate change may result in huge funding for the likely 'victim' nations. The funds would be of use only if the country has the proper capacity to utilise them. India with its advance technology in many fields could be of help to Maldives.

The long-term goal of the Government is also to achieve sound agricultural growth inspite of the adverse ecological terrain in island nations in the Indian Ocean. Presently, most of the food in Maldives is imported. They are planning to use hydroponics for growing high-quality food, fruit and vegetable. Some of the schools in Addu are already doing it and supplying them to resorts.

POSSIBLE SCENARIOS

There can be three possible drivers for India's engagement with Maldives: magnitude of climate change; the internal political and economic situation in Maldives; and India's policy towards Maldives. These drivers are marked by high uncertainty and high impact.

Climate change is one of the most important concerns of Maldivian foreign policy. Maldives foreign policy will depend on how severely or mildly the country is affected by the phenomenon of climate change over next two decades. If the manifestation of climate change is serious in Maldives, then its economy will be seriously affected, which will have political implications. This will also cause domestic unrest and large-scale migration will take place to various destinations including India.

With a stable internal political and economic situation Maldives can focus on tackling the phenomenon of climate change in a mature way by emphasising on mitigation and adaptation measures. However, in a situation of political and economic uncertainty, the country might try to externalise the issue and resort to a blame game. This will hamper its efforts in adopting corrective measures and affect bilateral relations with India as well.

If India wants to deepen its relationship with Maldives then it has to address this major concern of Maldivian foreign policy. An economically strong and politically stable India would be better able to address Maldivian concerns and help in mitigation and adaptation measures. On the other hand, an economically weak and politically unstable India would not be able to give due attention to Maldives, leading to decline in bilateral relations.

LIKELY SCENARIOS TILL 2030

Scenario I: High Water Mark

In this scenario, the phenomenon of climate change remains manageable.

There is no major adverse impact. India involves itself in successful adaptation measures in Maldives. The Maldivian economy continues to grow. The country opts for greater democratisation. There is greater understanding between India and Maldives. Climate change is only an irritant in bilateral relations. India participates in economic growth, provides health services and learning.

Scenario II: Low Water Mark

Climate change hits Maldives hard. Global warming takes place at a higher rate than expected. Sea level rises by 10 cm by 2025. Cyclones, storms, etc., occur more frequently in the Indian Ocean. When the severe cyclone *Gazab* hits Maldives, four islands are submerged. Life in inhabited islands is paralysed and there is widespread disruption of infrastructure and life in Male. Coastal areas in India are also affected because of which India is unable to offer adequate disaster relief to Maldives. Widespread riots take place on the streets of Male and the Maldivian Government is unable to control the situation. The government of the day falls but the interim government is also does not succeed in ameliorating conditions of people. India is blamed for not helping Maldives and for not doing enough to mitigate climate change.

Scenario III: Muddled Waters

The issue remains high on the Maldivian agenda partly because the effects of climate change are visible. Maldives keeps the issue alive to extract external economic aid/assistance. India is sympathetic to Maldives and helps it with assistance in health, education and infrastructure. However, because of polarisation of the polity in Maldives some parties take an anti-India stand and try to develop closer economic relations with China and Saudi Arabia (See Map 5.2 in Appendix which shows islands where Chinese have shown interest recently). Radicalisation of society increases. Mutual suspicion grows and India-Maldives bilateral relations follow a sine curve.

It is most likely that the muddled water scenario will continue for some years. Though the present Government is perceived as no-threatening, the shifts and turns in Maldivian politics may change the strategic landscape to India's disadvantage. Besides, the country is also facing a major economic crisis. Sometime back, the country had a serious foreign currency crisis. To make matters worse, former President Gayoom is back in politics. The growth of religious extremism has added to political uncertainty.

IMPORTANT BILATERAL ENGAGEMENTS ON CLIMATE CHANGE

1. Ambassador Shyam Saran, the then Special Envoy of the Prime Minister on Climate Change, visited Maldives in 2009 to exchange views on India's approach towards Copenhagen. It helped tremendously in having a free flow of views/ideas between the two sides leading towards the outcome in Copenhagen.
2. India has been participating in conferences and seminars, both bilateral as well as regional, that are being organised in Maldives. India's Bureau of Energy Efficiency has pledged assistance in capacity building to the Maldives for making it carbon neutral by 2020. Their proposal is being examined by the Ministry of External Affairs.
3. India has been contributing regularly to various activities pertaining to fighting climate change. Financial assistance to the Coastal (Disaster) Management Centre has been particularly significant. India is the main contributor to this Centre which is being established in Maldives.
4. Former President Mohamed Nasheed was invited to be the Chief Guest of the 'Delhi High Level Conference on Climate Change: Technology Development and Transfer' in October 2009. This ensured that India recognizes the efforts of Maldives to represent the issues afflicting small and vulnerable islands.

RECOMMENDATIONS

Climate change offers an opportunity for India to enhance its cooperation with Maldives, increase its footprint in the region and revitalise its foreign policy. At the same time, India should be prepared to accept climate refugees from Maldives. This would have an economic cost for India. It can help Maldives in mitigating the adverse impact of climate change and also in its economic growth without endangering its survival. For this purpose following recommendations can be made.

- Maldives is considering use of green technologies to reduce carbon emission. A large part of the carbon emissions in Maldives comes from diesel generators that the country uses for power generation. India can help Maldives to develop alternate energy. The concept of alternative energy can work for Maldives because it has small economy and limited energy needs. India can help Maldives in exploiting solar and wind energy (Indian corporates like Suzlon have significant expertise in the area).

- India can also help in mitigating infrastructure damage. Protection of the Male International Airport is of utmost priority to Maldives because this is the only gateway through which international tourists arrive. Though an Indian company—GMR—has already taken the contract to build a new airport in the same place and operate the existing one, it should be ensured that the airport functions in a proper way and no avoidable controversy is created.
- India can also help upgrade two other existing domestic airports.
- Economic diversification: Maldives is greatly dependent on tourism and the fishing industry. But fishery exports have been falling. Thus tourism remains the only major foreign exchange earner for the country. Indian software companies and other corporates can help Maldives in its economic diversification efforts.
- Ship-building has been an important industry in Maldives. Indian companies can launch joint ventures with Maldives in this area and contribute to the country's economic growth.
- Maldives can be developed as an international centre for conferences.
- Agriculture and Food security: Maldives has very limited capacity for growing food. Most items it consumes are imported. However, the country has been trying to grow food through hydroponics. The agricultural technologies in India are quite advanced. The country also has a number of research institutions. India can think of developing links with Maldivian institutions in agricultural field so that food security in Maldives could be enhanced.
- India can also help Maldives in protecting its water resources. Technology for rainwater harvesting and increasing storage capacity can be shared with Maldives. We can also help protect ground water from contamination.
- It is essential that Maldives develops sufficient capacity to adapt to climate change. In this India can help in developing human resources, institutions research and systematic observation of the climate change phenomenon.
- India can help in strengthening national and local capacities for effective early warning dissemination and response for tsunami and other hazards.
- For a country like Maldives, which faces adverse weather conditions, the construction of multi-purpose safe shelters can be useful. These buildings are used for vertical evacuation at the time

of natural disasters such as tsunami and flooding. These buildings can also be used for community and commercial activities during normal times. India can help construct such shelters.

- India can involve its multi-nationals like Larsen & Tubro and others who have established their credentials in the area of infrastructure development. They can be asked to take up coastal adaptation and other climate mitigation measures like construction of sea walls, etc., if necessary, with an element of interest rate subsidy.

- A number of proposals have been considered but not seen much progress primarily due to lack of a cohesive policy of tackling the various issues related to the climate change in Maldives. The current stakeholders (on Indian side) are the Ministry of External Affairs, Ministry of Environment and Forests, Bureau of Energy Efficiency, private investors and The Energy and Resources Institute (TERI). It would be useful if a five-year perspective plan on climate change cooperation with Maldives could be prepared with assured funding for achieving the desired impact. It can be termed the 'Climate Change Dialogue between India and Maldives' and have at least two annual meetings—one in Maldives and the other in India—at the Secretary/Ministerial level.

NOTES

1. 'Maldives President Says Melting Glaciers can Result in Serious Conflicts', *Thaindian News*, October 23, 2009, available at http://www.thaindian.com/newsportal/india-news/maldives-president-says-melting-glaciers-can-result-in-serious-conflicts_100264777.html, accessed on November 12, 2009.
2. 'Maldives President Discusses Climate Change with Manmohan Singh', *Thaindian News*, available at http://www.thaindian.com/newsportal/enviornment/maldives-president-discusses-climate-change-with-manmohan-singh_100264053.html, accessed on November 12, 2011.
3. Officials at the Foreign Ministry of Maldives, President's office, Housing and Environment Ministry, Peoples Majlis (Parliament), offices of three leading newspapers and some NGOs were interviewed for this study during April 3-17, 2011. Discussions were held with a number of officials of the Indian High Commission, including High Commissioner Shri DM Mulay. The prominent people interviewed included at that time the Speaker of the People's Majlis, Mr Abdullah Shahid; Minister of Foreign Affairs, Mr Ahmed Naseem; Permanent Secretary of Ministry of Foreign Affairs, Mr Mohamed Naseer; Foreign Policy Advisor, Dr Ahmed Shaheed; Mr Ibrahim Hussain Zaki; National Security Advisor, Mr Ameen Faisal; Minister, Housing and Environment, Mr Mohamed Aslam; Mr Ilham Mohamed, Transparency Maldives; Mr J.J. Robinson, *Minivan News*; Mr Abdul Lateef Adam, *Miadhu Daily*,

    Ms Mariyam Seena, Ministry of Human Resources, and Youth and Sports and editor of *Haveeru Daily*.
4. Nils-Axel Mrner, 'The Maldives Project: A Future Free from Sea-level Flooding', *Contemporary South Asia*, Vol. 13, No. 2, 2004, pp. 149-155. This is also based on anecdotal evidence. For instance, during the interviews, the editor of *Miadhu Daily* and even the National Security Advisor of Maldives said that sea levels have not risen.
5. Wang Zhaokun, 'Maldives Woos Chinese Investors Source: Ambassador Talks about Green-development Ambitions', *Global Times*, September 26, 2010, available at http://world.globaltimes.cn/asia-pacific/2010-09/577067.html, accessed on October 4, 2010.
6. 'Durban Renewal', *The Indian Express*, December 13, 2011, available at http://www.indianexpress.com/news/durban-renewal/886978/, accessed on December 14, 2011.
7. Nitin Seth, 'Now, India's Real Climate Battle Begins', *The Times of India*, December 13, 2011, available at http://timesofindia.indiatimes.com/home/environment/global-warming/Now-Indias-real-climate-battle-begins/articleshow/11088585.cms, accessed on December 14, 2011.
8. Nitin Seth, 'Small Islands Snub India, Back EU's Vision on Climate Talks', *The Times of India*, December 9, 2011, available at http://articles.timesofindia.indiatimes.com/2011-12-09/global-warming/30497547_1_climate-talks-small-island-states-climate-convention, accessed on December 14, 2011.
9. 'Floating Golf Course in Maldives to Counter Threat of Global Warming', *ANI*, March 12, 2010, available at http://www.thaindian.com/newsportal/health/floating-golf-course-in-maldives-to-counter-threat-of-global-warming_100333797.html, accessed on March 14, 2010.
10. 'Floating Golf Course in Maldives to Counter Threat of Global Warming', *ANI*, March 12, 2010, available at http://www.thaindian.com/newsportal/health/floating-golf-course-in-maldives-to-counter-threat-of-global-warming_100333797.html, accessed on March 14, 2010.
11. See First National Communication of the Republic of Maldives to the United Nations Framework Convention on Climate Change (UNFCCC), 2001, published by Ministry of Home Affairs, Housing and Environment, Government of Maldives.
12. 'Maldives Wants India's Help in Climate Change Battle', *PTI*, February 20, 2011, available at http://www.ptinews.com/news/527339_Maldives-wants-India-s-help-in-climate-change-battle, accessed on February 25, 2011.

APPENDICES

Map 5.1: Impact of One Meter Sea Level Rise on Various Maldivian Islands

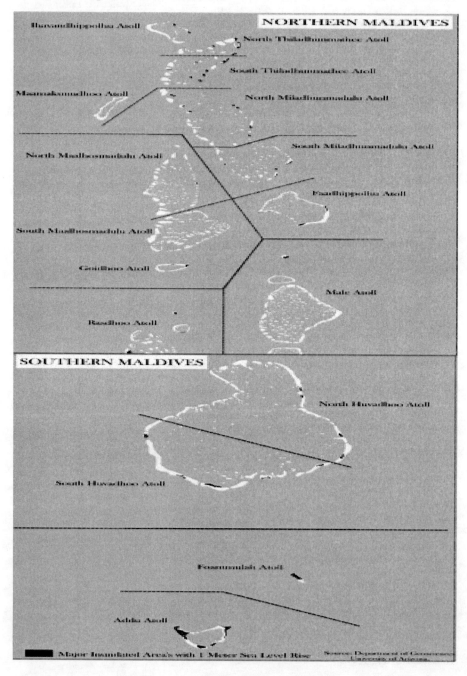

Map 5.2: Maldivian Islands where China has Shown its Interests

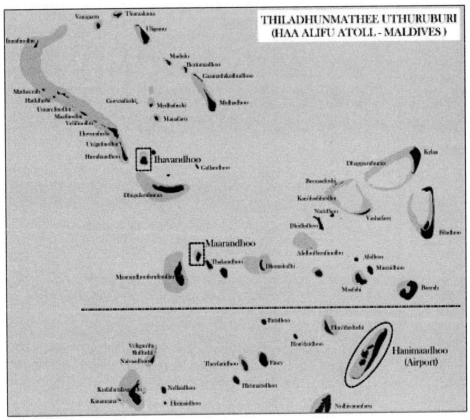

Chapter 6

MYANMAR
THE NEED FOR INFRASTRUCTURE INTEGRATION

Udai Bhanu Singh and Shruti Pandalai

INTRODUCTION

India has a window of opportunity in Myanmar, one that would aid in the successful realisation of India's Look East Policy (LEP). Myanmar's importance lies in its geo-strategic location and as a country in transition. The challenge is to ably leverage our LEP to successfully integrate our Northeastern Region (NER) with Southeast Asia by strengthening linkages with Myanmar. China can be kept at bay, or at least balanced, if we stick to this mandate. India needs to show clear political will to equip the NER economically and strategically and implement plans already in place, use the NER as a bridge to reach out to Myanmar and the rest of Southeast Asia, and develop it the way China has developed its Yunnan province. India needs to carry out a constant reappraisal of its Myanmar policy and deliver on promised infrastructure development in Myanmar.

Its strategic location at the tri-junction of East, Southeast and South Asia, and a shared border of over 1,640 km with four of India's Northeastern states, makes Myanmar a critical neighbour for constructive engagement. In a world which is shrinking constantly, India's Northeast can no longer be considered a buffer against external threats. The development of infrastructure connecting India and Myanmar has acquired its own salience. It demands as much government support as private sector involvement. Apart from Myanmar's geographic importance, India needs to act proactively in developing the country's extensive natural resources. Its hydrocarbon reserves and hydro-power potential are substantial. China has already secured its investments in the country, while India, despite its considerable involvement, is struggling to tie up the back-end operations of most of these projects. There is a need to develop the means to transport the gas through pipelines back to India, link the hydro-electric potential of Myanmar and NER through a seamless mechanism of inter-grid connectivity, and ensure that border trade does not suffer due to over-regulation and security lacunae.

Despite efforts being made to increase it, border trade has fallen below potential and prestigious projects like the Tamanthi Hydel power project have suffered delays. The Government of India needs to get the private sector involved in a wide range of areas in Myanmar. There is ample proof regarding the political will to back Indian investors in Myanmar; it is time for India to get its act together. Development of infrastructure on our own side of the border is a pre-requisite for effective economic integration with Myanmar.

The objective of this chapter is to highlight the prioritisation of infrastructure development in the Northeast for strengthening ties with Myanmar and the rest of Southeast Asia over the next 20 years. It will investigate: why India's ambitious plans for integration of the Northeast have not taken off; what are the projects on both sides which need immediate prioritisation; what are the institutional/political/economic impediments in trade and investment; what lessons do we need to learn from China; why isn't India using multi-lateral forums like BIMSTEC, ASEAN and Mekong-Ganga Cooperation more effectively to attract funding for projects from the ADB, World Bank and IMF?

It will ambitiously attempt to predict possible scenarios vis-à-vis Myanmar in the next two decades and recommend policy options that India can adopt in the near future.

STATE OF INFRASTRUCTURE DEVELOPMENT IN THE NORTHEAST REGION OF INDIA

Four of the eight states of Northeast India share borders with Myanmar.[1] In its geography, remoteness, natural resources wealth and level of development, the NER mirrors China's Yunnan province. Yet today the differences couldn't be starker. China has invested intensively in the infrastructure-building to connect Yunnan to Myanmar and potentially to the rest of South Asia. India needs to emulate this infrastructure roadmap with urgency.

Roads: In the past connectivity was undermined by neglect under colonial rule and then by the flawed logic that 'safety lay in not building the road'. Despite pressure from the trader lobby, India refrained from working on these projects due to security concerns. This alienated our own Northeast while doing nothing to prevent the Chinese from building roads and infrastructure right up to our doorstep. It is expected that the upgradation of the Stilwell road on the Indian side may be delayed (see Map 6.1).[2] The Shillong Statement on Roads and Highways has endorsed urgent infrastructure development and demanded a rethink of the Border Area Development Programme.[3]

As strategic consensus evolved, the Indian Government has now proposed to 'construct roads stretching to 1,417 km along the Indo-Myanmar border and establish more than 50 helipads to ensure accessibility and movement of forces through the treacherous terrain.'[4] However, officials from the Border Roads Organisation (BRO) have struck a note of caution. Logistically, not only is the NER remote, its soil does not support the type of stones required to construct tar roads. More often than not project costs do not include budgets for carrying heavy machinery and equipment to these areas, which then translates into delays. Local quarrying affects the geological balance of the region, making road construction fragile. This is further complicated by heavy precipitation in the NER leading to landslides and damaged roads.[5]

Railways: Railways, which have played an important developmental and integrating role elsewhere in the country, were denied to the Northeast and till recently were limited only up to Assam. India is now planning railway lines extending over 2452 km, connecting remote towns to the NER state capitals as part of the Northeast Vision 2020. Yet this is far from becoming a reality.

The obstacles are many—'difficult terrain, small working season, militancy, extortion, lawlessness and inadequate funding.'[6] The local contractors lack the capacity to undertake such large projects and the big companies do not have the incentive to work under adverse conditions. Where the state government provides security at work sites, as in Tripura, the project implementation is smoother. The Government also needs to re-assess the capacity of BRO in undertaking these massive projects. With its outdated techniques and reliance on local contractors, it is crumbling under pressure. Instead there is a view that the Government should consider securing the services of international companies with expertise in constructing roads in mountainous terrain (Swiss and German companies, for instance),[7] or involve big Indian infrastructure companies with provision of security.

Air connectivity: Despite its strategic and economic importance, air

Map 6.1: Stilwell Road (Ledo Road)

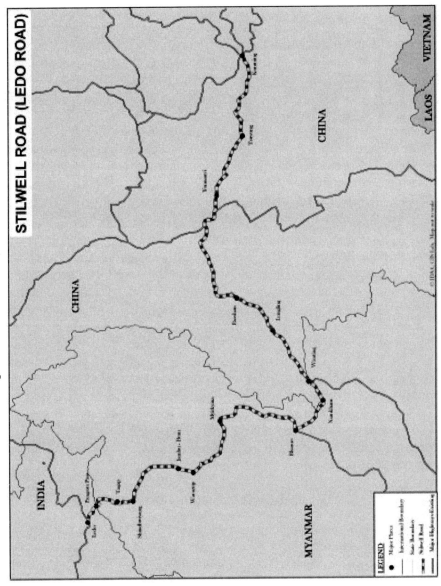

connectivity in the NER has 'deteriorated over the past 30-40 years, as privately run Dakota air-taxi services vital for connectivity in NER have been barred by civil aviation ministry on safety grounds and have inappropriately been replaced by wide-bodied aircraft that cannot take off on short runways'.[8]

In the absence of fully-equipped airports, helicopters that are often unsafe are pressed into service. There are currently 11 operational and 11 non-operational airports, and all air connectivity is routed via Guwahati. Three proposed greenfield airports—Itanagar, Tawang and Pakiyong (Gangtok)—will take time to get operationalised. People in Arunachal Pradesh have demanded that the MEA must not impose the norms of a 70 km distance from the border for construction of the greenfield airport at Tawang. Currently, Guwahati and Agartala airports have nightlanding facilities. Instrument landing systems are only available in Agartala, Dibrugarh, Dimapur, Guwahati and Imphal.[9]

Hydropower and Energy: The Northeast could be the powerhouse for the country having a hydroelectricity generating potential of over 60,000MW, but it currently generates only 8 per cent of that.[10] Almost all of it is generated in Arunachal Pradesh and Tripura. Per capita power consumption in the NER is one-fourth of the national average,[11] and many areas still have no access to power. Tripura generates surplus power which cannot be provided to power-deficient Mizoram due to the lack of a transmission network. Provision of power to other states is also difficult because only 66KVA power lines exist up to Assam. The current installed capacity of the NER (2,520MW),[12] is proposed to be doubled by the end of the Eleventh Plan (2007-2012). However, this target has not been achieved. The dismal situation is the outcome of inadequate investment in transmission and distribution grids and delay in implementation of projects. Attention needs to be paid to small hydro-power programmes for the NER.[13]

STATE OF INFRASTRUCTURE IN MYANMAR

The Myanmar Government has prioritised physical infrastructure building to boost its economy through state monopoly at least since 1988. Over the years, due to a shortfall in foreign exchange reserves, the scenario has changed. Power and communication sectors remained state monopolies while private enterprise was allowed to control road transport. The Government's policy shift towards a market economy is further loosening up state control to attract investment.

Roads: Although Myanmar forms part of the Asian Highways project[14], its transport sector has been beset by several problems. While the number of roads has increased there has been little increase in the freight carried or the number of passengers. It is estimated that Myanmar has only 0.005 km of road per square km while neighbouring Thailand has 0.17 km of road per square km.[15] The road network in areas adjoining India is even less dense.

Railways: Myanmar has metre gauge railway tracks, as does most of Southeast Asia. China has a standard gauge. When it becomes unviable to change the national gauges, the Trans Asian Railway (TAR) would have to resort to mechanized facilities to move shipping containers from one train to another at the break of gauge. While its rail tracks have slowly increased to 3,798 miles (6,110 km), there has been a decline in the rolling stock. The main line runs north-south from Myitkyina-Mandalay-Yangon with lines branching east and west in between. One line branches off at Thazi eastwards to Shwenyaung (Inle Lake) and then to Bago and Mottama. A second branch extends from Yangon to Pyay on the western side.[16] Myanmar has not yet realised the full potential of railways with only one-third of domestic freight being carried by rail, which is far below the figures for river transport, but more than the 20 per cent carried by road.[17] There are plans to equip the Yangon-Mandalay line with VHF communication system.[18] Myanmar has constructed 1048.95 miles (1687.76 km) so far and there are plans 'to build 250 miles [402.25 km] of railroads yearly'[19] with a view to establish a National Railroad Network.

Air Connectivity: Myanmar has three international airports (Yangon, Mandalay and Naypyidaw), and 30 domestic aerodromes. The Naypyidaw International Airport was opened on December 19, 2011. It covers an area of 111,500 sq m, has a 3.6 km long runway, and it is designed to receive 20 million passengers annually.

The country has some half dozen domestic airlines[20] and 15 international airlines operate in the country. Myanmar has also ratified seven aviation related conventions and five protocols. They have plans for Automatic Message Handling System (AMHS) by 2011, Performance Based Navigation (PBS) in line with ICAO guidelines by 2012, AIS implementation by the year 2016, and a plan to get ISO 9001 certification for quality management in AIS and MET fields in the near future.[21]

Hydroelectric Projects: Myanmar has a huge hydro-power potential which is still untapped. Most rivers run north to south—the Ayeyarwaddy (Irrawaddy), Chindwin, Sittaung and Salween. According to the Director General of the Department of Hydroelectric Power and Dams, U Win Kyaw: 'With eight major schemes under construction and 16 more planned, Myanmar is on a major programme of hydropower development. The government regards hydropower as a priority, both to meet domestic needs and for export to neighbouring countries. With only about 2 per cent of hydro resources currently developed, there is much work ahead.'[22] The total potential is estimated to be a gargantuan 100,000 MW and Naypyidaw understandably has plans for a big target of 35,000 MW for the future.

CHINA'S STRIDES IN MYANMAR

For India, the comparison with China is inevitable.[23] China, so far, has left no stone unturned in wooing the generals in Myanmar and their relationship has reportedly peaked as a 'strategic partnership', during the May 2011 visit of President Thein Sein to Beijing.[24] A glance at the infrastructure projects undertaken by China shows how far ahead it is vis-à-vis India in Myanmar.

Roads: China attaches both strategic and economic significance to making inroads into Myanmar. The infrastructure projects it has taken up are geared towards using it as a 'land bridge' to revive the 'Southwest silk road from Yunnan province.'[25] The link-up is aimed at 'developing the poor economies in the south-western part of inland China to trade with the growing economies of South East Asia and India.'[26] Importantly, the focus is the construction of strategic roads along the Ayeyarwaddy river trade route, linking Yunnan to the Bay of Bengal.[27] According to some reports, Chinese companies have built 190 miles of highway in Myanmar with a special emphasis on roads leading up to Arunachal Pradesh, which China persists in claiming as its rightful territory of 'Southern Tibet'.[28]

Railways: On May 28, 2011, China signed an MoU for a joint rail transport project that will connect Myanmar's border town of Muse and the western Rakhine state's Kyaukphyu (a port city project undertaken by the Chinese).[29] The 810 km rail line will make the special economic zone under construction more accessible to the mainland.[30] This route is among the several planned by Beijing to link its remote southwest region with ports in Myanmar and Southeast Asia, all aimed at trade, and oil and gas trans-shipment points to connect with pipelines already under construction.[31] These projects will obviously have strategic uses also.

Currently three Chinese projects are underway: Kyaukphyu-Kunming, slated for completion by 2015[32]; Kunming-Yangon (1,920 km) railway line; and a rail route from Myanmar's Shan state connecting Kunming with the northern Thai town of Chiang Rai.[33] Finally, two more routes connecting southwestern China with Myanmar's rail network are planned between the Chinese town of Dali with Myanmar's Mytikyina and Lashio, both large trading centres.[34]

Most of these routes are planned to line up with the 14,000 km UNESCAP Trans Asian Railway (TAR) network linking China to the rest of the world markets.[35] Above all this, China has contributed to upgrade Myanmar's rail stock with 30 railway engines being donated as 'Friendship gift' in 2010.[36] India's efforts so far haven't matched up.

Air Connectivity: China has invested $100 million in funding an airport near Naypyidaw.[37] Increasingly, both Air China and China's Southern Airlines have added more flights between Yangon and Kunming as well as Yangon and Guangzhou to facilitate increasing air traffic between both countries.

Hydropower: China, according to some reports, pumped in $5 billion in the hydro-power sector within the first five months of 2010.[38] The *EarthRights International Report* elaborates; 'At least 45 Chinese MNCs have been involved in approximately 63 hydropower projects in Burma, including several related substation and transmission line projects. Of these hydropower projects, the largest is the 7,100 megawatt (MW) Tasang Dam on the Salween River, which is to be integrated into the Asian Development Bank's Greater Mekong Sub-region Power Grid.'[39] Chinese private sector companies like YMEC have been involved in over 25 projects over the last five years.

Hydrocarbon Resources: According to a detailed investigative report published by EarthRights International in 2008: 'At least 16 Chinese MNCs have been involved in 21 onshore and offshore oil and natural gas projects in Burma. In August 2007, Myanmar confirmed the sale of natural gas from the lucrative Shwe gas fields off the Rakhine state coast to PetroChina, at a lower price than other competitors, thus clarifying China's influence in Burma's natural gas sector.'[40] China has undertaken two major projects: the $2.5 billion oil and gas pipelines from Kyaukphyu to Kunming (800 km in Myanmar) and the Kyaukphyu deep sea project. Both these projects are scheduled to be commissioned by 2013. Meanwhile, India's returns on investments in the A3 & A4 blocks have been hampered by the lack of serious negotiations on our part and the delay in laying the necessary gas pipelines to transport the gas back into India.

INDIA'S CONNECTIVITY WITH MYANMAR

India has been trying to bridge critical gaps in connectivity and trade with Myanmar. Officials in the Myanmar Government seeking to cement ties insist that India needs to get more pro-active. They point out: 'A lot of other countries are being connected to Myanmar through the projects funded by the Asian Development Bank, but not India. So, India needs to move fast.'[41] The Special Accelerated Road Development Programme for North East (SARDP-NE) could prove to be an important instrument to improve road connectivity to Myanmar.

A look at the state of connectivity of the four NER states sharing borders with Myanmar explains the need for urgency.

Other Recommended Networks are:

Manipur: Under the Trans-Asian Highway project, Moreh will be at the crossroads to open new channels of trade with ASEAN countries. The 160 km long Tamu-Kalewa-Kalemyo road inaugurated in February 2001 constitutes a significant component of the Asian Highway Network. Moreh in Manipur is a critical link in AH1 and AH2. The trilateral highway project covering 1,360 km of connectivity between India, Myanmar and Thailand too needs to be followed through and the Tamu-Mywaddy (Myanmar)-Mae Sot (Thailand) link established. It will further help link up to Dawei port in Myanmar (a significant deep sea port which could provide important shipping route to Indian ports). In addition, local incidents intermittently spark off tensions on the Moreh-Tamu border.

Yet, a field visit to Moreh some time back showed that this town is totally unprepared to handle such increased traffic flows because hardly any of the institutions and infrastructure required is yet in place.[42]

Arunachal Pradesh: Although there are demands for upgradation of the Stillwell road to two-lane standards (24 km in Assam and 33 km in Arunachal Pradesh), the project is likely to be delayed.[43] Earlier reports had indicated Myanmar's reluctance to develop the Stillwell road on its side of the border (194 miles from Myitkyina to the Pangsau Pass in Arunachal Pradesh, close to the Indian border) because of the difficulties encountered with the Kachins, but then it emerged that China had won the contract and work has already begun.[44]

Nagaland: Improvements to the Dimapur-Kohima-Imphal-Moreh road (mostly comprising NH-39) are required. Seamless connectivity to the Tamanthi hydel project entails upgrading the Jorhat-Mariani-Mokokchung-Tuensang-Noklak-Tamanthi stretch.

Mizoram: As part of the Kaladan Multimodal Project a two-lane highway of 117 km from Lawngtlai (Mizoram) to the Myanmar border is required. On the Indian side, Lawngtlai would be connected to Aizawl and then to Silchar in Assam. On the Myanmar side, Rhi-Tiddim and Rhi-

Falam roads (which will eventually link to Mandalay) need to be completed by 2012-2013 or else the infrastructure built at Zokhawthar (Mizoram border) will remain unutilised, adversely affecting trade.

Railways: India has authorised the EXIM Bank to lend $60 million to Naypyidaw to finance railway projects in Myanmar.[45] India's assistance is part of its ambitious Mekong-Ganga Cooperation (MGC) project to link New Delhi with Hanoi by rail.[46] India contributed a $56 million line of credit to Naypyidaw to construct modern railway facilities in its central and northwestern regions. New Delhi has also assisted in the upgrading of the central Yangon-Mandalay railway line. Indian Railways have begun initial preparations to extend a broad gauge track from Jiribam in south western Manipur to Moreh, on the border with Myanmar. This involves constructing the Jiribam-Imphal-Moreh line in Manipur and the Tamu-Kalay-Segyi line in Myanmar, as well as rehabilitating Myanmar's existing Segyi-Chaungu Myohaung line (see Map 6.2, for proposed rail network). However, the execution of the project continues to be slow.

Airways: India's air connectivity with Myanmar has been hampered by inadequate airport infrastructure in the NER. Currently, Guwahati, Imphal, Agartala and Dimapur have limited connectivity even with mainland India. There is no direct connectivity to any airport in Myanmar from any of the airfields in the NER. The Airports Authority of India (AAI) has been allocated only Rs. 9348 crore for development of airports in the Northeastern states, in the union budget 2011-12.[47] This explains why there are only bi-weekly flights from Kolkata to Yangon, that too by a single carrier.

Hydropower: India has plans to invest Rs 15,000 crore through the NHPC in Myanmar.[48] The investment is for two hydropower projects: the 1200 MW Tamanthi dam and the 600 MW Shwesayay dam on the Chindwin river in western Sagaing division of Myanmar. An MoU was signed in 2004 followed by an agreement in September 2008. But the delays in the granting of clearances by the department of hydropower implementation (DHPI) of Myanmar and by India's National Hydro-electric Power Corporation (NHPC) in tying up with local partners could put these crucial projects in jeopardy.[49]

The Kaladan multi-modal transit-cum-transport project centres around the Kaladan River which flows from Myanmar into Mizoram and back into Myanmar's Chin and Rakhine states, before finally draining into the Bay of Bengal. This mix of road and riverine transport would avoid the circuitous route through Assam and the Siliguri corridor, saving a distance of 673 km (418 miles).[50] It will give the landlocked NER access to the

Map 6.2: Proposed Rail Network

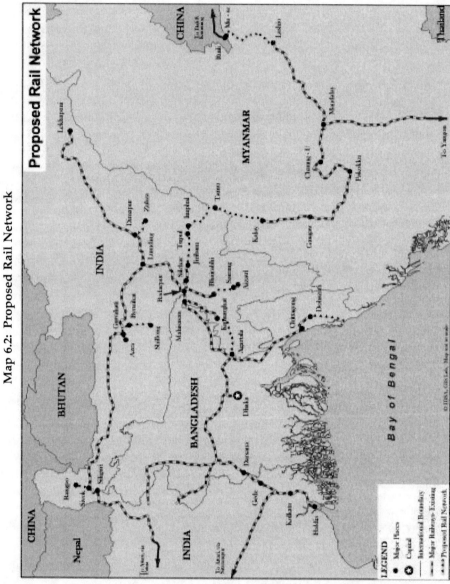

Indian Ocean, and Myanmar will get Sittwe port, which could develop over time into an important trans-shipment terminal, and the Kaladan, a channel for domestic navigation. If implemented efficiently it would be a win-win situation for all (see Map 6.3).[51]

TRADE AND ECONOMIC INVESTMENT IN MYANMAR

Trade: The implementation of the India-ASEAN FTA has meant slashing of duties on many products from Myanmar. Despite the various bilateral agreements and that India is Myanmar's fourth largest trading partner (after Thailand, China and Singapore) the absence of basic trade facilitation has meant that border trade between the two countries is minimal. India and Myanmar hope to achieve the target of $3 billion bilateral trade by 2015 (from $1.5 billion in 2010) by diversifying trade baskets and reducing barriers, especially tariffs.[52] Compared to India's trade figures of $1.2 billion[53] in trade with Myanmar in 2009-2010, China clocked $4.4 billion, making it Myanmar's second largest trading partner.[54]

Although it would appear a tough act for India to compete with China, it could be possible to reinforce mutual understanding at the official level by leveraging traditional links between the people of the border areas. For instance, a team of the Nagaland Government attended the annual conference of a Myanmar trading company in Yangon, following which a trading system will now link the Nagas of India with the Nagas of Myanmar.[55] Similarly, a Thai delegation visited Manipur to establish trilateral trade links between India, Myanmar and Thailand.[56]

Investment: Myanmar attracted a record $20 billion foreign investment in FY 2010-2011 which is more than what it has attracted over the past 20 years.[57] The investment was in oil and gas and electric power, manufacturing, real estate, hotels and tourism, mining, transport and communications sectors. It promulgated the special economic zone law. Market forces and the need to supplement Chinese aid compelled Myanmar to begin wooing foreign capital. Its Foreign Investment Law, 1989 sought to streamline procedures, provide guarantees and incentives, and allow repatriation of profit.[58]

As of 2010, India's investment in Myanmar stood at less than $250 million whereas Chinese investment totalled '$12.32 billion'.[59] At the two-day Unified Commanders' Conference in 2008, which was presided over by the Indian defence minister,[60] it was reiterated that the Chinese participation in infrastructure development in Myanmar could adversely 'affect our [Indian] security'. It would appear that Myanmar is also keen to prevent a Chinese dominance over its economy. It has divided the

Map 6.3: Kaladan Multimodal Project

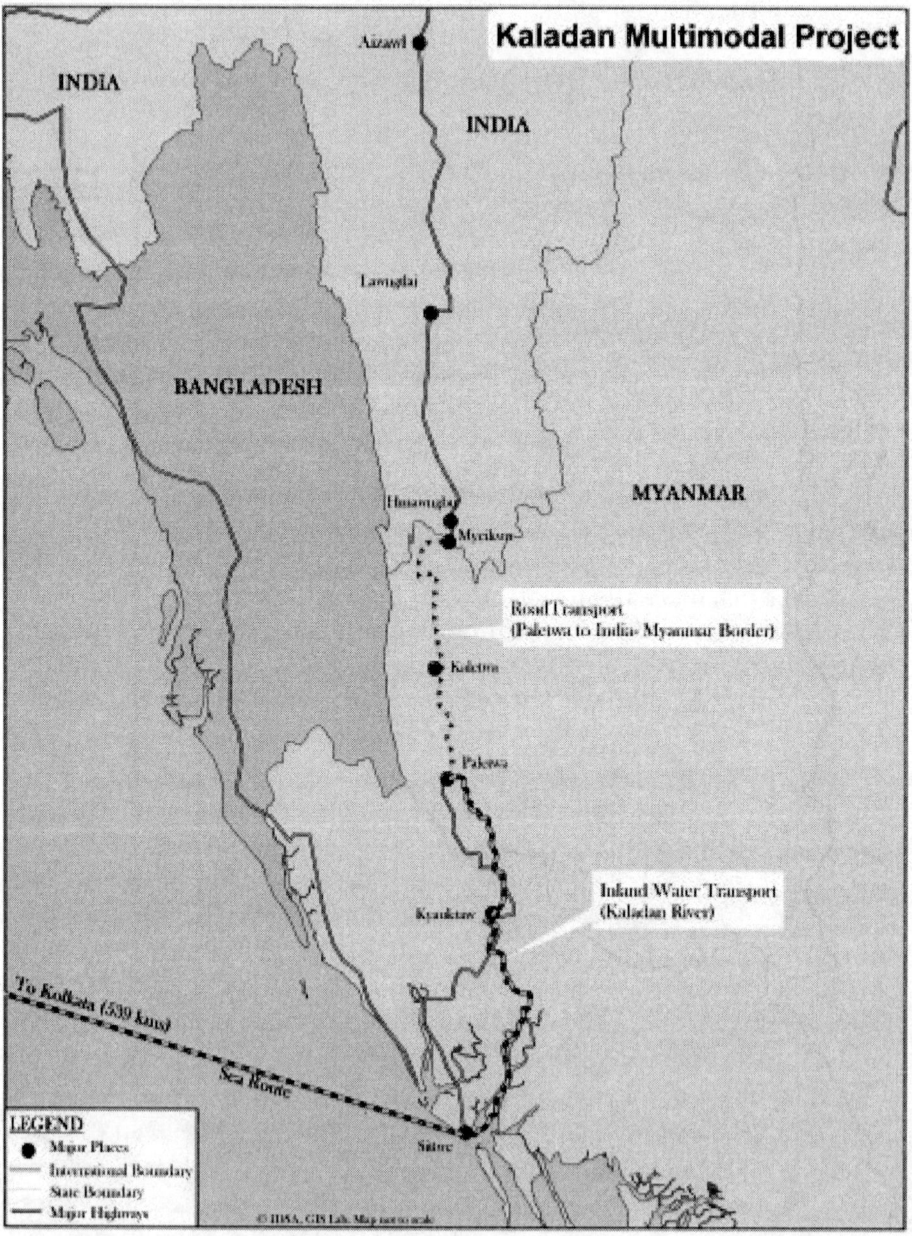

development of three of its important ports among three of its neighbours—China (Kyaukphyu), India (Sittwe), and Thailand (Dawei). The shared perceptions on China's behaviour could help evolve a strategy for dealing with China effectively. This approach could be more meaningfully pushed at the multi-lateral fora as well.

ENGAGING MYANMAR IN MULTILATERAL FORA

New Delhi can achieve its goal of better connectivity and closer relations primarily by fine tuning three instrumentalities: fast-track bilateral relations; incentivise the private sector to be pro-active; and leverage for better results through multilateral institutions such as BIMSTEC, Ganga-Mekong Cooperation Forum, ASEAN and the EAS, where India and Myanmar cooperate.

BIMSTEC: The Bay of Bengal Initiative for Multi-Sectoral Technical and Economic Co-operation (BIMSTEC),[61] constituted by countries of South and Southeast Asia is the ideal vehicle for pursuing the objectives of India's Look East Policy. Infrastructure projects like the Trans-Asian Rail network, the Trilateral Highway, the Kaladan Multimodal Transport Project, etc., and the BIMSTEC Tourism initiative and Regional Resource Co-operation Agreements (for oil and gas) could be developed for mutual benefit.[62] Despite many obvious advantages, the full potential of intra-regional trade presently remains unrealised because of tariff and non-tariff barriers, weak communication links, and lack of information regarding the supply capabilities and other barriers, and the fact that some SAARC member states still think locally rather than regionally.[65] Thailand, so far, has been a major cementing factor for ties between India and BIMSTEC and we should continue to give this relationship a lot of importance.[66]

The Mekong Ganga Cooperation Initiative: The Mekong-Ganga Cooperation Initiative (MGCI) provides India with the means for the socio-economic development of the region. However, over the past five years there have been few high level visits from the Indian side and, for all the initial diplomatic rhetoric, 'the MGCI has not received adequate attention to keep pace with future challenges and prospects.[67] Bureaucratic delays on projects, demands for training in IT and English education as well as knowledge exchange in terms of interaction between research institutes and people are needed by Myanmar, and these could be addressed through MGCI.

Key Drivers

Having analysed the various factors that influence the Indo-Myanmar

relationship, one can deduce the main drivers that will guide these relations over the coming decades. These are:
  i. India's political will and capacity to deliver especially vis-à-vis infrastructure projects in the NER and Myanmar;
  ii. security and infrastructure in the Northeast;
  iii. political and security situation in Myanmar; and
  iv. the external environment.

India's Political Will and Capacity: Perhaps the most important driver of the subset is India's resolve to implement and deliver on the LEP. This would include resolving the political and security situation in the NER, prioritising and increasing the pace of infrastructure development within India to enable the NER to build bridges with Myanmar and Southeast Asia and the delivery mechanisms to monitor and complete the projects promised to Myanmar as well as proactively engaging the neighbour. The thrust here would have to be on developing hydro-power, increasing inter-grid connectivity and transmission lines, improving rail, road and air connectivity, and the means to transport oil and gas—both within the NER and Myanmar. Trade-enabling measures like a rethink on tariffs, banking, and transaction and custom policies as well as developing border trade hubs and establishing linkages between the trade and industry organisations in NER with their counterparts across the border would be important factors. Project implementation remains a sore point in India's economic relations with most of its neighbours and this issue needs immediate attention.

Security and Infrastructure in the Northeast: The key positive drivers are: NER's strategic location and significance for the LEP, its cultural heritage, youthful population, and strong local communities. However, there are negative drivers as well: poor governance, inadequate transport and communication networks, perceived feeling of neglect by the centre (e.g., being on periphery and cultural differences), ethnic violence and insurgency, negative political culture, economic backwardness, and a porous international border.[64] For successful engagement with Myanmar, it is imperative that the negative drivers are addressed on priority and the positive drivers capitalised on. There is a huge potential for enhancing bilateral trade from the current figures of $1.5 billion. If infrastructure in the NER is upgraded and trading hubs are established in the bordering states then Indian exports to Myanmar can see a manifold increase from the current figure of about $200 million.

Political and Security Situation within Myanmar: The leadership, their orientation, priorities, goals for development and economic integration with the world as well as control over the internal security situation will be important. Myanmar already has a new Constitution and legislature in place. The National League for Democracy (NLD) has re-registered as a political party and Aung San Suu Kyi has successfully contested the April 2012 by-elections. The State Peace and Development Council (SPDC) was dissolved in 2011, but it would be unrealistic to assume that the military role will suddenly evaporate. National reconciliation in Myanmar requires not only political reconciliation but also ethnic reconciliation. Myanmar will need to do more to create a secure environment, not only within its territory but also assist India more effectively in overcoming the latter's insurgency problem by cracking down on insurgents, terrorists and smugglers. It is also important that the local youth are provided technical and managerial skill sets to be able to participate in and benefit from economic development of the country.

External Environment: This includes how other countries and multilateral fora respond to Myanmar; namely ASEAN, the West and China. Logically, Myanmar would like to benefit by engaging both China and India. But the fact is that China, having invested heavily in infrastructure sector in Myanmar, has much greater traction. Perceptions about China's intentions, involvement and influence and the cost-benefit analysis with regard to the leverages Myanmar can use vis-à-vis India and China through multilateral co-operation will also matter. This could also include perceptions regarding the potential of regional co-operation for Myanmar's development and whether its internal political dynamics are susceptible to outside pressures, particularly that from China.

VARIABLES OF THE DRIVERS

Each of these four drivers will have their own variables and their combination will create the scenarios for Indo-Myanmar relationship in the near future.

India's resolve will depend upon whether India allocates the required priority to these issues and deploys adequate resources to match its ambitions. Some of the questions that need to be answered are: can it transform its image with regard to project implementation and develop a result-oriented approach? Can India discard the zero-sum game outlook and integrate its Myanmar policy with the LEP? Can it develop a multi-dimensional relationship with Myanmar and not focus on democracy, rather focus on infrastructure, trade and capacity building? Can India manage its security situation in NER and build infrastructure on its own side of the border in order to be able to manage its policy proposals to

Myanmar? Will India's diplomacy proactively iron out any resistance since glitches are bound to appear in the relationship? There are two possible outcomes of the driver-variable interaction: (a) if India succeeds, the rewards will be an upsurge in trade and the success of its LEP; and (b) if India fails, the seriousness of its involvement and its intentions will be suspect, thus allowing China to gain an upper hand.

If natural resources are properly harnessed; universities and colleges function optimally and the youth acquire marketable skills; there is better governance with effective oversight mechanism; the various ethnic groups live in harmony; and infrastructure projects are put on a fast track so that they see timely implementation, the economy of the region will improve, insurgency will eventually fizzle out, and the Northeast will be able to reach out to Myanmar and the ASEAN. Should one or more of these conditions not be met then economic integration with Myanmar will remain a pipedream.

The political and security situation in Myanmar will depend on whether Myanmar gains political stability; private enterprise is encouraged; a robust civil society develops; political parties are permitted to play their legitimate role; local youth are empowered through education and skill-development programmes; a gradual transition to improved democratic governance with representation of all tribes comes about; and the leadership feels secure and confident about engaging with the external world. If all of these factors succeed then Myanmar's self-confidence will increase and there will be a pull-factor for development, which will make a case for greater engagement. Myanmar will then not feel threatened by India's increasing involvement and will not be bogged down by internal security issues.

The external environment will improve if ASEAN encourages Myanmar's complete integration into the system and sees India as an important ally. The attitude of the West will also determine Myanmar's behaviour and response to a great extent. However, with Hillary Clinton's visit in November 2011, a change has occurred in the West's approach towards Myanmar. This is expected to have its impact on Myanmar-China relationship as well and have positive ramifications for India.

Three scenarios emerge from the interactions between the key drivers and their dependent variables. It is important to reiterate that India's political will and capacity vis-à-vis prioritisation of infrastructure projects, both within India and in Myanmar, will be the most important driver.

Scenario I: Thus Far and No Further

India begins to lose interest in infrastructural development in Myanmar. India's ambitious plans to develop the geographically remote NER as a bridge to Myanmar also loses steam. There is slow progress in building of hydro-power projects like Tamanthi and proposals for increased connectivity, inter-grid power sharing, ease of banking, transaction and customs policies, setting of more hubs for border trade, and investment in technical training for locals on both sides of the border remain unimplemented. Myanmar too decides not to make any more democratic concessions and ethnic tensions once again come to the fore. The rest of the world goes into a wait-and-watch mode. It gives China an open field to invest and dominate Myanmar.

Scenario II: East Looks Bright

By 2015, India has completed all the projects it has undertaken in Myanmar while simultaneously making appropriate infrastructural investments in NER. The NER is on par with the most developed states in the country and has assimilated seamlessly with the Indian identity. The economic boom in cross-border engagement draws attention of states that had, so far, followed a policy of non-engagement and sanctions. This brings greater stability to Myanmar and the government is now in a position to make concessions to the Kachins and the Karens (minority ethnic groups) and other dissident groups. As the other ethnic groups and political parties see the rewards of economic progress and the possibilities of an equitable share in the political and economic pie, they begin to cooperate in the nation-building process. Democracy flourishes and the military is sidelined. Seeing this, the international community gives up its opposition and financial institutions also pitch in to bring Myanmar back into the mainstream. ASEAN delivers and Myanmar comes into its own as China is kept at bay.

Scenario III: Myanmar is Too Far!

India begins to withdraw from Myanmar. None of the infrastructural projects come through due to intra-government disagreements, failure in timely implementation and diplomatic differences. Pace of infrastructure development in the NER remains sluggish and the internal security situation remains volatile. Ethnic tensions in Myanmar get exacerbated leading to conflicts and resulting in a clamp-down. The world community does not feel that Myanmar is doing enough to change. There is no progress and a stalemate emerges. Myanmar becomes China's client state and is totally dependent on it, with the world having no opportunity to intervene. India's relations with Myanmar deteriorate.

POLICY RECOMMENDATIONS

India's policy towards Myanmar needs to remain one of 'constructive engagement' with a focus on prioritising infrastructure projects both in the NER and Myanmar and identifying linkages that would strengthen the relationship, both economically and politically. Some of the recommendations are as follow.

- **Timeline** of projects from the stages of proposal and implementation to delivery needs to be reduced drastically. India should consciously take up only those projects which have complete support of the Government in Myanmar. The Kaladan project, being very important, needs to be completed on schedule.

  India must proactively engage Myanmar diplomatically to avoid embarrassments like the delay and bickering over the Tamanthi hydel power project and ensure it is put back on track soon.

- **Connectivity,** first with the NER and then with Myanmar, needs to be prioritised and expanded. Old unused roads constructed during World War II can be identified on both sides and suitable link-up points could be established to provide alternate routes for trade and cargo traffic. Tamanthi requires road connectivity and transmission lines linking it to Nagaland and Mokokchung in Assam (Mokokchung-Tuensang-Noklak-Tamanthi). Other roads also need to be upgraded to develop multiple axes.

- Other recommended networks are:

Table 6.1: Upgradation of Roads Linking Northeast India with Myanmar

S.No.	Roads Upgradation
1	Jorhat-Mariani-Mokokchung-Tuensang-Noklak-Tamanthi
2	Guwahati-Shillong-Silchar-Imphal
3	Silchar-Aizawl-Tuipang
4	Aizawl-Zokhawthar, Rih-Tiddim, Rih-Falam
5	Tiddim-Mandalay (Myanmar)
6	Dimapur-Kohima-Senapati-Imphal-Moreh (see Map 6.4)

- **Construction** of major projects (such as the 169 km Moreh-Tamu-Kalemyo-Kalewa road) must have concurrent development of all associated linkages, e.g., petrol pumps, rest houses, signages, and connecting roads in place. The Government of India needs to revamp the 45 rickety bridges that are hampering the movement of cargo on this road. While the road itself was upgraded in 2011,

Myanmar 129

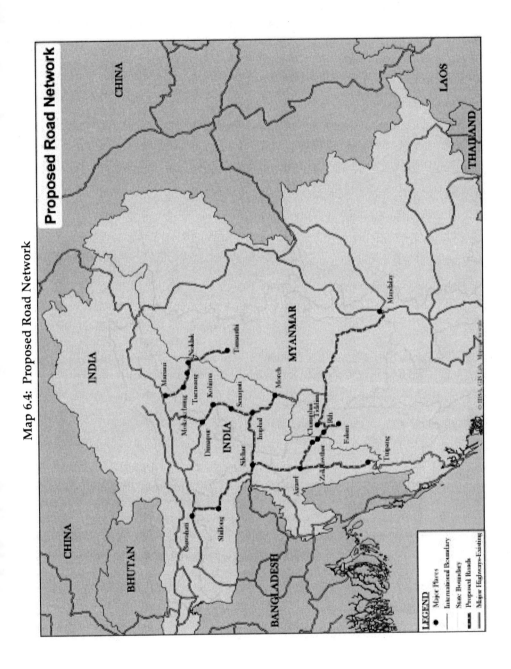

Map 6.4: Proposed Road Network

the bridges were not. The maintenance of NH 39 continues to be poor. Furthermore, the establishment of the transit facilities must be accompanied concurrently by development of other infrastructure such as land customs stations, warehousing, food testing laboratories, and weighbridge facilities under the ASIDE (Assistance to States for Developing Export Infrastructure and Allied Activities) scheme. Establishment of more trade routes with accompanying customs, banking and immigration facilities is a must to facilitate trade and commerce. The different departments responsible for providing the facilities need to synchronise/coordinate and deliver results in a timely manner.

- To ensure sustained connectivity, it is imperative to **develop more railway lines of uniform gauge** within the NER and using *break of gauge* to deal with the problem arising from a difference in gauge width (India/Myanmar), and develop link up routes within Myanmar territory. The terrain across the border in Myanmar is even more formidable. Rail lines will have to cross rivers and cut through rugged mountains and thick tropical jungle. Once the missing rail-links on the Indian side (Jiribam to Imphal-Moreh), and those on the Myanmar side (Tamu-Kalay-Segyi, plus the rehabilitation of the existing Segyi-Myohaung line), are taken care of the Trans Asian Railway (TAR) dream would be closer to realisation. In addition, in order to reduce the distance by rail, a feasibility study should be carried out to link Diphu with Maram or Karong in the Senapati district of Manipur, with the aim of extending it to Moreh via Imphal.

- The **power transmission** network can generate great mutual benefit. Once more power is generated in Arunachal Pradesh, high voltage transmission lines would be required within the NER and with Myanmar. This issue, if addressed immediately, could resolve the power crisis within the NER and can suitably be used to create inter-grid connectivity with Myanmar right up to Mandalay. Extraction of power from Tamanthi also needs to be planned. For this road connectivity to the Northeast will be an additional asset.

- **Private sector** should be given subsidies for projects, excise duty waivers and counter-guarantees through insurance for projects on either side of the border. This will take care of their security-related concerns.

- **Streamline trade payment arrangements and banking links:** Permit currency exchange within some distance from the border and then develop banks on the borders; start with *haats* and develop them into bigger trade centres. The example of Bhutan could be emulated here.

- **Link tourism circuits:** the NER's tourist spots could be linked with tourist spots in Myanmar by helicopter and railroad. The wildlife parks on either side of the border could be put on the tourist circuit and made more accessible for wildlife tourism.

- **Capacity building** on both sides of the border is important. The NER can overcome its dearth of skilled workforce by establishing more vocational training institutes and polytechnics which would give locals a stake in the development of their state. Similar expertise could be developed through training programmes for Myanmar locals across the border, who can be then absorbed in India-funded projects in Myanmar thus ensuring that there is no opposition to our presence. India and Myanmar should integrate small- and medium-scale industries on either side of the border, e.g., bamboo, rubber, fisheries, etc., to bring general economic prosperity.

- **Establish healthcare centres** close to the border areas. Initially, we can allow Myanmar patients to avail of healthcare facilities on our side. We can then establish similar healthcare centres on the Myanmar side. State capitals must have quality healthcare facilities.

- Effective policy requires an in depth understanding of the Myanmar mind. There is a need to **understand the ethnic dynamics** of the country.[65]

- India must **use its diaspora** as effectively as the Chinese do, including the networks built by Chettiar traders in Southeast Asia and the Meitis in places like Mandalay, and also involve local interests. The visit by members of the Indian Chamber of Commerce, Kolkata and representatives from Manipur, Nagaland and Mizoram to Myanmar in September 2010 was a positive step. Chambers of Commerce should also establish offices in Guwahati and other state capitals and have regular interaction with the Myanmar authorities and trade organisations.

It is imperative to develop the NER and first help it acquire an identity, which later can be slowly assimilated into a pan-Indian identity.

NOTES

1. The NER covers an area of 2.6 lakh sq km (7.9 per cent of India's total area) with a population of 39 million (as per the 2001 census, or 3.8 per cent of India's total population), and as per 2011 provisional census figures, the total population is 45.6 million and about 3.7 per cent of the total population).
2. The Stillwell road was built to enable the Allied forces to keep the Chinese troops supplied in the battle against Japanese occupation during the Second World War. While 61 km of the stretch lies in India, 1,033 km (642 miles) falls in Myanmar and 632 km (393 miles) is in China. For details see http://www.telegraph.co.uk/news/worldnews/asia/china/8243834/China-plans-to-rebuild-Burmas-World-War-Two-Stilwell-Road.html, accessed on February 25, 2011.
3. The Shillong Statement on Border Roads and Highways (February 9, 2007) states: 'The opening of International Trade Centres at several different points of the North-East's borders, is an urgent economic necessity and vital requirement for the Look East policy to bear fruit. With this in view, the Border Area Development Programme requires a fresh look and a new orientation'. For details see 'NEC's Sectoral Summits: A paradigm of Shift to Development of the North Eastern Region', Ministry of Development of North Eastern Region, Government of India, 2007, p.8, available at http://www.arunachalpwd.org/pdf/NEC's%20Sectoral%20Summits.pdf, accessed on February 21, 2012.
4. Alok Tikku, 'India to Build Roads Along Myanmar Border", *Hindustan Times*, February 27, 2011, available at URL: http://www.hindustantimes.com/India-to-build-roads-along-Myanmar/Article1-667585.aspx, accessed on February 27, 2011.
5. BRO officials interviewed at workshop on the 'Imperative of Infrastructure Development for developing Indo-Myanmar Relations, held at IDSA on March 30, 2011.
6. During his field trip to Myanmar, Dr Udai Bhanu Singh held interviews in Yangon and in Mandalay, arranged with assistance from the Embassy of India and the CGI, Mandalay during his field trip (May 7-16, 2011). Earlier, in February 2011, he had undertaken a field visit to Manipur and the Moreh-Tamu border. The people interviewed include the following: in the capital Naypyidaw, at the Ministry of Foreign Affairs, U Kyaw Swa (Director, Economic Division, International Organisations and Economic Department, MOFA), U Tin Yu (Deputy Director, Political Department, MOFA), Han Thein Kyaw (Head of Branch/Second Secretary, Political Department, MOFA); at the Ministry of Energy, HE U Htin Aung (Director General, Energy Planning Department); at the Ministry of Industry No.(2), U Than Htaik (Director General, Directorate of Heavy Industrial Planning); Daw Khin Mar Ye (Project Director), Tin Tin Htoo (Deputy Director, Directorate of Heavy Industries Planning), Khin Mar Yi (Director, Directorate of Heavy Industries Planning), and U Myo Zarni Win (Deputy Assistant Director). In Yangon, at the Indian Embassy, the Ambassador of India to Myanmar, HE V.S. Seshadri, Counsellors, Sripriya Ranganathan and Mayank Joshi, and the Defence Attache, Col. Rajesh Kumar. At the Ministry of Foreign Affairs, Yangon, Daw Yin Yin Myint, (Director General, Training, Research and Foreign Language Department & MISSIS Ex officio Secretary). At the Department of Civil Aviation, Ministry of Transport, Yangon, HE Tin Naing Tun (Director General), Win Swe Tun, (Deputy Director General), Kyaw Sein Hla, (Deputy Director, Air Transport Division), and Tike Aung, (Air Navigation Safety

Division). At the Myanmar Port Authority, Yangon, U Thein Htay, (Managing Director) and Mya Than, (Chief Civil Engineer, Civil Engineering Department). In Mandalay, Dr Madan Sethi, (Consul General, India), Khin Maung Soe (Lecturer, Chindwin College), Soe Myint Than (Senior Academic Advisor, Educational Outreach Center), and Ratan Sen (Myanmarese national of Indian origin, running a chemist shop in Mandalay).

7. The contrary view holds that this would serve to further demoralise the BRO.
8. B.G. Verghese, 'Imperatives of Connectivity', in Asian Institute of Transport Development, *Connectivity Issues in India's Neighbourhood*, Ed., New Delhi: Asian Institute of Transport Development, 2008.
9. *North Eastern Region Vision 2020*, Ministry of Development of North Eastern Region and North Eastern Council, Agartala, May 13, 2008.
10. Ibid.
11. It is 110 KWH in NER as compared to 411 KKWH nationwide.
12. With an effective output of 1,800 MW in 2006.
13. In fact, the strategic impact of developmental activities like hydro-power projects in a border state like Arunachal Pradesh was highlighted by Takam Sanjoy, an MP from Arunachal Pradesh earlier. See 'Arunachal for Dams', *North East Sun*, November 1-15, 2010.
14. It covers 15 countries and 65,000 km. See Myat Thein, *Economic Development of Myanmar*, Singapore: ISEAS, 2004
15. DLA Piper Rudnick and Gray Cary, *Threat to the Peace: A Call for the UN Security Council to Act in Burma* [Havel-Tutu Report], Washington D.C., September 20, 2005, p.12.
16. *Jane's Sentinel Security Country Risk Assessment*, June 29, 2011, available at http://sentinel.janes.com/public/sentinel/index.shtml, accessed on June 30, 2011.
17. Ibid.
18. Ibid.
19. *The New Light of Myanmar*, June 5, 2011, p.1, available at http://www.myanmararchives.com/newspapers/The-New-Light-of-Myanmar/2011/06_Jun/05-06-2011.pdf, accessed on January 23, 2012.
20. These are Air Bagan bound for Chiangmai, and Myanmar Airways International (since 1993) bound for Bangkok, Kuala Lumpur and Singapore. There are six other airlines for the domestic circuit: Myanmar Airways (since 1953), Air Mandalay (since 1994), Air Bagan (since 2004), Asia Wings (since 2011), Air KBZ (since 2011), and Yangon Airways (since 1996; suspended in December 2010 and restored in October 2011).
21. Presentation by Win Swe Tun, Deputy DG. in the Department of Civil Aviation, during the author's meeting with him at DCA, Yangon on May 12, 2011.
22. 'Hydropower Plays a Leading Role in Myanmar's Power Development Plans', *International Journal of Hydropower and Dams*, No. 2, 2005, cited in *Dammed by Burma's Generals: The Karenni Experence with Hydropower Development from Lawpita to the Salween*, Karenni Development Research Group, 2006.
23. Interviews conducted with various top officials in Myanmar.
24. 'Myanmar Official Media Hail President's China Visit', May 29 2011, *People's Daily*, available at http://english.peopledaily.com.cn/90001/90776/90883/7393992.html, accessed on May 30, 2011.
25. Kim Poon Shee, 'The Political Economy of China-Myanmar Relations: Strategic and

Economic Dimensions', *Ritsumeikan Annual Review of International Studies*, Vol.1, 2002, pp. 33-53.
26. Ibid.
27. Ibid.
28. 'High Altitude Border Roads: India Catching Up With China', April 11, 2011, available at http://www.himalayanaffairs.org/article.aspx?id=310, accessed on April 12, 2011.
29. 'China Railway Agreement with Myanmar on 810 Km Rail Project', May 30, 2011, *Myanmar Business Network*, available at http://www.myanmar-business.org/2011/05/china-railway-signs-agreement-with.html, accessed on May 30, 2011. Also see 'Construction of China-Myanmar Railway Could Start in December', available at http://www.monstersandcritics.com/news/business/news/article_1659676.php/Construction-of-China-Myanmar-railway-could-start-in-December, accessed on May 30, 2011.
30. Ibid.
31. Brian McCartan, 'China Outward Bound hrough Myanmar', *Asiatimes* , January 8, 2011, available at http://www.atimes.com/atimes/Southeast_Asia/MA08Ae01.html, accessed on January 8, 2011.
32. Ibid.
33. Ibid. This route, along with the one being worked out in Laos, will facilitate shipment of goods by rail between China, Cambodia, Thailand and Singapore.
34. Ibid.
35. Ibid.
36. Ibid.
37. 'Airport Just Latest Chinese Foray Into Burma's Transport Sector', *The Irrawady*, June 14, 2011, available at http://www.irrawady.org/highlight.php?art_id=20486, accessed on June 15, 2011.
38. 'Airport Just Latest Chinese Foray Into Burma's Transport Sector', *The Irrawady*, June 14, 2011, available at http://www.irrawady.org/highlight.php?art_id=20486, accessed on June 15, 2011.
39. 'China in Burma: The Increasing Investment of Chinese Multinational Corporations in Burma's Hydropower, Oil and Natural Gas, and Mining Sectors', EarthRights International (ERI), September 2008, available at http://www.earthrights.org/sites/default/files/publications/China-in-Burma-update-2008-English.pdf, accessed on January 23, 2012.
40. Ibid.
41. Interview with Daw Yin Yin Myint on May 12, 2011.
42. Field visit to Moreh-Tamu between February 12-13, 2011.
43. The upgradation to two-lane standards (24 km in Assam and 33 km in Arunachal Pradesh) will perhaps stretch to 2013 and beyond.
44. Subir Bhaumik, 'Will the Famous Indian WW-II Stilwell Road Reopen?', Februart 8, 2011, available at http://www.bbc.co.uk/news/world-south-asia-12269095, accessed on February 8, 2011.
45. Brian McCartan, 'China outward bound through Myanmar', *Asia Times Online*, Jan 8, 2011, available at http://www.atimes.com/atimes/Southeast_Asia/MA08Ae01.html, accessed on February 8, 2011.
46. India signed a pact for the project in 2000 with Thailand, Laos, Myanmar, Vietnam and Cambodia.
47. See the report in *Economic Times*, available at http://articles.economictimes.

indiatimes.com/2011-02-28/news/28642356_1_airport-development-union-budget-civil-aviation-sector, accessed on February 28, 2011.
48. 'India's NHPC to Invest Rs 15000 Crores in Myanmar', 2 August 2011, available at http://asian-power.com/power-utility/in-focus/indias-nhpc-invest-rs-15000-crore-in-myanmar, accessed on August 3, 2011.
49. 'India Suggests Exiting Out of Tamanthi Hydel Project to Escape from China Pressure', May 26, 2011, *The Economic Times*, available at at http://articles.economictimes.indiatimes.com/2011-05-26/news/29586113_1_hydel-tamanthi-project, accessed on May 26, 2011. Also see http://www.burmariversnetwork.org/dam-projects/tamanthi.html, accessed June 1, 2011.
50. Myanmar Port Authority figures. This would involve the construction of a port/inland water transport (IWT) terminal at Sittwe port, the development of Kaladan waterway from Sittwe to Paletwa (157 km), construction of IWT at Paletwa, and construction of a highway from Paletwa to the Indo-Myanmar border.
51. BGVerghese, in his autobiography, *First Draft: Witness to the Making of Modern India* (Tranquebar Press, New Delhi, 2010), cites the Tamanthi and the Kaladan multimodal project as two that hold out promise.
52. 'India, Myanmar to Double Bilateral Trade to $3 Billion', available at www.inewsone.com/2011/09/27/india-myanmar-target-to double-trade-by-2015/79432, accessed on September 27, 2011.
53. Official figures cited in 'India-Myanmar Relations, available at www.mea.gov.in/mystart.php?id+50044503, accessed on August 28, 2011.
54. 'China, Myanmar Forge Partnership, Ink Deals on Myanmar President's Maiden Visit', *Xinhua*, available at at http://news.xinhuanet.com/english2011-05/27/c_13897797.htm, May 27, 2011, accessed on May 28, 2011.
55. 'Trade Links for Burma Nagas', *The Morung Express*, available at , accessed on January 30, 2011.
56. It observed: 'Myanmar would be the confluence of India's Look East Policy and Thailand's Look West Policy', thus establishing a new link.
57. Myanmar's total foreign investment was $36.05 billion in March 2011, calculated since the year 1988 when it first invited foreign investment.
58. For details see Aung Than Tun, *Myanmar Laws Digest*, Yangon: INNWA Publishing House, 2001, pp. 81-82.
59. 'China, Myanmar Forge Partnership, Ink Deals on Myanmar President's Maiden Visit', *Xinhua*, available at at http://news.xinhuanet.com/english2011-05/27/c_13897797.htm, May 27, 2011, accessed on May 28, 2011.
60. *Asian Age* website, New Delhi, June 11, 2008, cited in BBC Monitoring Asia Pacific, Political, June 12, 2008.
61. BIMSTEC members include India, Myanmar, Thailand, Cambodia, Laos and Vietnam; it excludes China. Also see Tony Allison, 'Myanmar Shows India the Road to Southeast Asia', , February 21, 2001, *AsiaTimes Online*, available at http://www.atimes.com/reports/CB21Ai01.html, accessed on February 21, 2001.
62. Ibid.
63. Tridib Chakraborti, 'India's New Regionalism in Asia: Look East and the Northeast', in T. Nirmala Devi (e.d.) *India and Bay of Bengal Community: The Bimstec Experiment*, New Delhi: Gyan Publishing House, 2007.
64. Ibid.
65. Swaran Singh, 'Mekong-Ganga Cooperation Initiative: Analysis and Assessment of

India's Engagement with Greater Mekong Sub-region', available at http://www.jnu.ac.in/Faculty/ssingh/Mekong-Ganga.pdf, accessed on June 30, 2011.
66. Namrata Goswami, 'India's Northeast 2020: Four Alternative Futures', IDSA Occasional Paper No. 13, New Delhi: IDSA, 2010.
67. Sociologists, anthropologists and political analysts are required to study the social and political system. Steps such as promoting 'cross border growth poles' or 'growth triangles' should be encouraged. The share of border trade in the bilateral trade needs to increase if the NER is to develop. Whereas the bilateral trade in 2009-10 was $1207.56 million, the border trade amounted to only $13.73 million. The NER is landlocked and, despite its natural and human resources, the people of the region cannot have a share in the maritime trade. To the extent the increase in maritime trade does not stimulate NER economic growth (and ignores and even breaks traditional trade links), it perpetuates the perception that the benefits of LEP bypass NER as 98 per cent of the trade is conducted through ports.

Chapter 7

NEPAL
ISSUES AND CONCERNS IN INDIA-NEPAL RELATIONS

Nihar Nayak

India-Nepal relations are based on historical, cultural, geographical and economic linkages. Both the countries have periodically acknowledged each other's value and importance, and have also described the relationship as 'special' on various occasions. However, the India-Nepal bilateral relationship is currently at its lowest ebb due to anti-India sentiments in Nepal, in reaction to the perceived political interference by India. The Nepalese media, civil society groups and academicians have been very critical of what they call 'India's micro-management' in Nepal. The intensity of the anti-India feeling has become so deep that in October 2010, for the first time, the Indian Ambassador was attacked and was shown black flags in Nepal. Even Indian priests at the Pasupatinath temple and business houses are frequently targeted. This chapter makes an attempt to isolate the cause of the prevailing anti-India mindset, especially in light of the evolving political situation in Nepal.

ANTI-INDIA SENTIMENTS IN NEPAL

In this chapter, 'anti-India feeling' is defined as a mindset that regards India as a country that is acting against the interests of Nepal. This feeling is manifested in street demonstrations, articles in the media criticising India's intervention in internal affairs of Nepal, physical attacks on

Indians, showing of black flags to Indian delegations, circulation of posters detailing Indian activities, among others.

There are several factors—political, economic, social, geographical, social, and psychological—apart from some external factors that are responsible for the growing anti-Indianism in Nepal. This chapter ranks those factors according to their impact on India-Nepal relationship.

Political

Anti-India feeling in Nepal is largely politically motivated and has been present since the re-installation of monarchy in 1951. The monarchy used anti-Indianism as a rallying point, both to create a popular support-base for itself and to generate a sense of national unity amongst the people. The Nepalese monarchy viewed India's latent support for democracy with suspicion, even though it benefited immensely from such policies, because they led to removal of the Ranas. In fact, over the years, both the monarch and the democratic forces[1] have looked at India with suspicion, given their own interests. China has been seen as a potential support and as a countervailing force vis-à-vis India.[2]

Interestingly, the anti-India feeling among certain ethnic groups in Nepal emanates from the perception that India is still backing the monarchy clandestinely.[3] On several occasions, both the right- and left-wing political forces in Nepal (the royalists, communists and the Maoists) have generated anti-Indian sentiment for their own political benefit. Since the 1990s, these elements have been frequently using the Treaty of Peace and Friendship between India and Nepal signed in 1950, as well as the Kosi, Gandaki and Mahakali Treaties, the alleged border encroachments by India, poor treatment of Nepalese workers in India, and unresolved trade issues to foment anti-India feeling for their political benefit. Even many Kathmandu-based intellectuals and journalists indulge in anti-India rhetoric to get monetary benefits from external agencies known for their adversarial position towards India.[4]

Interestingly, this trend has reached new heights since the decline of monarchy in 2006 and emergence of the Communist Party of Nepal-Maoist (CPN-M) as the largest party in the Constituent Assembly (CA) elections in 2008. While this phenomenon was earlier confined to the elites in Kathmandu, it is now also being reflected in rural areas. Some Nepal army officers and the royalists believe that India is responsible for the end of the monarchy and the rise of the Maoists. Senior officers in the Nepal Army point to the fact that India's refusal to supply arms in 2005 after the royal coup d'état indirectly strengthened the Maoists. On the other hand, the Maoists accuse India of not letting them come to power and also hold it responsible for the political instability in Nepal and delay in the drafting of the Constitution. The most popular narrative in Nepal at present is that Indian bureaucrats, including those from RAW and IB, are responsible for the political instability in Nepal. They believe that the bureaucrats in the South Block lack the knowledge and understanding of Nepalese politics to tackle the political situation in the country.

There is also a general perception that India does not like the emergence of the CPN-M as the largest party. However, some sections argue that India tried to cultivate the Maoists just after the CA elections but they were betrayed by Maoists as they did not fulfil the promises they made to the Indians.[5] After the resignation of Prachanda, it was believed that India was not in favour of a Maoist government assuming power in Nepal. Maoists blame and accuse India of interfering in the internal affairs of Nepal and encouraging encroachment of Nepalese territory along the borders. The Maoists have also tried to convince the people that India does not want political stability in Nepal. In this context, they say that some Madheshi parties supported the Madhav Kumar Nepal government on India's behest. It is also argued that India does not support the integration of Maoist combatants into the security forces despite the fact that other parties—like the Nepali Congress (NC), Communist Party of Nepal-Unified Marxist Leninist (UML) and the Nepal Army—are also against bulk integration of Maoist combatants.

While this phenomenon was earlier limited to the elites in Kathmandu, it gained grounds in rural areas due to constant propaganda by the Maoists against India, especially in the aftermath of Prachanda's resignation as Prime Minister of Nepal. This was also reflected in the Nepalese media. Surprisingly, the rhythm of anti-India propaganda in the Nepalese media reduced to some extent after the re-assumption of power by the Maoists in August 2011, for the second time in the last four years. This is, firstly, because Baburam Bhattarai—who has a strong support base amongst the intellectuals and media houses in Nepal and is also perceived to enjoy Indian goodwill— became the Prime Minister of Nepal. Secondly, with little progress on the peace process despite a Maoist-led government, the people have gradually realised that it is not Indian intervention, rather intra-party factionalism in almost all the political parties, which is responsible for the political stalemate in Nepal. Thirdly, after repeated failures in seeking Chinese support for government formations in Kathmandu since 2008, the Maoists have realised that antagonising India would be costly for them. According to some observers in Nepal, as the author gathered during his fieldtrip, the Maoists believe that India is partial towards the Nepali Congress (NC) and their strategy has been to keep Maoists out of power at all costs. Therefore, their perception of India is conditioned by an unreasoned fear that India would not favour their success in Nepalese politics. Because of their popular support base among the masses, the Maoist leadership has successfully transferred their suspicions among wider population at the grassroots level. Interestingly, sympathisers of NC, UML and the royalist groups also consider India responsible for the rise of Maoists in Nepalese politics and therefore they would argue that the instability in Nepal is mainly due to unnecessary involvement of India in the internal politics of Nepal. This explains the prevalence of anti-India sentiments amongst their ranks. This explains the surge in anti-India sentiments in Nepal today.

Economic

Economic factors also add to the growing anti-Indianism. This phenomenon is especially noticeable in the rural areas. Every day, thousands of unskilled labourers from mid-western Nepal cross the Indian border in search of jobs and are harassed in various ways (inhuman living conditions, lower wages than their Indian counterparts, ill-treatment by employers, generalisation of Nepalese as gatekeepers, and misbehaviour by security force [SF] personnel while crossing the border and at airports). When they share these experiences with their fellow villagers, it inevitably gives rise to a negative perception of India.

In fact, many retired Gurkha soldiers from rural areas also narrate instances of harassment by Indian officers for retirement benefits. These voices were perhaps muted during the monarchy. However, with the emergence of the Maoists, who are perceived as a strong 'pro-people' party with the courage to stand up to India, these views are being expressed more openly. Another factor could be opening up of alternative job markets, other than India, for the Nepalese population. This has, to some extent, emboldened the Nepalese people to express their views openly against India.

Although these narratives have not impacted the flow of annual unskilled labour migration from Nepal to India (around 3 million)[6], it has certainly motivated skilled labour and the youth to think about other countries before coming to India. Despite India's accommodation of the highest number of Nepalese labourers in the last 19 years,[7] the Nepalese work-force has started migrating to countries other than India, which was its only destination until recently. According to the Department of Labour and Employment Promotion, Government of Nepal, around 1,193,023 Nepalese migrated to other countries, excluding India, between 1992 to mid-July 2008.[8] As a result, India may not be a favourite destination for the Nepalese people in terms of seeking jobs and higher education any more.

India's decision, in March 1989, to close all the border transit points except four in response to Chinese arms supplies is often cited as an example of Indian high-handedness. As far as bilateral economic relations are concerned, firstly, the growing trade imbalance between the two countries has led some political leaders, economists and traders to allege that this is a deliberate strategy by India to keep Nepal poor. Despite a revised trade treaty in 2009 between two countries, Nepalese traders have often complained that India has not complied with the list of Nepali-manufactured goods that were given duty-free access on a non-reciprocal basis in accordance with the trade treaty in 1996. Nepal's other major concern has been the non-tariff barriers on sanitary and phyto-sanitary measures (SPS) imposed by India. Secondly, Nepal is unable to export pharmaceutical products because these companies are denied registration in India. Thirdly, India does not allow Nepali entrepreneurs to send their machineries for repair and maintenance after three years of their import. Fourthly, Nepalese exporters are concerned about the restrictions on the export of industrial by-products, poor infrastructural facilities at the borders, congestion and delay while importing cargo from Kolkata port, and India's decision regarding the double seals on Nepali cargo coming via Kolkata port.[9]

Bilateral economic relations have also been affected by political developments in Nepal.[10] After the joint secretary level meeting on commerce and trade issues (IGSC) in New Delhi in March 2011, some Nepali officials said that the atmosphere was 'reminiscent of then King Gyanendra's direct rule era', when India took a very hardline position.[11] But Nepalese traders changed their views after the visit of Nepalese Prime Minister to New Delhi in October 2011, the subsequent visit of India's then Finance Minister Pranab Kumar Mukherjee to Nepal in November 2011, and especially after the discussion on bilateral trade issues at the Commerce Secretary level in December 2011.

Despite these developments, the ground reality remains as it was earlier and the changes are mostly on paper. Despite several rounds of discussions, logistical problems, the doublelocking system, and other kinds of cumbersome steps come in the way of clearance of the consignments for import and export by Kolkata port. Although all these issues were discussed during the Commerce Secretary level meeting, Nepalese traders are pessimistic about their implementation. Apart from the above, there is also poor inter-departmental coordination—commerce, transportation, custom, MEA; poor knowledge of the state governments on MEA initiatives and security agencies—while clearing consignments. It is often seen that the decisions taken at the bilateral level either do not percolate down to the lower levels or are diluted by the time they do so. There are also unnecessary delays in the process at the various checking points. As a result, traders pay extra charges for delay in receiving of the consignments and also for demurrage. According to observers in Nepal, there has not been any progress on the Bilateral Investment Promotion and Protection Agreement (BIPPA) since it was signed on October 21, 2011.[12] The radical faction of the UCPN-Maoist has been opposing this agreement at the moment. Moreover, Nepal's quest for an alternative trading route, via-Bangladesh, is an indication of unsatisfactory services while trading through Indian land routes and seaports. Recently, Bangladesh has agreed to allow Nepalese trucks to go up to Mongla to facilitate trade and tariff concession for certain products that Nepal wants to export.[13] Finance ministers of Nepal and Bangladesh have observed recently that 'Bangladesh and Nepal have necessary infrastructure for transit but a 17-km slice of Indian territory between the two borders lies in dilapidated condition.'[14]

The Issue of Water and Hydropower Cooperation

Water has been a contentious issue between the two countries because of the controversies surrounding the water treaties on Kosi, Gandak and Mahakali (see Annexure I).[15] As a result, Indian investors in the hydropower sector in Nepal face problems on several counts. There is a sentiment in Nepal that India has cheated Nepal in those treaties and Nepal's natural resources have been sold out without taking into account its interests. Deepak Gyawali has observed that in the case of Kosi and Gandak treaties, Nepal can do nothing as all management powers have been retained by the Indian side.[16]

Some Nepalese analysts consider the Mahakali treaty to be one of the best treaties between the two countries, which was ratified by a two-thirds majority in the Nepalese Parliament. Despite this, there is a feeling that the project is not moving forward because of Indian reservations over use of the term 'equality' (equal share of electricity and water) adopted in the agreement; therefore, India has not set up the headquarters, Chief Executive Officer and other technical aspects of the project deliberately. There is also lack of reciprocity from the Nepalese side due to political instability in Nepal. The Maoists are now demanding modification of the existing treaty to make it more equitable.

Despite the chronic power/electricity shortage, large sections of Nepalese, including Kathmandu-based intellectuals, are not satisfied with the level of investment made by India in the hydro-power sector. The Nepalese perceive that the benefits from these investments may not accrue to them. They want a 50 per cent share in the hydro investments and guarantee that the electricity generated from these projects would be distributed to the local population at the rate fixed by the Nepal Electricity Authority. They allege that most of the agreements related to hydro-projects are not transparent. This allows the opposition parties in Nepal to exploit the situation. Indian insistence on management control and refusal to allow independent assessment of downstream benefits also adds to Nepalese suspicions.[17]

There is also another group of intellectuals and political leaders who do not want India to benefit from electricity produced in Nepal even if India pays the best price per unit. 'Export of electricity is not ruled out but large generation primarily for export to a single buyer (India) is not, in this view, desirable.'[18] Therefore, they emphasise on small dams with the production capacity of 10-20 MW electricity for Nepal's own need.

There is a general impression that Nepal has not got a fair deal from India in the Kosi and Gandak water-sharing arrangements.[19] However, much of the popular resistance is politically motivated and prejudice-driven. Many of the critics, especially the Maoists, oppose the projects without even reading the MoUs and tend to project the companies from India as agents of Indian imperialism.

In many cases, Indian companies have been blamed for no fault of theirs. There have been allegations of Indian companies not taking the consent of the local population and discouraging local participation. However, it is the responsibility of the Nepalese state to consult the local people before allotting a project to a particular company. In most cases, this is not done, giving rise to feelings that the Indian investors are apathetic to local needs and concerns. The people in northern Nepal, where most of these hydro-projects are being planned, have little knowledge of India and the business MoUs. They are guided by the narrative of the local political leaders. As far as local participation is concerned, the Indian companies find it very difficult to involve local contractors in the construction work because of their lack of technical expertise.

On the whole, the Nepalese people are made to believe that the electricity generated from the hydro-power projects being built by India would be too expensive for their use and would be exported to India. Therefore, they often blame their politicians for selling the rivers to India without taking due care to protect the interests of the people of Nepal. However, one Nepalese scholar has observed that the 'rancour may not diminish as long as Nepal and India insist on project-centric cooperation. Both sides will pay a high political cost and their leaderships will be increasingly alienated from the people, the supposed beneficiaries.'[20]

In the aftermath of Prachanda's resignation in May 2009, the Maoists opposed Indian investments in the hydro-power sector and suggested that they would support it only if India supports a Maoist-led government in Kathmandu. The Maoists stalled construction work on the Upper Karnali, West Seti, Upper Marsyangdi and Arun III projects because they wanted to be paid for allowing the companies to work in the area. There is a faction within the Maoist party which opposes Indian projects and wishes to re-allot them to some other foreign concern. The water resources and energy department of the UCPN-Maoist had also threatened to halt development work in 14 different hydropower projects,[21] because these projects were 'export-oriented' and, according to them, against national interests.[22]

Despite all this and cutting across party-lines, it is accepted that India is a potential investor in hydro-power sector and a potential market as well. There are many who also believe that both the countries will benefit from bilateral cooperation in the hydro-power sector. A country like Nepal, which is not industrialised and earns much of its revenue from tourism, would benefit immensely by harvesting its huge water resources in a productive manner through active cooperation with India. Both the countries can fulfil their massive energy requirements by exploiting this natural resource. It will also help them in irrigating their lands and controlling floods.

So far, India does not have any strong competitors in the hydro-power sector in Nepal (See Annexure II for investors from other countries in the hydel sector). China is a potential competitor but since it is not a market for surplus hydro-power, it may not be willing to invest in mega hydro-power projects. India is the largest and nearest market for the surplus hydro-power from Nepal. Export to China would require huge investment for transmission across high mountain ranges. In comparison, the two border states of India with Nepal—UP and Bihar—have been facing power shortages and would be immediate markets for surplus energy from Nepal.

Nevertheless, China has been investing in small hydro-projects in Nepal, both for the purposes of goodwill and for strategic reasons. Moreover, China has abundant water resources in Tibet. However, given China's interests in the water resources of South Asia and especially Pakistan, it may in the future bid for mega projects in Nepal to further its business and strategic interests.

Social

Familiarity breeds contempt. Due to strong cultural linkages, certain sections in Nepal feel insecure about the demand for a separate Madheshi region. The Madheshis are commonly regarded as people of Indian origin and hence regarded as a pro-Indian constituency in Nepal. There is a suspicion amongst the Pahadis and major political leaders in Nepal that India is out to balkanise Nepal. Reportedly, during 2002-2004, India attempted to give a political colour to Madheshi grievances which encouraged Madheshis to organise themselves politically.[23] As part of this initiative, the Nepal India Friendship Association was reportedly formed with the active support of India and some development projects funded by India were diverted to the Terai region to nurture this constituency.[24] The Nepali Congress (NC) leaders—despite their pro-India stance—believe that India has weakened their party, by encouraging Madheshi leaders to break away from NC and form their own parties.

The Madheshis, on the other hand, believe that India's policy towards Nepal is Kathmandu-centric. They accuse India of neglecting the Madheshi movement. Upendra Yadav stated in a published interview:

> India, especially South Block and the Indian Embassy, have been against the Madhesh and MJF. They created the TMLP [Tarai-Madhesh Loktantrik Party] to weaken us. In fact, one of the reasons the pre-election alliance did not happen was because India was trying to boost up TMLP.[25]

A senior leader of the Sadbhavana Party also remarked to this author during the fieldtrip that 'Eighty per cent of India's aid is being utilised in the hilly region.' Of late, some Madheshis have also accused India of engineering divisions in the MJF in June 2009. Keshav Mainali, President of the *Chure Bhawar Ekta Samaj* (CBES) observed: 'It is only as and when India wants controversial issues to erupt that it shows up in Madhesh. India's stand on Nepali Madheshi issue has been self-contradictory.'[26]

There is also a view in the Terai that the Madheshi groups have failed to take any concrete decision about their future because of India's support to the liberal democratic parties, who oppose ethnic-based federalism.[27]

One scholar observed that even the Madheshi political and rebel leaders do not support Indian intervention because it can hurt their political future in their constituencies. Some of them consider the Madheshi issue solely as an internal issue because there is nothing in it to make it a bilateral issue.[28]

There is also a new trend of growing anti-Indianism amongst people living close to the border on the Nepalese side. This feeling is visible among the Terai and hill Madheshis who are mostly dependent on India for their livelihood. While the livelihood of some villagers is dependent on farming, others earn money by trafficking of illegal goods. Those who are dependent on farming allege encroachment of farm land by Indian farmers and security forces. Those who are dependent on trafficking of illegal goods complain of harassment by Indian security forces. Both the sections make their hatred towards India quite plain.

Role of External Forces

The role of external powers in fomenting anti-India feelings in Nepal has not been investigated so far. There are reports that both China and Pakistan are providing financial support to media houses who add fuel to the anti-India fire in Nepal. Pakistan has made its presence felt in Nepal since the 1960s and its intelligence agencies have used Nepalese territory to export terror to India, taking advantage of the open border between India and Nepal. Therefore, Pakistan's ability to foment anti-Indianism through sponsorship should not be underestimated. Some Madheshi leaders indicated to the author that due to growing anti-India feelings in the Madheshi region, China, US and other countries have been trying to build their constituencies in the region. Some analysts in Nepal admitted that the Nepalese often shared their resentment against India with officials from the Western embassies in Kathmandu.

There is a common view in Nepal that India's insensitivity or over-reaction to Nepal's assertions of sovereignty (even when they do not affect legitimate Indian interests) has fuelled anti-Indianism over the years. Nepalese analysts give several examples of India's misconceived Nepal policy. These include: India's inconsistency in supporting various Nepalese political players and thereby giving one or the other a sense of political insecurity; the recurring effort to micro-manage Nepal's democracy (an effort which can be said to date back to the 1950 Treaty); its intrusive profile in Nepal's internal politics (a historical pattern rather than occasional aberration); and a hegemonic intent which is all too apparent to most Nepalese, despite New Delhi's professions of respect for Nepal's sovereignty. Other irritants include: the Indian Embassy in Kathmandu lobbying for an Indian company to get the Machine Readable Passport (MRP) contract without following due process; holding up the Kantipur printing consignment at the Kolkata sea port; the undiplomatic manner of treating Nepalese leaders, i.e., allegedly threatening a CA member of the Maoist party; and statements on linkages between Nepalese Maoists and Indian Maoists without sufficient evidence. These have further contributed to the recent anti-Indianism in Nepal.

The Nepalese urge that India needs to recognise changes in the demographic and economic profile of Nepal that have taken place over the past decade. Nepal now has an expanding middle class which was practically absent earlier. This segment of the population has few personal or familial relationships across the border, unlike either the feudal top strata or the poorer Madheshi belt. These changes call for a restructuring of the India mindset.

People in Nepal perceive that India does not have any consistent foreign policy towards Nepal. Till date, India has hardly clarified its stand on controversial bilateral issues in any public forum. The absence of any high-level political engagement from the Indian side has added to misunderstandings and misperceptions. During the last 12 years, seven Nepalese Prime Ministers have visited India while no Indian Prime Minister has gone to Nepal on an official visit. India does maintain very good relationship with many leaders of Nepal cutting across party lines; however, it is yet to formulate a comprehensive and clear-cut policy towards Nepal. The present security centric approach has to make room for a more mature, sensitive and people-centric approach towards Nepal.

Geographical Issues: The Case of Open Borders
The 1950 Treaty and the unsettled border disputes at Kalapani and Susta have contributed substantially to the anti-Indian sentiments in Nepal. The issue of open borders has also been a point of debate in Nepal in recent years.

A large section of people in Nepal believe that the open border is a historically unique arrangement. It symbolises the deep trust and friendship between the two countries. The livelihood of thousands of economically-backward people on both side of border depends on the open border. Contrary to the belief in India, the Nepalese people argue that the India is benefiting more from it than Nepal. The fact remains that the Nepalese farmers benefit from the cheaper agricultural inputs and household products from India while the Indians benefit from better medical facilities and cheaper education in medical colleges across the Nepalese border. Given the socio-cultural linkages, the open border helps in cementing ties between peoples of the two countries.

The open border and 26 transit points reduce the time and cost of the transportation of goods from India to Nepal. Thousands of Nepalese workers, who send remittances to Nepal, cross the border without any documents at any point of the border in search of jobs. Quoting a survey report conducted by the World Food Programme (WFP) and the EU, some commentators point out: 'Thirty nine per cent of Nepal's total households with one or more migrants have India as their destination. On the Indian side, availability of Nepalese labour takes care of the labour scarcity in different parts of India. In comparison, less number of Indian workers go to Nepal in search of jobs. The open border has benefited immensely the poor people of both countries. In the absence of passport and visa requirements, the poor people on either side can easily cross the border in search of gainful economic activity.'[29]

Of late, both countries feel the arrangement does not take into account new security challenges and that the border now requires better regulation. The open border is used by terrorists, smugglers, drug peddlers (*ganja* from Nepal and *charas* from India), smuggling of small arms from both sides, etc. Most importantly, Indian Maoists, illegal armed groups operating in the Madheshi region, and organised criminal gangs take advantage of the open border and take shelter on either side to evade the law enforcement agencies of respective countries. Apart from that, of late, some religious fundamentalist groups have increased their activities along the border region. This could pose a serious security challenge both to India and Nepal in future.

Considering these challenge, both the countries have formed a joint Border Monitoring Committee and deployed their security forces along the borders. However, given the political instability in Nepal, these mechanisms are not sufficient. The infrastructure for patrolling and management of the border is very poor. The joint patrolling arrangement is not operational at this moment.

Both sides believe that there should be some regulation of the border but there are also other views. One section in Nepal, including the Maoists, argues that the open border has been responsible for the underdevelopment of Nepal and that it should be closed. On the contrary, people living in the border districts of Nepal feel that it should be regulated and kept open.

Psychological

There is also a psychological factor at play the asymmetry in size between the two countries. Nepal feels vulnerable and insecure because it is landlocked, and its sense of insecurity is ironically fuelled by the very cultural affinities which are also touted as a great asset in the relationship. Trailokya Raj Aryal argued in an analytical piece in *Republica* on April 25, 2010: 'With so many similarities between Nepal and India, naturally, Nepal had no other options but to contrast itself with India.'[30] There is a tendency to define Nepalese identity as distinctly different from that of India. In Nepal, it is fashionable to project oneself as anti-India, especially in Kathmandu, as a mark of Nepalese nationalism and patriotism.

FUTURE SCENARIOS

Drivers

After analysing the factors responsible for growing anti-India feeling and the main determinants of the India-Nepal relations, three major drivers are identified on the basis of high impact and high uncertainty: political situation, economic opportunities and aspirations, and external actors.

Political Upheaval

The main players influencing the political situation in Nepal are the mainstream political parties, the civil society and the Nepalese army. The nature of politics will largely depend upon the interaction among all these forces in future. As things stand today, Nepal is experiencing a political deadlock because of the differences between major political parties on issues ranging from the form of government, nature of federalism, integration/rehabilitation of Maoist combatants, to the competition between the major political parties to lead the national unity government (see Annexure III, following this chapter). There is a serious trust deficit between the major stake-holders in Nepal. The NC and UML suspect that the Maoists have a long-term agenda to capture state power by infiltrating their cadres into the army, bureaucracy and other institutions. Some sections within the Maoists suspect that the NC along with the Nepal Army and India is trying to suppress them. The Madheshi parties are reluctant to support any NC and UML-led government due to their differences over autonomy issues. Moreover, all political parties are divided from within. This has affected the present peace process and delayed the process of Constitution writing. The mistrust between the Nepal Army and the Maoists has also had a negative impact on the integration/rehabilitation as well as the reconciliation process. In the prevailing atmosphere of uncertainty, Nepal has already had four Prime Ministers heading coalition governments with simple majority in the CA-cum-Parliament between April 2008 and August 2011. A prolonged state of instability could lead to serious governance problems, ethnic unrest in eastern and southern Nepal, an economic and energy crisis, and labour migration to other countries.

The political situation in Nepal will play a critical role in determining Nepal's future and its relations with India and the wider world. Nepal will stabilise if the political parties strike a consensus and deal with all contentious issues effectively and the Maoists assure all concerned about their commitment to the democratic process. However, if the present state of dissention continues, Nepal will become further unstable; it could even witness a fresh round of political violence.

Economic Opportunities and Aspirations

Nepal's economy and infrastructure development has been badly affected due to political instability since 2008. Since then, the annual budget of the country has been either delayed or hurriedly prepared without taking public interests into consideration. As a result, Nepal has witnessed frequent closure of factories, capital flight, loss of employment and entrepreneurial opportunities, labour migration to other countries, banking problems, trade deficit, energy crisis and double digit inflation. For example, the Nepali banking and financial system is under a liquidity crisis.[31] However, some commentators in Nepal are of the view that there is a natural resilience in the Nepali economy because the country's banking and economy are less dependent on the international monetary system and are more linked with the Indian market. Therefore, there is a possibility that the Nepali economy could grow despite the political turmoil, if it links up further with the Indian economy.[32] Nepal is rich in human capital, tourism, agro-facilities and water resources. Nepal can also earn enough from IT outsourcing, tourism, hydropower and commercial agriculture. It could also emerge as a transit point between China and India.[33]

A depressed economy badly affected by chronic political instability could push Nepal deeper into chaos and even restart the civil war. However, if the right measures are taken on the economic front by the political leadership and Nepal links up effectively with the growing Indian economy then its economic condition will improve. It would create an enabling condition for political reconciliation and lead Nepal to peace and prosperity.

External Powers

A politically divided Nepal has been a playground for external actors seeking to maximise their leverages in Nepalese society and politics. India has often been cited as an external actor that has been an important factor in the Nepalese political dynamics. It is even said that India has been able to determine the course of Nepalese domestic politics for a long time. Earlier, the fall of first Maoist government led by Prachanda as well as the delay in the Maoists' return to power later were ascribed to interventionist policies of India. Similarly, China has, for long, sought to countervail Indian presence in Nepal and expand its area of influence through developmental activities and cultural exchanges. There are indications that China's posture is not exclusively nfluenced by its 'obsession' with Tibet, but may be part of a new strategic policy for South Asia and in keeping with its global aspirations. The emergence of the Maoists as a major political force and the declaration of Nepal as a republic have also led to increasing engagement of Nepal by the US, the UK and other Western countries. These external actors allegedly have their own favourites in Nepalese politics and have the ability to influence Nepalese politics. The UNMIN, which allegedly favoured the rebel Maoist group, played a role in complicating the relationship of the Maoists with the rest of the political parties.

If the external actors play a constructive role, like, for example, India did during the Comprehensive Peace Agreement in 2005, it will have a positive effect on Nepalese politics. Surprisingly, the Nepalese elite and politicians tend to perceive that constructive role as intervention in the internal affairs of Nepal. However, if they work at cross purposes and raise their own constituencies without being mindful of the effect their actions will have on the prevailing political instability, then the situation in Nepal will continue to be volatile.

SCENARIOS

Scenario I: Win-Win Situation: Political Stability

The Constitution is accepted by all the political parties and ethnic groups. The Maoist Party gradually transforms itself into a moderate and responsible party. The Maoist government seeks India's help for stabilising Nepalese politics and economy. Coalition governments govern Nepal and regular peaceful elections take place. The UCPN-Maoist adopts 'national unity government' and alternately leads the government and stays out of it. The Nepal Army backs political consensus on integration/

reconciliation. Maoists maintain a balance between India and China by addressing the sensitivities of both the countries. India and Nepal revise the 1950 Treaty and implement the Mahakali Treaty with the participation of the ADB and private sector companies from India. The Indo-Nepal border is better regulated. India's security concerns are addressed by Nepal and bilateral relations improve considerably. External actors play a constructive role and help Nepal develop its economy. Nepal stabilises as a normal democratic republic.

Scenario II: Nepal Muddles Through

In spite of their differences, political parties evolve a consensus to finalise the Constitution. The Maoists lose popularity due to intense intra-party factionalism and split into two groups. Some sections from the UML join the moderate faction of the Maoist party. Madheshi and smaller parties emerge as king-makers. No party is in majority position as per the provisions of the Constitution to form a government, andthe country witnesses frequent coalition governments. The economic situation deteriorates due to political instability and there is a reduction in the inflow of remittances. Due to political divisions, the government does invest much in India-Nepal relations, which remain plagued by suspicion and mistrust. The government introduces major reforms in banking and industrial sectors to control the growing underpayment problem. The labour-intensive industry fails due to the energy crisis. Certain groups blame India and external actors for political instability while external actors stay aloof. Ethnic unrest in both eastern and southern Nepal continues. Chinese influence in Nepal increases manifold and it tries to checkmate India at every level.

Scenario III: Chronic Political Instability

The Constitution-making process fails. Various ethnic groups become assertive. Serious internal conflicts among political groups arise; the situation borders on civil war, wherein different armed groups try to carve out their areas of dominance resulting in high degree of political instability and economic deprivation. The ex-King Gyanendra joins politics and becomes the leader of all three pro-royalist parties by merging them into one. The Army fails to bring order. Ethnic tensions rise in the Terai region and eastern Nepal. India is blamed for the Terai unrest. External forces play favourites with some political group or other to India's discomfort, some powers try and gain influence at India's cost. India's relationship with the Nepal Army is affected due to Madheshis' demand for a separate autonomous region and, subsequently, a separate state. The Nepal Army veers towards China and US as an alternative source of weapons supply. As the Nepali polity is stressed due to prevailing political instability, there is more anti-Indian sentiment, both artificially generated by some sections of the polity as well as by India's own erroneous handling of the relations.

Scenario IV: Red Nepal

The CPN-Maoist consolidates its hold over power and forms the government with a clear majority. The NC becomes the second strongest political party followed by the UML. Both of them split due to internal differences. The UML and other smaller parties lose their importance in Nepalese politics. Maoist-indoctrinated cadres infiltrate the Army. The Maoists adopt intimidating tactics to consolidate their position in the rural and urban areas. The political parties and civil society get divided on ethnic lines. Terai-based regional parties openly start supporting armed groups. The Army does not cooperate with the Maoists because of its traditional enmity towards the latter. The Maoists revive their armed young cadres, the Young Communist League (YCL) and begin to use the YCL cadres and, eventually, the People's Liberation Army (PLA) in armed clashes against political rivals. India tries to be helpful but is kept out of the loop by the Maoists. Protracted instability induces China to support the Maoists as a factor for stability. This provokes India to neutralise the Chinese influence. Political instability leads to further deterioration of law and order as well as the economic condition. To contain China's growing influence, the US and EU provide financial aid to Nepal and ask India to be more sensitive to Nepal's needs. Considering the overall negative impact that the continued tensions are likely to have on its image in the neighbourhood and beyond, India relents. However, it loses considerable amount of trust and political capital.

RECOMMENDATIONS

It is obvious that every country has its own interests and it tries to pursue the policy which serves its interests. But, when it comes to the matter of a stable relationship between any two countries, both need to find convergence of interests. Some recommendations for improving the relationship, which will also help in addressing the main issues being examined in this chapter, are listed below.

- India needs to formulate a comprehensive and long-term Nepal policy. Shaping of perceptions should be an integral part of this strategy. Instead of playing favourites amongst the political parties, India should engage with all of them and with other stakeholders like the Army and civil society. It needs to be recognised that Nepal will have to be helped to grow along with India lest it should be a drag on India's own growth.

- India has to resist the temptation to micro-manage Nepalese politics. It is too messy to do so and the outcome will be just the opposite of the one that it desires. It will take considerable time for Nepal's democracy to stabilise and its leaders to start thinking of the country before them. They have to be allowed to make mistakes and learn.

- Conventional security certainly cannot be the sole basis of India-Nepal relations. Therefore, the 1950 Treaty should be revisited to not only address Nepal's concerns but also to include India's concerns about non-conventional threats that have emerged in recent years.

- One cannot erase the anti-India sentiment in Nepal; however, this can be minimised considerably. Firstly, India has to identify the anti-India forces and engage them. These elements are also present within the Nepal Army. It is perceived in Nepal, as the author gathered from his interlocutors during his fieldtrip, many top officers of Army are, perhaps, not very happy with India's arms supplies because the arrangement does not allow them to make money. Secondly, India should try to correct the perception through a Track-II dialogue with Nepal, which should extend beyond Kathmandu. India's 26 pension paying camps across Nepal should be utilised for this purpose. A special emphasis should be given to the Terai region to counter Chinese influence in the region. Thirdly, India should highlight its developmental activities in Nepal.

- Surveys by academic and non-governmental organisations should be commissioned to identify projects—both small and large—which most people want to be implemented. Only those projects which find public acceptance must be taken up. We need to connect to Kathmandu via rail and run special trains till Raxaul or Gorakhpur (Nautanwa-Sunouli) for people visiting Nepal. That will generate goodwill for India and strengthen people-to-people contacts further. The train can be named the 'Nepal-India Maitri' train.

- There is a need to shape the perceptions of the people of Nepal regarding the benefits to be gained by them from joint hydro-power projects. Efforts must be made to dispel unreasonable fears/suspicions about India's intentions. The welfare and development orientation of the projects need to be highlighted. Transparency levels about project details have to be improved in order to allay peoples' misconceptions. Last, but not least, keeping Nepalese sensitivities in mind, India must be ready to revise/modify some of the existing contentious water treaties with Nepal. For future hydro-power treaties, funding from multinational agencies and involvement of companies from third countries as lead developers may help.

- In case of hydro-cooperation, it should make a beginning with low-risk, quick-yield, less-controversial projects. Gradually, medium-size hydro-electric projects can also be started. Participation of the private sector in hydro-power development and power trading should be encouraged, and finance can be mobilised jointly by involving the private sectors of both countries.

- Closing the border is an impractical proposition due to the nature of the terrain and the likely, adverse, public reaction on both sides of the border. However, given the emerging security situation, there is a need for regulation of the border due to the prevailing political and economic situation in Nepal and the costs involved. Nepal may not fulfil India's expectations on the joint-patrolling issue. Therefore, the capacity of the Sashastra Seema Bal (SSB) needs to be enhanced for effective patrolling and regulation. Special attention should be given to the intelligence-gathering capacity related to border issues of security forces in the region. In terms of infrastructure, there is an urgent need for developing motorable border roads in most, if not all sectors, to facilitate bike patrolling by the SSB; India could also reduce the distance between SSB posts (presently there is one post at every 10-15 km), provide lighting facilities in sensitive areas, watch-towers every kilometre, and fencing of some sections of the border which are not being used for cultural, economic and social purposes. An adequate number of border posts with well-regulated markets and public services need to be developed. Given the heavy transaction at Bhairwa, there is an urgent need of a world-class Integrated Check Post (ICP) there and on other important trading routes/points between both the countries.

- Many people on both sides of the border do not have proper documents to prove nationality. As is the case on the Nepal-China border, where locals have border passes, a similar system can be introduced on the Indo-Nepal border also.

- Reciprocity in all matters will not work. Nepal would expect India to be generous while retaining its right to criticise India. Prickliness on our part will have to be replaced by large-heartedness and accommodation. The greatest change has to seen in the behaviour of our diplomats and officials who deal with officials and people of Nepal on a regular basis.
- India should undertake capacity building programmes—commando training, intelligence gathering, supply of terrorist tracking modern equipments, etc.—with the Nepal armed and civil police for aviation security and for dealing with trans-border criminals.
- Besides continuing to undertake big projects which are in the pipeline, e.g., hydro-power projects, transmission lines, construction of roads and bridges, etc., there is immediate need to give a fresh look at the likely dividends from cooperation in new sectors. From the business point of view, growth of small and medium enterprises (SMEs) in Nepal has better prospects for balanced growth that can favourably impact on the middle and lower population strata.
- Extension of educational facilities on the Indian pattern should be considered as a long-term strategy. This will help mould young minds to be inclined towards India in the long run. Both academic and vocational institutions should be facilitated.
- Despite the Maoists success in 2008, China is yet to take them into confidence due to their long association with India during their armed struggle period. Therefore, India's engagement with Maoists at this moment will keep them away from China. India must engage all the factions of Maoists at the political level to get them away from China. Along with engaging the Maoists, India should re-engage with the Nepal Army.
- Since 2005, the relationship between India and the Nepal Army has not been warm. India needs to strengthen its defence cooperation with Nepal and also address the factors responsible for eroding of the relationship.

NOTES

1. Trailokya Raj Aryal writes that Nepali politicians do fuel 'anti-Indianism to safeguard our own interests'. See 'Rethinking Anti-Indianism in Nepal, *Myrepublica*, April 25, 2010, available at http://www.myrepublica.com/portal/index.php?action=news_details&news_id=17877, accessed on April 27, 2010.

2. Leo E. Rose, *Nepal: Strategy for Survival*, Bombay: Oxford University Press, 1971.
3. S.D. Muni, Anti-Indianism in Nepal: Need to Relate with Popular Aspirations', *The Tribune*, December 29, 2010, available at http://www.tribuneindia.com/2010/20101229/edit.htm#4, accessed on December 30, 2010.
4. This view was expressed during the author's interview with some Nepalese scholars in Kathmandu in June 2011.
5. Pradeep Giri, Leader of the Nepali Congress, in his interaction with the author in Kathmandu in June 2011.
6. India still ranks first in accommodating Nepalese labourers. But, owing to the open border, the data available in the various documents is not accurate. Moreover, most of the labour migration to India is seasonal and unskilled. There has been a new trend that those who cannot manage to visit other counties, migrate to India as a country of last resort. They feel that if work norms remains same everywhere, then it is better to opt for the destination which provides more money in exchange of the same amount of labour. There are also issues of dignity, harassment at the India-Nepal border, and poor protection to the Nepalese labourers in India in the absence of job visas. For example, a migrant in India remits on an average only Nepalese Rs 9,000 per year, whereas migrants to the Gulf States are able to send an average of Nepalese Rs 90,000 per year. See Michael Kollmair, Siddhi Manandhar, Bhim Subedi and Susan Thieme, 'New Figures for Old Stories: Migration and Remittances in Nepal', *Migration Letters*, Vol. 3, No. 2, October 2006, pp. 153-155. Nepalese students who come to India for higher studies also face a similar situation. Their first priority remains to go to places like the USA, Europe, Japan and Australia.
7. In 1993, the Government of Nepal granted permission to its citizens to work in the foreign country, other than India.
8. Dinesh Raj Sharma, 'Labour Migration Issues and Challenges in Nepali Context', Paper presented at the International Conference on 'Challenges of Governance in South Asia, Kathmandu, December 15-16, 2008. Mr Sharma is Founder President of Nepal Natural and Human Resources Development Association, Lalitpur, Nepal.
9. Bishwambher Pyakuryal, 'Revised Indo-Nepal Trade Treaty', *Republica*, Kathamandu, October 28, 2009. Also, the author's interaction with some traders in Kathmandu and Birgunj in June 2011.
10. It is alleged that India has had its political favourites and tries its best to keep them in power. India feels that Nepal should provide special concession to Indians on investments, guarantee protection to India's interests in all sectors of Nepal's economy, no sharing of India's sphere of influence with other countries, anytime access of Nepalese authorities by Indian officials without adhering to diplomatic protocols, and allegiance to India.
11. 'Nepal-India Trade: India Resumes Hard-line Approach', *The Kathmandu Post*, March 16, 2011, available at http://www.ekantipur.com/the-kathmandu-post/2011/03/15/money/nepal-india-trade-india-resumes-hard-line-approach/219486.html, accessed on March 25, 2011.
12. Author's telephonic conversation with a senior functionary of the NEFFA on January 31, 2012.
13. 'Nepal Seeks Help in Power Generation', January 31, 2012, available at http://www.bdnews24.com/details.php?id=217248&cid=4, accessed on February 4, 2012.
14. Ibid.
15. DN Dhungel and SB Pun (eds), *The Nepal-India Water Relationship: Challenges*, UK: Springer, 2009. Also see Annexure I for details.

16. 'The Right of the River', interview with Dipak Gyawali in *Himal South Asian*, March 2011, available at http://www.himalmag.com/component/content/article/4312-the-right-of-the-river.html, accessed April 10, 2011.
17. Rajeev Ranjan Chaturvedy and David M. Malone, 'Hydro-diplomacy: A Neglected Opportunity for Nepal and India', *The Hindu*, available at http://www.hindu.com/2011/06/28/stories/2011062858541100.htm, accessed on June 27, 2011.
18. Ibid.
19. Akhilesh Upadhayay, 'A Barrage Too Far?' *Outlook*, available at http://www.outlookindia.com/printarticle.aspx?201797, accessed on April 10, 2011.
20. Ibid.
21. For details see Annexure II.
22. 'Govt Bid to Assure Investors', *Kathmandu Post*, September 24, 2010, available at http://www.ekantipur.com/the-kathmandu-post/2010/09/24/money/govt-bid-to-assure-investors/213136/, accessed on September 30, 2010.
23. Author's interaction with a Madhesh-based Maoist leader, who would like to remain anonymous, in Kathmandu in 2010.
24. Krishna Hari Pushkar, 'Seeds of Ethno-civil Car in Terai', *Nepal Monitor*, December 20, 2007, available at http://www.nepalmonitor.com/2007/12/seeds_of_ethno-civil_war_in_nepal_terai.html, accessed on December 28, 2007.
25. Prashant Jha's interview with Upendra Yadav, 'Koirala Must Resign', *Nepali Times*, No. 401,May 23-30, 2008. Also, author's interaction with Mr Yadav in June 2011 in Kathmandu.
26. Keshav Prasad Mainali, 'India's Stand on Madhesh Isue is Self-contradicting', *Telegraph Nepal*, July 1, 2008, available at http://www.telegraphnepal.com/news_det.php?news_id=3654, accessed on August 5, 2008.
27. Author's interaction with a senior leader of the NSP in Patna on ebruary 29, 2009.
28. Krishna Hari Pushkar, 'India's Neighbourhood Intervention in Madhesh', *Nepal Monitor*, February 14, 2008, available at http://www.nepalmonitor.com/2008/02/inviting_indias_neighbourhood_intervention_in_madhesh.html, accessed on February 25, 2008.
29. Hari Bansh Jha, '1950 Treaty: A Visionary Approach', May 17, 2010, Paper no. 3815, South Asia Analysis Group, available at http://www.southasiaanalysis.org/%5Cpapers39%5Cpaper3815.html, accessed on June 10, 2010.
30. Trailokya Raj Aryal, 'Rethinking anti-Indianism in Nepal', April 25, 2010, available at http://archives.myrepublica.com/portal/index.php?action=news_details&news_id=17877, accessed on February 22, 2012.
30. According to the Nepal Rastra Bank, the country's economy in 2004-2005 earned over US$922 million in remittances from overseas workers and accounted for 12.4 per cent of the national GDP. The 2010 National Living Standard Survey (NLSS) report indicated that Nepal has recorded an 18 percentage point decline in absolute poverty in the six years between 2003-2004 and 2009-2010, leaving just 13 per cent Nepalis below the poverty line due to rise of remittance to 55.8 per cent from 31.9 per cent, as reported in NLSS III, 2010.
31. 'US, EU Recession Will Not Ht Nepal', *The Himalayan Times*, August 16, 2011, available at http://www.thehimalayantimes.com/fullNews.php?headline=US%26sbquo%3B +EU+ recession+will+not+hit+Nepal&NewsID=299563, accessed on August 30, 2011.

32. China had earlier pledged to initiate the process of constructing the strategically vital Larcha Dry Port by the end of 2011 in Sindhupalchowk. However, there is no information available yet as to whether it has been finished at the time of publication of this chapter. It was stated that once operational, the dry port was expected to ease the flow of goods imported from the northern neighbour through Tatopani customs and substantially bring down the transport cost of the imports. China has also committed to construct another dry port at Rasuwa, which lies just opposite to Kerung in Lhasa.

ANNEXURE I

Contentious issues raised by the Nepalese commentators on the Kosi, Gandaki and Mahakali Treaties

- The Kosi Treaty does not say anything about the total area (in Nepal and India) that would be irrigated from the Kosi barrage nor does it say anything about the quantum of hydroelectric power to be generated from it. It did not have any provision for providing water to Nepal for irrigation.
- Power generation from the Gandak treaty is very poor, about 3-4 MW. The canals supply water to Uttar Pradesh and Bihar.
- India refuses to recognise the downstream benefits of the Mahakali project (not clear, India is downstream low riparian country) and wants to buy the generated electricity on a marginally cost-plus basis as opposed to the cost principle that Nepal insists on.
- The ownership status of the head and tail reaches of the Mahakali remains contested. Nothing is clear either about the price at which generated electricity will be bought and sold or the principles by which such a price is to be fixed.

ANNEXURE II

Hydel Projects undertaken by different Countries in Nepal

Dudhkoshi 2 (138 MW) by Maytas Estates (India)

Dudhkoshi 4 (350 MW) by Nanda Devi Agro Farmers (India)

BudiGandaki Ka (130 MW) by Naulo Nepal Hydroelectric (Nepal/India)

Phulkot Karnali (210 MW) by PES Energy (India)

West Seti (750 MW) by West Seti Hydro (Nepal/Australia)

Chainpur Seti (454 MW) by Jindal Power (India)

Upper Karnali St 1 (184 MW) by Everest Power (India)

Upper Karnali (900 MW) by GMR (India)

Arun III (402 MW) by Satluj Jal Vidyut Nigam (India)

Tamakoshi-3 'A' (880 MW) by SN Power (Norway)

Lower Arun (400 MW) by Lower Arun Hydroelectric (Brazil)

Likhu-4 (120 MW) by Green Ventures (Nepal/India)

Upper Marshyangdi (600 MW) by Himtal Hydropower (Nepal/India)

Project Development Agreement expected

Upper Karnali (900 MW) by GMR (India)

Arun III (402 MW) by Satluj Jal Vidyut Nigam (India)

Lower Arun (400 MW) by Lower Arun Hydroelectric (Brazil)

Likhu-4 (120 MW) by Green Ventures (Nepal/India)

Upper Marshyangdi (600 MW) by Himtal Hydropower (Nepal/India)

Balefi (50 MW) by India

Tamakoshi-3 'A' (880 MW) by SN Power (Norway)

Annexure III

Major Political Parties' Position on Contentious Issues in Nepal as on February 2012

Major Parties	Maoist integration	Form of government	Electoral system	Federalism	Economic policy
UCPN-M	Brigadier General in new Directorate and Mass integration/ 5000 to 6000	President to be elected directly by the people	Proportional representation on the basis of caste and ethnicity	Ethnic identity based	New transitional economic policy
NC	3,500/suggested in CPA	Parliamentary system, President elected indirectly	Majoritarian	Geographic, cultural, social, economic	Open market
CPN-UML	As suggested in CPA, no integration	Prime Minister elected directly by the people	Mixed	Geographic, economic and natural resources	Mixed economy
UDMF	No integration	President to be elected directly by the people	Proportional representation	One Madhesh One Pradesh	Not clear

Note: CPA = Comprehensive Peace Agreement. UCPN-M = United Communist Party of Nepal-Maoist; NC = Nepali Congress, CPN-UML=Communist Party of Nepal-United Marxist Leninist, UDMF-United Democratic Madhesi Front
Source: Compiled from reports of Nepal-based English media.

Chapter 8

PAKISTAN
CHRONIC INSTABILITY AND INDIA'S OPTIONS

Ashok K Behuria and Sushant Sareen

THE BACKDROP

Pakistan is in the throes of a major socio-economic and political crisis. Ethnic and sectarian violence show no sign of abating. The internal security situation seems to be in a state of disrepair. The economic situation is worsening day by day. At the political level, the Pakistan People's Party (PPP)-led alliance government is spending much of its time trying either to ward off threats to its continuation in office (courtesy judicial activism or scandals like Memo-gate), or to keep the alliance together. The Nawaz Sharif-led Pakistan Muslim League (PML-N), the main opposition party, is threatening to create a grand alliance against the government. The Pakistan Tehrik-e-Insaf (PTI), led by Imran Khan, has emerged as an alternative political force—allegedly backed by the military and banking on the twin anti-incumbency factors, both at the central level against the PPP and at the provincial level against the PML-N—threatening to eat into the popular vote bases of both the PPP and the PML-N. Most militant and political groups, including the Jamaat-ud-Dawa (front organisation of the Lashkar-e-Taiba) and the Ahle-Sunnatwal Jamaat (front organisation of Sipah-e-Sahaba) have come together under 'Difa-e-Pakistan (Defence of Pakistan)' banner with express political intent to participate in the coming elections. Last, but not least, the civil-military tension again come out into the open, in the wake of the Memogate episode.

In the face of continuing political turmoil in one form or another,

Pakistan-watchers the world over now doubt the capacity of the military to keep the state together. Against this backdrop, issues like Pakistan's viability as a state, its internal faultlines, socio-economic and political dynamics, problems related to water scarcity, and likely impact of the developments in Pakistan on India, need to be analysed. The main objectives of this study are: (i) to provide a detailed analysis of the recent developments in Pakistan; (ii) to study their impact on India; (iii) to visualise future scenarios; and (iv) to recommend policy options for India.

INTERNAL CONTRADICTIONS AND SOCIO-POLITICAL DYNAMICS

A Case of Unsettled Identity; Anti-India Sentiment to Stay

Ever since its formation, Pakistan has been unable to decide whether it is a 'state for the Muslims' or an 'Islamic state'. Even if advocates of the latter strand have been able to project Pakistan as an 'Islamic Republic', 'a bastion of Islam', and the only confessional state built in the name of Islam in modern history, this debate is yet to be resolved. This basic contradiction gets amplified by the inability of Pakistan to evolve an identity of its own, based on territorial or political sentiments.

The conscious decision of the Pakistani elite over the years to define Pakistan in opposition to India has made this basic contradiction even more complex. This contradiction has translated into a pathological and obsessive enmity with India, which will continue to provide support for a negative and regressive form of nationalism and further legitimise the radical constituency in Pakistan in days to come. The anti-India sentiments peddled over the years have been bolstered through a misquoted reference to call for jihad against India by the Prophet (reference to *Gazwa-e-Hind*) in the *Hadees*. The resultant drive to take on India (eat-grass-make-bomb and use terrorism as an instrument) will continue to define the strategic calculus of Pakistan. There is no indication of Pakistan changing this discourse.

Resort to Islam plus the anti-India rhetoric in times of national crisis, will continue to be the dominant feature of the Pakistani elite's (especially the military's) strategy to unite the country and divert popular attention away from their weaknesses.

Inter and Intra-sectarian Faultlines to Widen

Culturally, the people of Pakistan follow a sub-continental brand of Islam (which tolerates diversity in spite of intense sectarian differences), but the narrative of the state, steadily propagated during the post-Partition years, gravitates towards a relatively more orthodox version of Islam. Immediately after Partition, a Deobandi Sunni version of Islam held sway at the political level in Pakistan. However, since the late 1980s, it has been informed by the Wahabi/Salafi/Ahle-Hadis versions of Islam, thanks to the deliberate radicalisation process to counter spread of communism in Afghanistan as well as the flow of funds from Saudi Arabia and other Gulf countries.

These conservative strands seek to steamroll diversity and force all sects to adopt a version of Islam which rejects plurality within it. This has led to violent inter- and intra-sectarian conflicts, i.e., Shia-Sunni, Deobandi-Barelvi, and Ahmadiyas versus all others. According to some sources, since 1989 there have been 2,582 sectarian incidents in Pakistan, in which 3,719 persons lost their lives and 7,727 were injured.[1]

The intra-sectarian divide within the Sunni fold has erupted in a major way since the mid-1980s; in the last seven years alone, since 2005, 209 persons have been killed and 560 injured in 29 terrorist attacks on Barelvi shrines in the country.[2] The Barelvis had, in the past, rallied around Sunni Tehreek, a militant political outfit, that which pledged to protect Barelvis from attacks by Deobandi militant groups. However, on April 12, 2006, the entire top leadership of Sunni Tehreek was wiped out in a suicide attack at a conference organised to celebrate the birthday of Prophet Mohammad at Nishtar Park, Karachi. Following this, in May 2009, several Barelvi groups came together to form Sunni Ittehad Council (SIC), which staged a long march from Islamabad to Lahore on November 27, 2010, despite an official crackdown, ostensibly to demonstrate their opposition to Deobandi militancy. Interestingly, Pakistan Sunni Tehreek (PST) organized a rally in Karachi on January 29, 2012 and announced that it would convert itself into a political party and participate in the coming elections. It is all set to launch itself as a political party after its March 23, 2012 rally at Minar-e-Pakistan, Lahore.

The attacks on Barelvis are likely to increase, in spite of all this. After the attack on the Sakhi Sarwar shrine in Dera Ghazi Khan on April 3, 2011, one of the suicide bombers, apprehended before he could detonate the explosives, revealed that he received training with 350 other teenagers at a camp in North Waziristan.[3] This suggests that such attacks will go on in future, despite the Army's widely publicized efforts at de-radicalisation.

Attacks on the Shias have continued unabated for a long time. Shia *Imambarghas, Muharram* processions and other such congregations have been attacked with astounding regularity since the 1980s. Several Sunni extremist organisations have come up with the avowed aim of targeting the Shias.[4] These outfits are affiliated to Al Qaeda and are becoming deadlier day by day. The Shias of Parachinar (called Turis), Kurram Agency in the Federally Administered Tribal Areas (FATA), Hazara township in Quetta, Balochistan, and Gilgit-Baltistan have been particularly attacked by these outfits since the mid-1980s. Shia doctors are being targeted in Pakistan with increasing regularity and as per Amnesty International reports, 72 such attacks took place between 2001 and 2007.

The Ahmadiyas[5] have been at the receiving end of the increasing radicalisation of Pakistani society, where most Islamic sects have come together to attack them. They continue to suffer at the hands of sectarian bigots, who often go unpunished. The assassination of Salman Taseer by his own security personnel, especially after he criticised attacks on the Ahmadiyas, and later of Shahzad Bhatti, the Minister for Minorities Affairs, in broad daylight show how far the virus has spread through the Pakistani body-politic. Interestingly, during the Memogate crisis, there was move by one of the prominent Urdu language dailies, *Ausaf*, to brand it as a conspiracy by Ahmadiyas to destabilize Pakistan, because Mansoor Ijaz hailed from that community.[6]

The inter- and intra-sectarian divides are likely to widen further in future as the state tends to favour a particular sectarian philosophy (Deobandi-Wahabi) at the cost of others. Therefore, these faultlines are likely either to stay as they are, or they may even get worse in the coming days.

System of Diarchy

A system of diarchy operates at the structural level within the political system of Pakistan, whereby the military dominates the foreign and the security policy and the civilian political establishment handles other municipal functions. The military is unlikely to concede ground to the civilian authorities on strategic issues, despite occasional outbursts from the civilian side not to allow a 'state within the state'. The civilian political forces are also hopelessly mired in inter- and intra-party dissensions, driven by their petty selfish interests while they have been in power. Some of them have also made themselves available for manipulation by the military, which was visible in the 'Operation Midnight Jackal' in 1989, the Mehran Bank scandal in the early 1990s, and when the Army tried hard either to topple the PPP government or defeat the PPP in the polls by sponsoring forces opposed to it. Moreover, the political leadership is corrupt and venal, and does not have any vision for Pakistan's future.

Thus, by default, as a well-organised professional institution, the military is likely to continue to wield enormous power without accountability. It is also likely to be regarded by the people, despite their declining faith in it, as the only institution that can safeguard the interests of Pakistan, in the face of the perceived threat from India, carefully drummed up by the establishment to lend legitimacy to its predominance in Pakistan. Since the departure of Pervez Musharraf, the military has partially regained its image amongst the people and it has been able to control the defence, security and foreign policies of Pakistan. The fact remains, however, that the people of Pakistan have started looking at the military as a predatory institution which needs to be kept under tight leash. With the proliferation of the media in Pakistan, any assertion by the Pakistan military is likely to be subjected to greater public scrutiny, which may act as a check on its ambition to usurp power in future.

Nevertheless, the ongoing system of diarchy is likely to continue, which will inhibit the process of generation of a national consensus, and constrain the capacity of the Pakistani state to address the critical internal economic and security challenges it is confronted with. However, it needs to be mentioned here that the military—with its coercive agencies and its influence on certain sections of the media—may continue with its efforts to generate antipathy towards India and draw legitimacy from it by projecting itself as the only institution which can defend the territorial integrity as well as the ideology of Pakistan.

Ethnic Faultlines in the Society

The faultlines between the Punjabis and non-Punjabis (the Sindhis, Balochis and Pakhtuns), the Sindhis and Mohajirs in Sindh, and the Pathans and Mohajirs in Karachi remain unresolved till date. The Seraikis and Hazaras are also beginning to assert their ethnic identities. As the country passes through political instability and the internal security situation shows no sign of improvement, no effective political measure has yet been taken to address these issues. The gross ethnic imbalance in the Army, bureaucracy and other institutions of governance (where the Punjabis dominate, followed by the Pakhtuns) has aggravated the ethnic situation further. The summary rejection by the Baloch people of the devolution package announced by the Zardari administration—entitled the *Aghaz-e-Huqooq-e-Balochistan* (roughly translated as 'beginning of recognition of the rights of Balochistan')—shows that the sense of alienation is too intense to be reversed.

Grievances against Punjabi Dominance and Economic Disparity

Disparity between the state of Punjab and other states has been a point of contention for a long time. The Baloch argue that they have been colonised by the Punjabis because their land is rich in natural resources. They feel that the Punjabi-dominated Pakistani state has systematically exploited their resources and federal allocations for the Baloch people have been much too low compared to what they contribute to the national economy.

The Sindhis also argue that there is a conscious move to reduce them to a minority in their own land. They allege that in spite of their overwhelming contribution to the Pakistani economy (99 per cent of the coal reserves, 56 per cent of oil, 71 per cent of natural gas, and 68 per cent of total direct and indirect taxes), they are subjected to step-motherly treatment. The Seventh National Finance Commission (NFC) Award (2010) in Pakistan tried to address the issue of distribution of resources among the provinces by widening the criteria for distribution and allocating more resources to the provinces; however, Sindh and Balochistan continue to complain of unfair treatment.

Even within Punjab and Khyber Pakhtunkhwa (KP), popular movements by ethno-linguistic groups, backed by political forces, are appearing on the horizon. The demand for separate provinces by the Hazaras (less than 3 per cent of the population)[7] and the Seraikis (10.53 per cent of the population)[8] is a case in point. The Seraikis, who are largely concentrated in southern Punjab and northern Sindh, allege that the Punjabis are controlling their resources and keeping the region poor and underdeveloped. Therefore, they would like to move away from the politics of Lahore or as they call it 'Takht-e-Lahore' (the throne of Lahore).

The feeling of alienation vis-à-vis the Punjabi-dominated state apparatus will continue to fuel nationalist sentiments/movements in Sindh and Balochistan, while other sub-nationalist identities (Hazaras, Seraikis and others) will become more assertive. By 2030, one may witness the formation of more provinces in Pakistan, which may change the political landscape in the country. However, even then, Punjab (with a population of about 44-45 per cent) is unlikely to lose its predominance in the overall power equation in the country.

Economic Situation

Questions regarding the economic viability of the Pakistan as a state were raised even before the state was born. Despite inheriting the most extensive irrigation network in the world, and even after extracting a very favourable concession on water sharing with India through the Indus Water Treaty (1960), the Pakistani state has not been able to generate favourable conditions for sustainable economic growth. It has been dependent on external aid right since its formation in 1947.

External Dependence

The phases when the Pakistani economy boomed have coincided with periods when Western aid flooded into Pakistan. Figure 1 below shows the inter-relationship between official development assistance (ODA) from US, FDI, and the GDP of Pakistan. Interestingly, each time Pakistan suffered an economic crisis, the security and political situation in the neighbourhood deteriorated, and it led to an infusion of external aid to rescue Pakistan, in view of its geo-strategic position. During 1999-2004, major debt relief given by international institutions, largely effected by the US, saved Pakistan from an imminent economic crisis. As the data indicates, the total debt relief provided to Pakistan during this period was to the tune of $18 billion. Moreover, the data (Tables 8.1 and 8.2) in ODA indicates that the net ODA accounted for an average of about 10.6 per cent of the total government expenditure during 1999-2007.

Table 8.1: Debt Forgiven or Reduced (1999-2004)

(in millions)

Year	Debt forgiven or reduction (current mn US$)
2002	300
2003	708
2004	482
2005	0
2006	0
2007	1.3
2008	4.8

Source: World Bank Data, Interactive webpage on http://databank.worldbank.org/

Weak Fundamentals

The fundamentals of Pakistani economy remain weak. According to Pakistan government figures for July 2010-March 2011, the tax-to-GDP ratio was as low as 9.4 and total public debt was about $124 billion (debt-to-GDP ratio is 55.7), out of which the external debt was about 59.5 billion. The forex reserves remain comparatively low at $17.1 billion. The FDI inflow was low in 2010-11—$1.08 billion, a 29 per cent decline over the previous year—while government expenditure continued to mount.

At the moment, it seems that there are structural problems that make

170 India's Neighbourhood

Figure 8.1: GDP Growth, Net ODA (as % of GNI) and FDI (as % of GDP) (1960-2011)

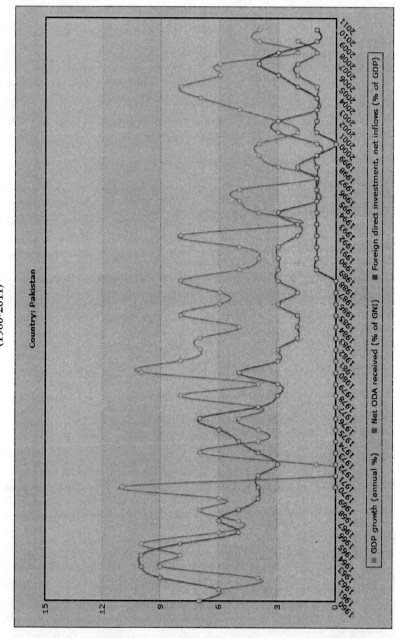

Source: World Bank Data.[9]

Table 8.2: ODA Received by Pakistan 1999-2009

Year	Net official development assistance received (current mn US $)	Net ODA received (% of central government expense)
1999	733	6.5
2000	700	5.7
2001	1941	17.6
2002	2092	16.9
2003	1071	7.5
2004	1440	10.3
2005	1607	10.1
2006	2140	11.1
2007	2243	9.6
2008	1539	5.04
2009	2780	10.29

Source: World Bank Data: Interactive webpage on http://databank.worldbank.org/

it difficult for Pakistan to avail of external aid. The internal political dynamic in Pakistan today seems to have come in the way of structural readjustments in Pakistani economy, as per IMF and World Bank recommendations. Nawaz Sharif's party has taken advantage of the popular outcry against imposition of Reformed General Sales Tax (RGST).[10]

Challenges

Pakistani economy is passing through a deep economic recession with a high inflation rate. The ability of the state to generate revenue for its burgeoning expenditure is constrained by its inability to generate political consensus in favour of the reforms it seeks to initiate. Deficit financing has been done mainly through borrowings from the State Bank of Pakistan (printing currency) which has fuelled inflation. The food inflation hovered around 20 per cent in March 2012.

There is a shortage of about 5,700 MW in the energy sector. The state is unable to finance the companies it has awarded contracts to for generation of power in order to meet the deficit. The state-owned enterprises, known for their under-performance, are a drain on the public exchequer and are weakening the economy further. If this trend continues, very soon there will be no money to pay for the import of fuel, gas, milk and cooking oil. Under these circumstances, the state is compelled to cut down its developmental expenditure and cannot finance the much-needed new education, sanitation and healthcare projects. The IMF is adamant about the benchmarks/conditions it wants Pakistan to fulfil. The promised loan of $3-4 billion by Friends of Pakistan, to help it handle the economic crisis, is not forthcoming.

Pakistan is in a far worse situation than India was in the early 1990s; yet, there is no consensus to bring about structural adjustments as suggested by the IMF, namely reduce total expenditure, increase revenue (through RGST, agricultural tax, income tax, property gain tax, etc.) to bring down deficit from 7 per cent to 4 per cent.

There is a perception in Pakistan that relatively poorer people are paying more for government expenditure than the rich in Pakistan. The government has no option but to tax the rich, but it is afraid of the political fallout of increasing taxes further because the state is primarily run by the rich and famous with no accountability and no sense of responsibility towards society. In Pakistan, consolidation of political power relies on transfer of government resources to the people associated with the government. The structure of governance is such that all revenues are directed towards the elite. Pakistan is in urgent need of a wholesale structural change. With the internal security situation continuing to be fragile for nearly a decade now, no dramatic change is going to take place on the FDI front.

Natural disasters like the earthquake in 2005 and widespread floods in 2010 have furthered weakened the capacity of the Pakistani economy to stand on its own. In view of the increasing incidences of natural calamities, like earthquakes and floods, Pakistan's dependence on outside help and support will grow. The changing demographic conditions are also posing unique challenges for Pakistan. Issues like rapid population growth, youth bulge, rising urban population and massive unemployment may compound the economic crisis faced by Pakistan.

Moreover, the security paradigm is not in sync with the economic and political capacity of the Pakistani state, which is today over-stretched and over-burdened by the Army-driven strategic thinking and policy framework. Pakistan's economy cannot afford the expenditure which is required to build the paradigm defined by the security establishment, i.e., to achieve parity with India by all means. Worse still, the blowback of the policy of using non-state actors and terrorists as instruments of state policy has had an extremely adverse impact on the economy.

In one year (between 2010-2011), Pakistan's ranking on the global competitive index, drawn up by the World Economic Forum (WEF), fell by 22 points (from 101st to 123rd place). The report stated: 'The most important positive impacts on Pakistan's competitiveness would come from improving the security situation, greater investment in people (as opposed to defence) and improving business environment.'[11]

Today, and for the foreseeable future, Pakistan's economic condition will be critically dependent on the Western aid and market access. Nevertheless, given Pakistan's geo-strategic location and its critical relevance for any global effort aimed at countering terror, it is unlikely that Western aid will ever come to a grinding halt unless something dramatic happens, or Pakistan adopts a suicidal policy vis-a-vis the US. It is true that the Pakistani economy will continue to be under stress in future, and it will have an adverse impact on the society and politics of Pakistan.

However, a long-term depressed economic situation may not necessarily lead to a total collapse of the state. This is because Pakistan has developed the habit of operating at a subsistence level, and thus there might not be too much internal pressure on the state to transform itself. This is not to deny that economic pressures along with persisting political turbulence and growing radicalisation of society may lead to a state of anarchy where the state and the military will lose control over large terrains of the state; yet, they may retain the power to survive nominally at the centre—very much a case of Pakistan not in control of itself and pulling in different directions.

Rising Radicalism and the Portents for Political Stability
The rising tide of radicalism in Pakistan has certainly threatened the stability of the state. It has widened fissures in the social fabric of the state and led to a situation of war of all against all. Some of the radical outfits have come together to take on the state. The killing of investigative journalist Syed Saleem Shahzad,[12] allegedly by the security agencies in May 2011, indicated how the system itself might be seeking to cover up the extent of jihadi penetration into the armed forces.

Radicalisation of the Deep State
The Pakistan Army seems to be divided over the issue of fighting the militants and jihadi elements. In the aftermath of the killing of Osama bin Laden by American security forces in Abbottabad, close to the Pakistan Military Academy, brought out into the open the collusion between the security forces and militant and terror groups in Pakistan, which kept Osama away from the US gaze for almost a decade. However, rather than focusing on a sincere and transparent investigation into the incident, the Pakistan Army seems to be spending more time and energy on

apprehending officials and civilians who helped the US in acquiring necessary ground intelligence on bin Laden.

Pakistan has sent back a majority of US Army officers training its paramilitary forces and is hunting down US intelligence operatives in Pakistan, which is interpreted both as a step to assuage public opinion at home and, especially, some sections within the Army who are deeply critical of *Operation Geronimo*. According to media reports, at the 139th Corps Commanders' Conference on June 9, 2011, the Pakistani Army Chief had a tough time convincing his colleagues about the need to continue to work with the US.

The press note from the Army at this time suggested that Pakistan was reviewing its position on intelligence sharing and the presence of US troops in the country. After the aerial attack on the Pakistani military outpost at Salala, along the Afghanistan-Pakistan border, Pakistan stopped US supplies and demanded an unconditional apology from the latter, which it refused to comply with. The heightened tension between the US and Pakistan has continued since November 2011. Even if the official line of the US has been to work with the Pakistan Army, the disillusionment of the American public with Pakistan is bound to have its impact on bilateral relations, especially when the preparations for the next presidential elections are in full swing.

Overall, there are tremendous pressures from within the Pakistan Army against continued cooperation with US, which indicate that the constituency favouring the militant elements has grown over time inside the armed forces. This will further weaken the resolve of the Army to counter the radical forces. The problem lies basically in Pakistan's dual approach: dealing with some factions of the Tehrik-e-Taliban Pakistan (TTP) by force and, simultaneously, sponsoring the Afghan Taliban and India-focused jihadi outfits. Playing favourites would only deepen the existing fault lines and 'militant-ise' the society further. The state will become more and more fragile as radical elements make inroads into the institutions of the state.

Impact on Society

Growing radicalism would only polarise society further. One has seen in the recent past how the political parties were muted in their criticism against the brutal murder of Salman Taseer. One may witness further witch-hunting of liberal elements, if the trend is not arrested. The Pakistani state apparatus, which is practically driven by the Army, has only two choices: (i) incrementally concede ground to radical forces and establish a Sharia-driven Islamic state in Pakistan (which could lead to massive bloodshed for want of a consensual view of Islam); (ii) leave all pretence and fight the monsters it has created (which will also prolong the present state of instability). Either way, Pakistan's future appears gloomy. Moreover, there is no indication that in either of the scenarios the Pakistan military will give up its anti-India stance, failing which its strategy of using terrorism as an instrument against India is likely to continue.

Given Pakistan's growing identification with the Sunni Wahabi school of Islam, and its long-standing patronage of these groups to fight covert wars in Kashmir and Afghanistan, the state has not taken (and is not likely to take) any convincing step to address the sectarian dimension of the problem. Most of these groups have an intensely sectarian outlook and their cadres have participated in sectarian attacks orchestrated by groups like Sipah-e-Sahaba Pakistan or Lashkar-e-Jhangvi. There have been few arrests of militant Sunni leaders but this has not curtailed the activities of these groups.

Madrassa reforms attempted by Musharraf could not quite take off due to stiff resistance from the conservatives. The way the state caved in to the reactions by religious groups on this issue suggests that madrassa reform is well nigh impossible in Pakistan. While it may be true that all madrassas do not preach violence, they are intensely sectarian in outlook and they do provide cadres for militant groups.

THE ETHNIC SITUATION

The state of Pakistan has not been able to federalise itself to accommodate the demands of various provinces, which are dominated by particular ethnic groups. The alienation in Balochistan is almost complete, it is unlikely that Baloch freedom fighters will be able to secede without external assistance or cataclysmic geo-political changes. However, given their determination and total disillusionment with the Pakistani state, the Baloch insurgency is likely to keep Pakistan internally engaged for a long time. The effort of the Pakistani military to soften its stand by announcing the withdrawal of the Army from the troubled areas in Balochistan, dropping the idea of building a cantonment and recruitment of Baloch into the armed forces has not been received well, primarily because the security forces continue to use brutal force to quash the insurgency.

Sindhi disaffection has been simmering for a long time and may surface at any time. According to the Sindhis, the divide between urban prosperity and rural deprivation is nowhere as wide as it is in Sindh. Due to the concentration of commerce and industry in its capital city, Karachi,

Sindh has the highest per capita income in Pakistan while its people are amongst the poorest. Most Sindhis believe that for them the most repressive form of colonialism began after the creation of Pakistan. Sindh accounts for 99 per cent of Pakistan's coal reservoirs (96.297 billion tonnes) located in Lakhra, Soondha, Thar, Meeting-Jhampeer and Badin. Among these, the Thar coal reservoirs are the largest in the world. Sindh also accounts for 48 per cent of the natural gas production in Pakistan. There are 10 gas fields in the province in the following areas: Kandhkoat, Khairpur, Mari (the largest), Suri/Hundi, Golarchi, Khaskheli and Leghari. It also produces 62 per cent of total oil produced in Pakistan. Almost the entire fish exports from Pakistan go from Sindh and Balochistan (worth US$ 199 million in 2005).

The Sindhi sense of alienation or xenophobia has been the result of the increasing differentiation of Sindhi ethno-national identity from the hegemonic Pakistani national identity, on the one hand, and growing distance from other neighbouring ethno-nationalities, on the other. However, the trend in Sindhi politics suggests that the hold of the nationalists has been extremely marginal despite the strong ethnic consciousness amongst the Sindhis at large. This is largely because of the hold of the feudal and political elite of Sindh, who have found a way of participating profitably in the political mainstream. The evolution of the PPP and its successful dent into Punjab and other provinces has added to their hopes of dominating the Pakistani political landscape through a party which is basically regarded as a Sindhi political party. This has dented the Sindhi nationalist movement and, therefore, apart from adding to the political turbulence in Pakistan in an episodic manner, it may not pose any critical challenge to the Pakistani state, unless, of course, the abiding sense of Sindhi alienation is manipulated by an external force seeking to destabilise Pakistan.

The inter-ethnic dissension in Karachi (among the Mohajirs, Sindhis and Pathans), which has assumed violent proportions in recent months, will continue to re-appear periodically in future. This will affect the economy as well as political dynamics in the state at both provincial and national levels.

The other so-called 'oppressed nationalities' of Pakistan (PONM), in the absence of a clear-cut agenda, will alternately bargain and agitate for their rightful share. Excepting perhaps the Baloch insurgency, other autonomist/para-secessionist movements are unlikely to pose any critical challenge to the Pakistani state. However, in the absence of any convincing centripetal pull (clearly-defined national identity, legitimate system of governance, efficient delivery of public goods, just distribution of resources, and accountable administration), centrifugal tendencies will keep appearing in the Pakistani federation from time to time.

TALIBANISATION AND STABILITY OF PAKISTANI STATE

Pakistan's ungoverned borderlands in FATA are host to some of the most radical forces like TTP, Lashkar-e-Jhangvi, Brigade 313, Al Qaeda, and Islamic radical outfits from the neighbourhood like Xinjiang, Uzbekistan and Tajikistan.

FATA has indeed provided sanctuary to radical forces of all kinds. The Pakistan Army's periodic thrusts into this region and increasing drone attacks have failed to contain the radical Islamist tide. The tribal leadership is falling into the hands of a comparatively younger generation of extremely radical elements who no longer feel inhibited to attack the Pakistani military. In fact, among the radical groups fresh alignments are taking place, based on the central question of who is siding with the Pakistani military and who is not. These elements have coordinated their activities and have successfully penetrated into the Pakistani hinterland and recruited local jihadi operatives from there to launch attacks against the Pakistani state. Notwithstanding the ongoing dialogue between the military and the TTP, some groups have chosen to attack the security forces, violating the directions issued to them by the TTP leadership in certain cases.

This problem is compounded by the reluctance of the Pakistani state to mainstream this region by introducing universal franchise and establishing an effective local representative system of administration. The state has distinctly failed to establish its writ over this terrain. It has helplessly watched the socio-political dynamics of the region evolve in a manner which has helped radical Islamist forces emerge as the neo-elite, replacing the earlier tribal structures which privileged the tribal elders. These elements now threaten to take their attacks to the heart of Pakistan.

They have launched attacks on Marriot Hotel in Islamabad, the General Headquarters (GHQ) in Rawalpindi, ISI headquarters, Federal Investigative Agency (FIA) in Lahore, Police Training School in Mianwali, the Sri Lankan cricket team, and now Pakistan Naval Station (PNS) Mehran, which would not have been possible without coordination with the local militants and jihadi penetration into the armed forces.

The inter-linkages among Afghan Taliban, Pakistani Tehrik-e-Taliban, Jihadi outfits and Al Qaeda are well known. These elements are likely to assert themselves more aggressively after the US pull out from Afghanistan. However, there is a dominant view in Pakistan, culled from interactions with seasoned analysts in Pakistan, that once the US forces leave Afghanistan and the situation stabilizes there, these insurgent forces could be diverted towards Afghanistan or India, and the situation in Pakistan would improve.

CIVIL MILITARY RELATIONS: CAN THE ARMY HOLD PAKISTAN TOGETHER?

The military would, at the best, allow a controlled democracy in Pakistan. There is a system of quartet at work now where there are four major players in Pakistani power politics, i.e., the political executive (the President and the Prime Minister), the Army, an increasingly assertive opposition, and the judiciary. At the moment, the judiciary is playing an assertive role in the process of democratisation thanks to the incumbent chief justice, Iftikhar Muhammad Chaudhry—especially because of the support he enjoys from the civil society and the main opposition party, the PML-N. While the Prime Minister will have constitutional powers, the opposition party or parties will assume lot of significance in view of the impending political instability in future. With the emergence of Imran Khan as a third force in Pakistani politics, no political party is likely to attain majority; the politics of coalition will make Pakistani politics unstable thus providing the Army with a chance to act as an arbiter and retain its pre-dominance. The lack of unity among political forces to impose civilian controls on the Army will keep civil-military relations tilted in favour of the latter. The Army is also likely to continue to raise the Indian bogey to legitimise its position and maintain its dominance in Pakistani polity and society.

There is, of course, a strong possibility that the Army may, despite large-scale purging of radical elements undertaken by Musharraf during his tenure, get dangerously divided along ideological lines. In case of greater assertion of radical elements within the Army, it is likely to assume an orthodox Islamist position to retain its influence in Pakistani politics. It appears certain, however, that even in such a situation the Army will dominate Pakistani power politics for a long time, primarily because there is no hope of the civilian forces ever coming together in a programmatic manner to clip its wings.

The situation as it obtains today does not make one believe that the Army can keep the country together, despite its ability to rally people around the 'Indian threat'. It is not immune to radical elements and its monopoly over means of coercion is gradually eroding over time. The Army may be able to hold temporarily but, in the long run, it is improbable that it can save Pakistan all by itself. It may at best officiate over a state pulling in several directions, where it may not have control over the entire state, but reserves enough strength unto itself to retain its centrality in a 'Lebanon-ised' state. If it Islamicises itself, it has to either evolve a consensual version of Islam, which is impossible in the Pakistani context, or co-opt the position of the most militant Deobandi-Wahabi strain, in which case it will have to face the wrath of the other sects.

Much will depend, therefore, upon the Army's willingness act against the radical forces, to arrest the ongoing descent into further radicalisation, and to allow civilian government to assume critical responsibility in areas like foreign, economic and security policy. Otherwise, the trend is that this virus of radicalism will affect the Army's unity and its capacity to conduct itself in an effective manner.

DURAND LINE AND PAKISTAN'S STRATEGY IN AFGHANISTAN

Historically, Afghanistan's reluctance to accept the Durand Line as the border has been a major concern for Pakistan. Both the countries have shared a tense relationship in the past and have encouraged covert operations against each other. Pakistan aims at establishing a government in Afghanistan that does not question the Durand Line. However, this is less likely to happen. Even the friendly Taliban during their rule refused to do that. The sense of unease in the Pakistani establishment on this count is well-articulated by former foreign secretary, Riaz Muhammad Khan, in his recent book *Afghanistan and Pakistan, Conflict, Extremism, and Resistance to Modernity* (OUP, 2011).

Pakistan, through its links with Afghan Taliban, seeks to play a much larger geo-strategic game in Afghanistan in the changed circumstances, in order to establish its influence in Kabul and even extend it into the Central Asian region. It also intends to control the trade and commercial routes to Central Asia through Afghanistan and reduce India's influence in the name of acquiring 'strategic depth'.

In reality, however, radical forces in Afghanistan have had a reverse strategic depth in Pakistan and a triumphant Taliban, after the US pull-out from Afghanistan, may not like to be projected as a proxy of either the Pakistan Army or the Pakistani state. The Taliban, a Pashtun-dominated force, is likely to reflect the Pashtun sensitivities with regard to the Durand Line.

THE ISSUE OF WATER

Pakistan does have a water scarcity problem which is primarily due to poor internal management, as has been acknowledged by its leadership as well as reasonable analysts in Pakistan in the past. However, it is creating an easy scapegoat in India in order to turn popular attention away from administrative mismanagement of important issues, including the issue of water scarcity.

The Indus Water Treaty of 1960 is a proof of India's generosity as an upper-riparian. Despite the fact that India has abided by the terms of Treaty, Pakistan has time and again raised the issues of unfair treatment, stealing of water, and violation of the terms of the Treaty. However, as the opinion of the neutral expert in the case of Baglihar dam showed, much of Pakistan's suspicions were ill-founded.

Pakistan's reference of Kishenganga to the court of arbitration and the anti-India propaganda being launched at the popular level (purportedly at the behest of elements within the Army) over the water issue shows that this trend is likely to continue as a diversionary tactic.

The issue of the inter-provincial competition for water resources within Pakistan is unlikely to pose any challenge to the state of Pakistan. The Indian bogey will keep the issue from boiling over. However, it is likely to have adverse impact on inter-ethnic and inter-provincial relations.

Apart from adding another issue to the already overloaded Indo-Pak dialogic track, the issue of water is likely to raise popular emotions on both sides and act as an additional spoiler in any future peace process between the two countries.

What should be India's Strategy?

India's strategy should be to proactively disseminate all relevant information (starting from glacial decay to the data on the flow of water in the Indus system) among the strategic community in both the countries in particular and the wider public in general. Simultaneously, at the bilateral level, India should encourage Pakistan to adopt better water management techniques and programmes and urge it to desist from raising the India bogey on the matter. There is a view in Pakistan that the two Indus Water Commissions are not discussing the issues enough and there is less enthusiasm on both sides to engage each other constructively. Therefore, the only mechanisms (the commissions) in the Indus Water Treaty to create mutual confidence are being increasingly overtaken by political propaganda (especially in Pakistan) and undermining the sanctity of the existing bilateral arrangement. Therefore, both countries should evolve an innovative way of upgrading the talks and making them open and transparent.

As an important element of trust building between the two nations, India must also try to persuade Pakistan to rein in elements spreading unfounded rumours over the issue and take measures against them in the interest of peace and understanding.

OVERALL IMPACT ON INDIA

In Pakistan one finds all the symptoms of a failing state—chronic political and economic instability, penetration of jihadis into the armed forces, declining economy and the rising tide of radicalism—which are likely to weaken the capacity of the state to control the menace of Islamic radicalism that the state has nurtured over the years.

These radical forces, operating in an autonomous manner in Pakistan, are providing refuge to fugitives from India. It is worrisome that these forces sustain themselves through proceeds from narcotic trade (drugs trafficking) and fake currencies (Fake Indian Currency Notes or FICN). Given the declining capacity of the Pakistani state to control them and the Pakistani military's penchant for using these forces as assets for launching asymmetric wars against India, they may be allowed to target India from time to time, either taking care not to leave any evidence behind or by executing attacks through Indian collaborators. This may also have an adverse impact on the internal communal situation in India. Some fringe groups among the Muslims, and even the Hindus, have already started adopting militant methods. India has to carefully isolate links between the radical forces in Pakistan and those in India, and take every possible measure to contain their spread, at the same time strengthening its internal security apparatus to meet this challenge effectively. The Muslims of India need to be mainstreamed without creating the impression that they are being pampered. The state must ensure that they are not discriminated against and are being given equal opportunity to prosper and develop on the basis of a level playing field for all communities.

There is a possibility of jihadi forces either expanding their influence over much of Pakistan or gradually infecting/infiltrating the ranks of the Army. In either case, India has to prepare itself to deal with more non-cooperative and less reasonable elements in future. As the possibility of Mumbai-type attacks cannot be ruled out in future, India has to carefully weigh the options of (i) active engagement (ignoring the provocations),

(ii) total disengagement and benign neglect, and (iii) active counter-measures.

Despite instances of successful popular upheaval to get rid of military dictators, the system has reverted to its earlier shape, sooner rather than later. Ironically, soon after Musharraf's departure from the political scene, the military re-emerged as the predominant institution in Pakistani polity. The political forces have failed to clip the wings of the military and bring it under civilian control. Broadly, there is no political consensus on this issue and Pakistan clearly lacks the will to transform itself. Thus, an undemocratic and Army-controlled Pakistan will continue to challenge India's defence and security policy in the days to come. India's policy towards Pakistan should be to take this basic fact into account while diplomatically engaging Pakistan.

As far as India-Pakistan relations are concerned, despite the restart of bilateral talks, Pakistan is unlikely to take a flexible position on the issues of terrorism, Kashmir and trade. The military will continue to be in full control of the making of security and foreign policy of the country; its maximalist views on India do not correspond to the views of the leading politicians of Pakistan, from Zardari to Nawaz Sharif. Nevertheless, it is in India's interest to keep the dialogue alive, without hoping for miracles to emerge from this process of engagement. This will help India sustain linkages with civilian forces in Pakistan.

In view of the critical importance of the Pakistani military on the foreign policy decision-making process in Pakistan, India ought to give serious thoughts to opening a back channel with the military. This can be initiated openly either at the institutional level (military-to-military, interaction with military personnel through think tanks, etc.) or though backroom channels, if taking an open posture on various issues would be considered politically risky for the time being. Such interactions could melt the ice between India and Pakistan, and lead to some fruitful exchanges on the issues of people-to-people contact, cultural exchanges and trade. At the same time, policy makers in India may weigh the option of developing leverages within Pakistani society as a possible countermeasure against the Pakistani military's efforts to export terrorism to India. Such leverages should be continually nurtured without giving an impression that they are being used as opportunistic bait from time to time.

There is a view in certain quarters in India that issues of radicalism, extremism, poor governance, centre-state tension, corruption, and even economic challenges are common to both India and Pakistan. However, the difference is that India has managed to evolve a more responsive, representative and inclusive system whereas Pakistan has developed as a quasi-military state, where democracy has often been the handmaiden of the assertive and generals largely unaccountable to the people.

SCENARIOS 2030

Key Drivers

There are four key drivers which would continue to shape Pakistan's future. They are: (i) the equation among different actors (the military, the civilian political forces including the civil society, non-state actors, etc.); (ii) socio-economic pressures; (iii) role of external players; and (iv) its relationship with India. These drivers score high in terms of their impact and their ability to cause uncertainty.

Equation among Different Actors

The main actors who would play a significant role in shaping the future of Pakistan are the military, the civilian government and the political forces, civil society, and the radical non-state actors. The military does play a dominant role among all these actors and its disproportionate influence in Pakistani polity has led to the evolution of a Praetorian state.

If the military continues to dictate Pakistan's security and foreign policy, and the civilian government remains largely ineffective, it will fragment Pakistani society and perpetuate the prevailing state of instability. However, a healthy equation among all these actors will take Pakistan in a positive direction. For example, if the military plays second fiddle to the government and wholeheartedly takes on the menace of terrorism, with the full backing of the civil society, then Pakistan will evolve over time as a normal state, at peace with itself and the world.

Socio-economic Pressures

Pakistani society is now torn by ethnic and sectarian divides, as is borne out by the worsening ethnic situation in Balochistan, the inter-ethnic power struggle in Karachi, and rising sectarian violence. If this situation prevails then the internal security situation will deteriorate, which would definitely have its impact on the overall economic situation of the country. A prolonged economic decline coupled with the problem of deepening societal divisions will weaken the capacity of the state and turn Pakistan into a state at war with itself. Alternately, if there is greater social, ethnic and sectarian harmony, brought about either by innovative policies of the government or intervention of civil society bodies, this will create the climate for better economic growth, and Pakistan will emerge as a forward looking regional economic hub.

Role of External Powers

Pakistan's critical dependence on external aid and assistance is well known. Its economy is in a state of crisis and it has not yet reached a point where it can manage on its own without help from outside. In this case, its relationship with the wider world remains a critical variable in determining its future. The US has played a major role in rescuing the Pakistani economy from disaster over the last decade. However, the US-Pak relationship is under strain, and if it deteriorates further it will also adversely impact Pakistan's relationship with other Western countries that are providing aid and assistance to it.

Pakistan will, in all likelihood, seek help from its traditional friends like China, Saudi Arabia and some other countries in the West Asian neighbourhood. However, if one goes by past trends , such help will not enable Pakistan to tide over the crisis and the country's economy will be under stress. On the contrary, if Pakistan develops its own vision of a liberal and democratic future, builds on convergences, especially in countering terror and not using it as an instrument of state policy, it will keep receiving the critical assistance it so urgently requires in order to stabilise its economy and establish itself as a progressive state.

Relationship with India

The relationship with India is a critical driver in shaping Pakistan's future. Pakistan has clearly invested a lot in its policy of using terrorists as instruments in its ongoing proxy-war/low intensity war with India since 1947. Its Afghan policy as well as its overarching emphasis on defence and security of the country is also heavily influenced by its perception of India as the number one enemy. This has prevented Pakistan from having better trade and commerce with India. On the whole, an adversarial relationship with India has had grave consequences for Pakistani society, polity and economy. If Pakistan changes this mindset and embarks on a path of friendship and cooperation with India, it will create the right context for the resolution of outstanding issues between them. This could indeed be a game changer and change the face of Pakistani society, polity and economy forever.

Based on the ability of these drivers to influence the future course of events in Pakistan, the following scenarios may emerge.

Scenario I: Pakistan of Jinnah's Dream

The political forces take stock of the worsening situation and come together, develop a common agenda and engage in constructive politics and evolve a strategy to fight out the menace of radicalism. The military confines itself to the security realm and plays second fiddle to the civilian government. The non-state actors lose their appeal and are handled effectively. The relationship with the US and the wider world improves. International aid and assistance help Pakistan build its economy. Pakistan sheds its anti-India obsession, engages India in trade and commerce and the peace process proceeds well. The Pakistani economy improves and Pakistan stabilises as a normal state.

Scenario II: A Hybrid Jihadi State

The military adopts a jihadi line due to infiltration by jihadi elements. The political forces stay divided and are unable develop a common agenda to fight the jihadi menace. The elections return hung assemblies and lead to political uncertainty. Pakistan's relationship with the wider world declines as non-state actors with an anti-West and regressive international outlook start controlling parts of Pakistan, which then act as nerve centres of international terrorism. International support dries up. Pakistan's traditional friends like China and Saudi Arabia insulate themselves against the corrosive influences from Pakistan and stay aloof. The Pakistani military adopts a confrontational posture vis-à-vis India in an effort to bring about internal cohesion. The internal ethnic and sectarian faultlines manifest themselves and centrifugal forces dominate distinct areas under their control. The threat of nuclear materials falling into terrorist hands seems real. The central authority weakens and Army lacks the capacity to hold the state together. Pakistan splinters.

Scenario III: Muddling Through: A Banana Republic?

The military is dominant and fights only those militant elements who challenge its might. These groups continue to defy the military. The military continues to play a double game and hobnobs with some militant groups to use them as strategic assets. The civilian political forces stay divided and fragmented. They continue to be guided by their narrow political ambitions. The relationship with the US and the wider world remains lukewarm. Pakistan's traditional friends like China and Saudi Arabia are unable to help Pakistan tide over the crisis. The economy remains perpetually in a precarious state. The relationship with India continues to be driven by irrational hatred and fear of India. The peace process continues haltingly but without any traction. Both autonomist and secessionist groups assert themselves. Pakistan hurtles towards internal chaos and there is a civil war like situation within the country.

PROGNOSIS

If the current trends were to continue, Pakistan may develop into a hybrid and semi-theocratic state—partly democratic and partly under the military's control with more emphasis on an extremely radical and less tolerant version of Islam, which is anti-West and anti-India in its orientation. In this case, the institutions of governance in Pakistan will be less effective in addressing the fundamental issues (radicalism, sectarian violence, declining economy and poor law and order situation) confronting the state today.

In its present state, Pakistan is in absolute need of critical help from outside and it has to make itself deserving of the same. Its closest friends at the international level, who have shown some favour towards it in the past, and with whom it does not have a confrontational relationship, are Saudi Arabia, the UAE and China. However, these countries have not demonstrated enough willingness, either individually or together, to harness adequate resources required by Pakistan to pull itself back from the brink. The combined help provided by them in the past has been a pittance compared to the help that has flowed in from the West.

If Pakistan fails to manage its relationship with the US and the West, because of the rising tide of anti-West sentiments at home (partially encouraged by the military to show its independence), the resource crutches furnished by the international community may not be made available to it for eternity. The Pakistani economy does not have the resilience to recover on its own and rudimentary help from its friends may help it in averting a short-term crisis, but its long-term future looks quite grim. Pakistan's traditional friends like China and Saudi Arabia may provide Pakistan short-term help but are unlikely to invest much in either Pakistani economy or security.

In this situation, the only factor that might compel some international attention and assistance is the American concern regarding Pakistan's nuclear arsenal, which runs the risk of falling into wrong hands if the country passes through a long-term political and economic crisis. Given Pakistan's propensity to play the India card in moments of crisis—both to generate internal unity/solidarity and to attract international attention/concern—it is highly likely that a failing Pakistan may adopt an increasingly confrontationist posture vis-à-vis India.

Pakistan can still manage the crisis it is confronted with, and become a normal state, if it:

i. Sheds its irrational fear of India, and improves its relationship with India by eschewing its subversive agenda vis-à-vis India.
ii. Evolves an unequivocal and irreversible policy of confronting radical outfits of all hue and snaps its links with them.
iii. Finds a way of overcoming civil-military dissension at home and building a forward-looking political consensus to ensure internal peace and prosperity.
iv. Relates to international community as a responsible state committed to fight terrorism in all its forms and manifestations.

RECOMMENDATIONS

The Indian strategy to cope with the uncertainty in Pakistan should be as follows:

- Pakistan's pathological obsession with India has to be taken note of, and an antidote to it needs to be evolved in the interest of a better relationship with Pakistan. While an adversarial relationship with Pakistan may not affect India's growth/development trajectory, improvement in relations will unlock tremendous potential for regional prosperity. Therefore, it is essential to develop lasting linkages with all sections of Pakistani population, including political parties, interest groups, ethnic leadership and the military, and convince them of India's good intentions.
- There is a small but articulate and active constituency of liberal elements in Pakistan whose voice is being drowned in the prevailing cacophony of anti-Indianism and radical Islam. Efforts must be made to reach out to them and to nurture and expand this constituency.
- The soft power of India has appealed to the new generation of youth in Pakistan. It has the potential to transform popular imagination and spread liberal values in Pakistan. This power should be used with care and through it message of India's goodwill can be communicated to the people of Pakistan. Due attention must also be paid to permit transmission of comparatively liberal Pakistani channels in India to acquaint Indian audience with the liberal constituency.
- India, with the third largest Muslim population in the world,

could encourage propagation of a liberal Islamic ethic, at an ideological level, as a counter to the radical version of Islam in Pakistan. Facilitation of interaction amongst liberal clerics in both the countries can open up avenues for progressive interpretation of Islam.

- Apart from the structured dialogue at the official level, multiple tracks at the unofficial level must be encouraged to complement formal channels of communication. Unilateral relaxation of visa to facilitate greater movement of people without lowering guard on the security front will be a definite step forward in this regard.

- A healthy dialogue on river water sharing with Pakistan at all levels will help remove popular misperception of India's intent in Pakistan. Facts and figures on the Indus Water Treaty should be shared with wider public in both the countries to counter the anti-India propaganda by some vested interest groups in Pakistan. This does not mean that India should re-negotiate the Treaty or give unilateral concessions.

- In view of the shrinking standards of education in Pakistan, India may also offer scholarships to Pakistani students and take active measures to encourage them to join Indian institutes of learning, especially in the vocational sector. This will help create permanent constituencies in Pakistan with a sense of obligation and goodwill towards India.

- While it is impractical to imagine that Pakistan would shed its pathological obsession with India overnight, such steps may incrementally change Pakistani perceptions about India and ensure better relations in the longer run. But this would only happen if the Pakistani political and military leadership take right measures to arrest the free-fall of the state. The possibility of holding a regular and purposive dialogue with military at whatever level possible may be explored.

- On the trade front, there seems to be a change in certain quarters in Pakistan over the issue of promoting trade and commerce with India, which can be gleaned from a recent report of the planning commission of Pakistan. It is also reported that Pakistan may continue with its efforts to grant MFN status to India. India can thus take pro-active measures like lowering of non-tariff barriers, facilitate interaction among business communities, and encourage Indian business houses to invest in Pakistan, in order to strengthen economic cooperation between the two countries. This may not

- happen in the short term but efforts towards it should begin in right earnest.
- There is a strong view in certain quarters in India that it should develop an entire portfolio of measures to penalise Pakistan unless it mends its ways. India may thus develop leverages within Pakistan, among constituencies amenable to Indian influence, in case it chooses to adopt counter-measures to deter Pakistan's asymmetric strategies vis-à-vis India.
- So far, India lacks leverages within Pakistani society and, in reality, it has little influence over Pakistani politics. Therefore, politicians and military leaders do nourish anti-India sentiments and forge it into politics, expecting, thereby, to reap a good electoral harvest. However, India must try proactively to develop pro-India constituencies in Pakistan and the suggestions above can go a long way in ensuring this.

NOTES

1. Data provided by South Asian Terrorism Portal, based on open source information. For details see http://www.satp.org/satporgtp/countries/pakistan/database/sect-killing.htm.
2. According to the data compiled by the Center for Islamic Research Collaboration and Learning (CIRCLe), a Rawalpindi-based think tank, a majority of these attacks have taken place in FATA (Orakzai [31 per cent] and Khyber [21 per cent] agencies) and the Khyber-Pakhtunkhwa province (Peshawar 24 per cent). However, in terms of casualties, Punjab has suffered the most (Lahore has witnessed 10 per cent of the attacks and 47 per cent of the casualties). Data provided by CIRCLe, based in Islamabad. For details see http://terrorismwatch.com.pk/images/Timeline%20Of%20attacks%20on%20Shrines%20In%20Pakistan.pdf, accessed on January 11, 2012.
3. ARY Digital TV's detailed coverage, available on youtub.com at http://www.youtube.com/watch?v=Ywx6R_K0uKw&feature=related, accessed on January 11, 2012.
4. Chief among them are Lashkar-e-Jhangvi (LEJ), Sipah-e-Sahaba Pakistan (SSP) and now, the Tehrik-e-Taliban Pakistan (TTP). LeJ has split itself into numerous sub-groups to avoid detection and also for effective implementation of its plans and programmes (Jundullah, Asian Tigers, Lashkar-e-Jhangvi-Al Almi, Junoodul Afsa, Punjabi Taliban etc.).
5. They were declared non-Muslims in 1974 during Zulfikar Ali Bhutto's rule and later General Ziaul Haq's Ordinance XX issued in 1984 subjected them to further persecution.
6. Naved Masood Hashimi, 'Sir Zafarullah Khan se Mansoor Ijaz Tak: Qadiyaniyat ke Libade Mein Chhupe Asal Kirdaron ki Kahani', *Ausaf*, January, 2012.
7. The demand for separate Hazara province is also gathering momentum. The proposed province will consist of the districts of Abbottabad, Haripur, Mansehra, Batagram and Kohistan.

8. According to Pakistani Census in 1998, 10.53 per cent of the population registered Seraiki language as their mother tongue. The Seraikistan province, as demanded by its advocates, will include 19 districts from Punjab (Sargodha, Multan, Dera Ghazi Khan and other districts in the Bahawalpur division), and two districts of Multan and even Tank and Dera Ismail Khan in Khyber-Pakhtunkhwa province.
9. The chart here is taken from the interactive World Bank website http://databank.worldbank. org/ddp/home.do, accessed on December 12, 2011.
10. Under the RGST, the earlier exemptions on basic food items (wheat, rice, pulses, vegetables, fruits, live animals, meat and poultry, etc.) have been kept intact. Also retained are exemptions on expenditures on philanthropic, charitable, educational, health or scientific research purposes as well as on life-saving drugs, books and other printed materials, including newspapers and periodicals. Those drawn into the tax net include textiles (including carpets), leather, surgical and sports goods, defence stores, stationary items, dairy products, pharmaceuticals (other than life-saving), agricultural inputs, agricultural machinery and implements, and aviation/navigation equipment, including ships and aircrafts, etc. For details see http://www.fbr.gov.pk/newst/stgos/2010/GSTBILL2010.pdf, accessed on January 11, 2012.
11. *The State of Pakistan's Competitiveness Report 2010-2011*, by Competitiveness Support Fund (CSF) can be accessed at www.competitiveness.org.pk/downloads/SPCR2010.pdf. CSF is a joint initiative of Ministry of Finance, Government of Pakistan and United States agency for International Development (USAID).
12. Shahzad had written about the links between certain sections of the armed forces and jihadi groups in the wake of the attack on the Pakistan Naval Station (PNS) Mehran, by the TTP and promised to reveal more in an upcoming piece in the *Asia Times Online*.

Chapter 9

SRI LANKA
CHALLENGES AND OPPORTUNITIES FOR INDIA

Smruti S Pattanaik

INTRODUCTION

The politico-strategic and economic environment of the country is predicated upon political stability, growth potential, investment climate and a skilled work force. The end of war has also unleashed its productive potential and created an environment free from violence that is conducive for investment.[1] The war-ravaged Sri Lankan economy is making a steady recovery. However, Sri Lanka's political and economic stability in future would depend on how it would deal with the ethnic issue and address the grievances of the Tamil community. Nevertheless, there are some positive trends in Sri Lanka's economy, generated by the end of war, and these are likely to attract investors.

In 2010, Sri Lanka recorded highest quarterly GDP growth since 2002 following the end of the civil war. The three major sectors of the economy—agriculture, services and tea—registered an impressive growth in the second quarter of 2010, compared with the same quarter in 2009. Agriculture grew by 5.1 per cent, industry by 9.2 per cent, and services by 8.8 per cent. Sri Lanka earned the highest ever proceeds ($1.37 billion) from export of tea in 2010.[2] According to the 2009 data of the Central Bank of Sri Lanka, the employment figures in various sectors were: agriculture—32.6 per cent; manufacturing industry—25.1 per cent; and services—42.3 per cent. At present, the country is growing at more than 8 per cent (it was 8.1 per cent in 2010 and an estimated 8.5 per cent in

2011) and it has an inflation rate of 6 per cent.³ A road map for 2011 announced by the Central Bank states that the nation's balance of payments is likely to show a surplus of $900 million in 2010 and the estimated remittances from Sri Lankans working overseas would go up to $4.1 billion, up by 24 per cent compared to the previous year.⁴ Sri Lanka faced a balance of payment crisis in 2009 due to war as its economic growth was only 3.5 per cent.

Sri Lanka has three major commercial ports: Colombo, Galle and Trincomalee. Apart from these, Hambantota in the south, being developed by China, is coming up as a major commercial port. Oluvil on the eastern coast is also being developed as a major commercial port and a base for fishing vessels. It is likely that, in the next two decades, Sri Lanka will emerge as a major maritime commercial hub. The Government is also taking steps to develop infrastructure and rail network that will feed the process of industrialisation, boosting its economy. Connectivity is bound to fuel economic growth in Sri Lanka and several infrastructure projects are also proposed.⁵ An Indian company—IRCON—is building the Madu-Talaimannar and Medawachchiya-Madu railway lines and reconstructing the Omanthai-Pallai segment and Pallai-KKS railway line. India has pledged a credit line of $800 million for these projects and signed a credit agreement for $416.39 million for the Northern Railway construction project. It is also building Palaly Airport and Kankesanthurai Harbour. Table 9.1 shows the financial commitments of different countries that are involved in developmental projects in Sri Lanka.

Sri Lanka has also signed Multilateral Investment Guarantee Agency agreement with the World Bank and foreign investment in Sri Lanka is protected by Article 157 of the Sri Lankan constitution. *Mahinda Chintana*, unveiled by the President during his 2010 election campaign, seeks to develop Sri Lanka as a regional hub for air and sea transportation, trading, energy and knowledge-based service by making the country the 'wonder of Asia' by increasing per capita income to above $4,000 by 2016.⁶ It is likely that the government will make all efforts to sustain economic growth as it believes the road to peace is through economic development. The sustainability of economic growth will depend on peaceful resolution of ethnic conflict.

Sri Lanka is encouraging investment and trying to project itself as a commercial hub after the end of three decades of conflict. Under Section 17 of the Board of Investment (BOI) Act⁷, BOI, Sri Lanka is empowered to grant special concessions to companies satisfying the eligibility criteria, which are designed to meet strategic economic objectives of the government. Such concessions are granted under the Agreement that

Table 9.1: Foreign Finance Commitments to Sri Lanka in 2010 (USD Million)

Donor	Loan	Grant	Total
Bilateral	2,402.5	104.6	2,507.1
Japan	396.6	42.3	438.9
China	821.4	7.5	828.9
India	483.8	-	483.8
Australia	105.2	10.5	115.7
France	16.3	-	16.3
Iran	111.2	-	111.2
Russia	300.0	-	300.0
Saudi Fund	46.1	-	46.1
Netherlands	-	0.1	0.1
USA	-	44.2	44.2
Korea	40.0	-	40.0
Other	81.9	-	81.9
Multilateral	762.3	19.0	781.3
ADB	366.7	5.5	372.2
World Bank	347.4	-	347.4
IFAD	24.2	-	24.2
OPEC Fund	24.0	-	24.0
UN Agencies	-	13.5	13.5
Total	3136.9	123.6	3,260.5

Source: Ministry of Finance and Planning, *Annual Report 2010*, Government of Sri Lanka, p. 245.

modifies, exempts and waives identified laws in keeping with the BoI regulations. These laws include inland revenues, customs, exchange control and import control.

To attract investors Sri Lanka allows 100 per cent investment in housing, infrastructure, hospitals, voice and data communication system, transport, etc. It welcomes investment in manufacturing household electrical products, textile, rubber industry, agriculture, mining and processing, gems and jewellery, tourism, leisure and hotel projects.[8] Sri Lanka, according to Economic Intelligence Unit Report, is the eighth fastest growing economy of the world.[9] It has six free trade zones, also called export processing or investment promotion zones located in Katunayake (1978), Biyagama (1986), Koggala (1991), Pallekelle (1996), Mirigama (1997), and Malwatte (1997). There are over 155 foreign export processing enterprises operating in these six zones.[10]

Sri Lanka received $236 million in foreign direct investment (FDI) in the first quarter of 2011, up 160 per cent from a year earlier, led by tourism. The utilities sector received the second highest investment which was around $62 million, followed by $7 million in apparels sector.[11]

The Government has liberalised the tax regime and allowed foreign companies to remit their corporate profit and dividends, stock market profits without prior approval of the Central Bank. The Government has also lifted restrictions on local investors to borrow money from foreign sources as well as invest abroad. Sri Lanka needs to double its savings for micro-economic stability. It is true that remittances have increased in spite of the global economic downturn.[12] However, dependence on tourism and remittances can make its economy vulnerable to external factors.

However several administrative constraints continue to fetter the business environment in Sri Lanka. The following indices (Table 9.2) give an idea about the existing business environment in Sri Lanka amongst 183 countries.

Table 9.2: Doing Business in Sri Lanka[13]

Topic Rankings	DB 2012 Rank	DB 2011 Rank	Change in Rank
Starting a Business	38	35	-3
Dealing with Construction Permits	111	110	-1
Getting Electricity	95	97	2
Registering Property	161	158	-3
Getting Credit	78	75	-3
Protecting Investors	46	74	28
Paying Taxes	173	171	-2
Trading Across Borders	53	53	No change
Enforcing Contracts	136	136	No change
Resolving Insolvency	42	44	2

Source: International Financial Corporation (IFC) & World Bank data at http://www.doingbusiness.org/data/exploreeconomies/sri-lanka/

Sri Lanka, however, has an edge in some areas. It has an efficient labour force. Labour force participation in the third quarter of 2010 was 48.2 per cent, of which males constituted 63.7 and females 28.7 per cent. Of the total labour force, 32.9 per cent are employed in the agriculture sector, which includes forestry and fishery; 24.3 per cent in industry (manufacturing, construction, mining, quarrying, electricity, gas and water supply); and 42.8 per cent are employed in the service sector.[14] The unemployment rate is 4.9 per cent of which male unemployment stands at 3.6 per cent and female unemployment at 7.7 per cent.[15] Sri Lanka is a major exporter of textiles to Western countries, but it is yet to optimise its potential. It has been able to export $900 million worth of garments —a 50 per cent increase over the previous year—but its share in the GDP is not impressive. Moreover, the EU has denied it preferential trade under General System of Preferences (GSP) plus accusing it of gross human rights violations which has affected its exports. Overall, Sri Lanka has favourable geographical and demographic conditions and it aspires to high economic growth and building economic infrastructure at a rapid pace. If it can manage its internal political situation, it would help the country to attract foreign investors and usher in an era of stability. To some extent, foreign investors are discouraged by politically motivated decisions of the Government to favour local companies over foreign ones. This is also one of the reasons why the Government is not prepared to sign Comprehensive Economic Partnership Agreement (CEPA) with India.

Tourism is a major source of its economy apart from agriculture. The Sri Lankan Government has identified the country's east coast as having potential for tourism business. The Government is targeting attracting 2.5 million tourists annually by 2016. Sri Lanka had declared 2011 as the year of tourism and witnessed a 46 per cent growth in tourism. The Government also expected to attract US$ 3 billion FDI in the tourism industry and increase tourism-related employment from 125,000 at present to 500,000 by 2016.[16]

The country faces a budget deficit and revenue generation remains impaired. The domestic savings ratio (as a percentage of GDP) was 18.7 per cent and the national savings rate in Sri Lanka was 24.7 per cent, according to the 2010 annual report of the Central Bank. The Government is heavily dependent on borrowings from both domestic and foreign commercial sources, international sovereign bonds as well as loans from bilateral and multilateral sources for specific projects and programmes.

The Government needs to diversify its export market which, at present, is focussed on Western countries for its garment business. Its labour laws do not allow dismissal of labourers, electricity prices are high, and roads and communication networks are not yet developed. It also needs to ensure a balanced growth by persuading the service industry to focus on export-oriented growth. Given the large-scale infrastructure development initiatives the country has undertaken, it is hoped that the Government will take measures to improve investment climate in the coming days.

INDIA-SRI LANKA BILATERAL FREE TRADE AGREEMENT

According to the Sri Lankan Central Bank Report, India was the largest foreign direct investor in Sri Lanka in 2010 with $110 million followed by Malaysia with $72 million and the United Arab Emirates with $66 million.[17] India is the fifth-largest destination for Sri Lankan exports[18], and the largest source for Sri Lankan imports, which account for 17.8 per cent followed by Singapore at 10.4 per cent and China at 10.1 per cent. The bilateral Free Trade Agreement (FTA) between the two countries has done exceedingly well. In spite of initial hiccups, the FTA has managed to address Sri Lanka's apprehensions of trading with a big country. The two countries have a CEOs' forum that engages the public and private sectors in a dialogue to generate ideas to deepen and broaden the bilateral economic relationship. Both the countries have already signed a Business Promotion and Investment Agreement in 1997. India can impart training to labourers working in the tea and garment industries. There could be joint ventures to produce ready-made garments as labour is cheap in India.

Sri Lanka's export base has expanded. Export of new products following reduction of tariff rates by India includes insulated wires, cables, pneumatic tyres, ceramics, vegetable fat and oil, and furniture. The trade between the two countries showed some decline in 2008-2009 due to the global financial crisis and after India withdrew the quota on *vanaspati* import from Sri Lanka. However, the quota was restored later. Companies like Brandix, one of the largest textile industries, has invested in India and has established a unit (over 1,000 acres) near Bengaluru. Similarly, leading Sri Lankan companies like the furniture firm Damro, Aitken Spence and Jetwing have also invested in India following the FTA. Among the Indian companies, the service sector has emerged as major attraction. Sri Lanka wants Indian investment in ports, power and telecommunications sector. The two countries can invest in joint ventures in manufacturing, services and infrastructure sectors in Sri Lanka.

India's National Thermal Power Corporation (NTPC) is collaborating with the Ceylon Electricity Board for building a 500 MW coal-fired plant at Sampur (Trincomalee). For this purpose, India has pledged $200 million and is negotiating a joint venture agreement, a power purchase agreement, and an agreement with the Board of Investment of Sri Lanka. These agreements have the potential to strengthen mutually beneficial relations. Joint venture agreements would lead to industrialisation and provide employment opportunities to the youth and, to a certain extent, assuage the disenchantment of the people with regard to gainful employment. Sri Lanka has proposed establishing a joint information mechanism on the possibility of oil and gas fields straddling the India-Sri Lanka maritime boundary. All these agreements, once operationalised, can enhance economic cooperation between the two countries.

India's private sector is playing a significant role in forging close economic ties. India's ICICI Bank has already opened a branch in Sri Lanka; L&T is engaged in civil construction; Bharti Airtel had earlier announced a $200 million investment by 2012 and it remains to be seen whether the goal has been achieved; and Cairn India has received approval to invest $400 million in oil exploration. The NTPC, the Aditya Birla group, the Mahindra group, HCL, and the TATA group are also in the process of investing in Sri Lanka.

The two countries are engaged in discussion to sign Comprehensive Economic Partnership Agreement (CEPA) to take their bilateral FTA to next level, which would mainly include the service sector. The principal sectors that would benefit from CEPA are tourism, computer software, advertising, financial and non-financial services, health, hotel, retail services and tourism. This will create employment opportunities.

COMPREHENSIVE ECONOMIC PARTNERSHIP AGREEMENT (CEPA)

The natural progression from the FTA would be the signing of Comprehensive Economic Partnership Agreement (CEPA) which would help the two countries to build economic synergy and interdependence.[19] A draft agreement was prepared after 13 rounds of intense negotiation between February 2005 and July 2008. However, some of the politically connected small business houses in Sri Lanka are opposed to this agreement.[20] Given the closeness of these business houses to the President, businessmen supporting the agreement are reluctant to express their support openly. After the elimination of the LTTE, the political space has unfortunately been monopolised by Rajapaksa's party (Sri Lanka Freedom Party [SLFP]). What has helped the government is the weakness of the main opposition party (United National Party [UNP]) that is riddled with factionalism. It appears that the Sri Lankan Government is having second thoughts on CEPA and has not countered the propaganda against the agreement. Anyone who supports CEPA is painted as anti-national and a smear campaign is launched by vested interests to portray them as being pro-India. Similar concerns were also expressed prior to the signing of bilateral FTA but strong political will of the two governments weathered the opposition, and now the FTA has worked out to Sri Lanka's advantage.[21] There are some concerns however regarding the dispute settlement mechanism proposed under CEPA. However, many in Sri Lanka feel that once the agreement is implemented some of the problem areas can be resolved through negotiations. Attempts are now being made to take sectoral approach to deal with the issue of large investment in the services sector.[22]

The rise of Sinhala nationalism—given the manner in which the war ended—has created further constraints. Some people from the industry and others who were involved in negotiation feel extremely disappointed that—given the opportunities that exist between the two countries—the Government is taking a political decision rather than taking into account its economic potential and the benefits that may accrue to Sri Lanka. The nationalists, who are the biggest supporters of the President, are in no mood to forge close economic ties with India, which is perceived as the country that, at one point of time, supported the LTTE. The Government is encouraging this lobby. However, this group has not yet come up with any concrete alternative, and is not clear on what problems it has with CEPA.[23] The Rajapaksa Government has relied on political jingoism and has portrayed him as a saviour of the Sinhala nation. It appears that he is not interested in implementing the CEPA since it does not augur well with the prevailing nationalistic discourse in Sri Lanka. Not caving in to India's demands also strengthens his image as a nationalist. Moreover, at the political level, any concession to India is seen as surrender to the supporter of the Tamils. The government is adopting delaying tactics for political reasons. Thus, many experts who participated in CEPA negotiation feel the Government of India needs to pressurise the Rajapaksa Government on this issue. However, there are others who feel this issue may be gently pursued behind the scenes without making too many noises in public.[24]

The CEPA with India will boost economic growth engine of Sri Lanka to fulfil Rajapaksa's dream of making Sri Lanka the 'wonder of Asia'. The service sector is largely unexplored and would need foreign investment to optimise its potential. CEPA would have been an ideal solution to expand trade in services and would have given a stake to the private investors. However, a sector-wise approach to the service sector, however cumbersome it may be in the short term, seems to be a way out of the current political quagmire.

The Ceylon Chamber of Commerce, that represents major industries, favours expansion of investment, trade in services sector and argues that CEPA takes into account the concerns of all the stakeholders.[25] Given India's geographical proximity, it is likely that India would be a major investor, which would benefit Sri Lanka immensely. CEPA will also send positive signals to other investors to seek business opportunities in Sri Lanka.

The success of the FTA has been to the mutual benefit of Indian and Sri Lankan businessmen and they are ready to take advantage of increased investment and opening of service sector. Problems with regard to the export of palm oil and *vanaspati* are cited as instances by the vested interest in Sri Lanka to argue against CEPA.[26] Interestingly, instead of countering this lobby, the pro-CEPA lobby want India to exert pressure on the Sri Lankan Government for its early resolution.[27]

The Sri Lankan Government is using the China card to counterbalance any pressure from New Delhi. While China is providing loans, Delhi is providing grants and has invested in joint ventures, which create long-term joint stakes. But there are bureaucratic delays in implementing the Indian projects. In contrast, the Chinese bring in their labour, fund their projects and hand them over faster to the Sri Lankan government.[28] The money invested by China is to be paid back over the long-term at higher rate of interest.[29] The Government portrays it as investment rather than loan. Some Sri Lankan analysts perceive that the Chinese move stealthily in establishing commercial ties and the Government of Sri Lanka are using their presence as a balancer vis-à-vis India.[30] China's supplies of weapons and its support to Sri Lanka in the UN Human Rights Commission are well publicised. This has created a politically-enabling environment for Chinese investments.

POLITICAL SOLUTION KEY TO BETTER INDIA-SRI LANKA RELATIONS

Mahinda Chinthan, which the President unveiled before his election, does not offer any solution to the ethnic conflict. It speaks of certain steps to be taken to bring about national consensus in the chapter entitled 'Undivided country, a national consensus and Honourable peace' and emphasises a 'fresh approach'. The Government has conducted several rounds of talks with the Tamil National Alliance (TNA) without any concrete proposals. The TNA has, in fact, been frustrated at the slow pace of the talks and the Government's reluctance to discuss issues related to the Tamils. Interestingly a section entitled 'A New Path for Natural Cohabitation' refers to an eastern revival, a northern spring, development projects and resettlement of the north and east, but is silent on political solution. It is unlikely that the ethnic issue will be resolved over the next 20 years. The situation may deepen the Tamil sense of alienation and has the potential to lead to militancy. This is because the Government is yet to initiate serious discussions to resolve the issue.

The talks with the TNA so far have centred on the issue of missing persons and rehabilitation, which are important issues but not central to the core ethnic problem that has much to do with political marginalisation.

Moreover, the so called 'home-grown solution' to the ethnic problem, being emphasised by Rajapaksa, has not been sincerely explored nearly three years after the war came to an end in 2009. The Tamils would argue that even though the Government has been arguing for a national consensus on the issue, its approach defeats the purpose of consensus building. For example, Rajapaksa has built an aura of triumphalism around the victory over the LTTE and this has shaped the ultra-Sinhali nationalist discourse. Moreover, many of his statements reveal that he is emphasising more on economic revival, which, he hopes, would reduce the salience of the ethnic issue, even amongst the Tamils. His reluctance to admit that war crimes were committed—which could facilitate reconciliation—has created serious doubt among the Tamil population on whether they can get any justice from the Government. The Government is also resorting to increased militarisation of the Tamil majority areas with the establishment of cantonments, and it is also rehabilitating Sinhalese population in the Tamil-dominated areas. It is employing Sinhali labourers, instead of local Tamils, to work in developmental projects in the north. All these do not create political confidence among the Tamils.

Both the Sri Lankan Government and the Tamil political parties have, from time to time, discussed the resolution of ethnic conflict with the Government of India and political parties in Tamil Nadu. The Tamils of Sri Lanka are in a desperate situation; at one level, they feel let down by India and, at another level, they look towards India as their 'protector' as they continue to distrust the sincerity of the Rajapaksa Government.[31] Even though many in India feel that New Delhi does not have leverage over Colombo, many 'moderate' civil society activists in Sri Lanka, including the TNA, perceive that India can pressurise the Rajapaksa Government as it has a 'credible' international voice and is increasingly playing a global role. The argument here is that India cannot play a global role if it is not in a position to influence regional peace. They hold that dialogue with the Tamil leaders, who were elected in the last provincial council elections, is important and the age-old grievances of the Tamils need to be addressed for durable peace. India has already expressed its strong support for a united Sri Lanka. However, India's continued support to the Rajapaksa Government, they argue, should not be at the cost of the Tamil community. India must aim at durable peace in Sri Lanka as that would be important for its security, and any prolonging of the conflict would invite extra-regional intervention.

India has emphasised the need for a structured dialogue with Tamil parties and other stake-holders and has extended financial support for rehabilitation and resettlement of the Tamils who were displaced during the war. The Government of India has also announced that it will build 50,000 shelters for the internally displaced persons in the northern and the eastern provinces. However, this project has been delayed as the Government of Sri Lanka has not provided the list of beneficiaries for whom these houses are meant. Modalities for providing housing assistance under the 'owner driven model' are pending for approval. It is likely that Indian projects would be further delayed as the Sri Lankan Government feels that these will give India a political foothold in the Tamil-dominated area and strengthen its relations with them. Though Rajapaksa reiterated that he was willing to go beyond the 13th Amendment to the Sri Lankan Constitution with regard to the Northern Province of the country, talks are yet to be initiated with various stakeholders on this count. At the same time it is clear that he is unwilling to concede land, police and investment powers to the provincial councils. The 13th Amendment is opposed by the ultra-Left JVP and other Sinhala nationalists, including the rightist parties consisting of Buddhist monks who feel that the end of war has provided them with an opportunity to re-establish Sinhala hegemony. Sri Lanka has referred to the Tamil problem as an internal matter at the United Nations Human Rights Commission and said that the issue would be resolved by Sri Lanka independently with the application of a home-grown solution.[32]

In Sri Lanka, anyone who argues in favour of devolution as a political solution in Sri Lanka is labelled as an LTTE sympathiser. This leaves hardly any space for a counter-narrative to deal with the increasing triumphalism that is promoted by the Rajapaksa Government, which portrays him as Dutugemunu, a Sinhala king (167-137 BC), who had defeated the Tamils. Rajapaksa was born and raised in Weerakatiya village in the southern rural district of Hambantota and has a rural background. He panders to the Sinhala Buddhist constituency and has politically cashed in on this political base. He is unwilling and, perhaps, constrained to make any concession to Tamils because he thinks any political understanding with the Tamils would be seen as a sign of weakness and undermine his position in Sri Lankan politics. Some Sri Lankan analysts argue that he can create a favourable public opinion in favour of devolution if he sincerely wants. However, he chooses somehow to float with the triumphalist mood sweeping Sri Lanka today.[33]

To deal with any possible revival of separatist militant movement in the future, the Army has established cantonments in Tamil areas and uses surveillance to monitor the activities of the Tamils. This has created unnecessary fear among the Tamils and undermines their confidence in the Sri Lankan state. Such increased militarisation may lead to social problems. The sense of helplessness, frustration, defeat and political alienation prevailing amongst the Tamils may translate into militancy if such coercive methods persist. The state's decision to use military as a major agent of reconciliation—for it is building roads and schools and has become the face of the Government in the north—is resented by many Tamils.[34]

India can play a role in facilitating a political solution between the government of Sri Lanka and the Tamil community. However, the political initiative to address the issue should be taken by the Sri Lankan government. The elimination of the LTTE, a fascist organisation that was responsible for silencing moderate Tamil voices, provides an opportunity to all stake-holders to come together work towards to a framework for settlement. Knowing that the direction of ethnic peace will impinge on Indo-Sri Lanka relations in the next two decades, it will be challenge for India's diplomacy to enable a meaningful process of reconciliation. India does have its leverages with political groups in Sri Lanka and can play a constructive role if there is right political will in this direction. Of course, India's efforts will be constrained by the fact that other than urging the Sri Lankan Government, it cannot play a direct role in the process unless invited by the Government and the Tamil parties. Both the countries will have to handle this issue carefully.[35]

THE TRILINGUAL FORMULA

In Sri Lanka, the Official Languages Commission (OLC), constituted in 2005, had recommended making both the Tamil and Sinhala languages compulsory for all the new recruitments made by the Government. In 2009, Rajapaksa announced the tri-lingual policy, proposing a 10-year action plan for the same. Unfortunately, there is lack of sufficient infrastructure for implementing the three-language formula, which also needs an enabling political environment.[36] As of now, few Tamils want to go to Colombo and teach the Tamil language. Moreover, the Government continues to send official communications in Sinhala language, which is an irritant for the Tamils. The language of each community is strongly linked to their socio-cultural and literary heritage, and due recognition of each language would go a long way in assuaging the feeling of being discriminated against. The trilingual policy, if pursued in right earnest, will definitely have a positive impact on the political cohesion of the country in the next two decades. After all, it was the Sinhala-only Policy of 1956 which sowed the seeds of the ethnic conflict in Sri Lanka. The Government needs to provide more resources to fund the language programme. Exhibition of sensitivity and empathetic attitude on the issue of language would provide a healing touch.

THE ISSUE OF DEVOLUTION/AUTONOMY

The negotiating parties need to move slowly on the issue of devolution/autonomy because in its truest sense it will only come with the passage of time. There exists significant distrust between the two communities, given the lack of communication and interaction over last three decades. The Government should release and hand over the civilian land and property to their rightful owners in the high-security zone in Palaly, presently occupied by the security forces. The Government needs also to resolve the issue carefully—not only have land records have been destroyed but also because many abandoned their houses and fled to foreign countries because of the war. It also needs to decide the fate of the people who continue to be in the custody of the armed forces. These measures, if adopted, will help in building confidence between the two communities.

The Muslim population of Sri Lanka also have a role to play in the devolution debate. It needs to be mentioned that there are around 100,000 Muslims who were internally displaced during the war. Three decades of war have alienated the Muslim population from the Tamils as the Muslims were brutally killed and driven away from the Tamil-dominated areas due to their suspected disloyalty to the 'Tamil cause'. Therefore, there is a need to take their views into consideration to ensure that they do not feel marginalised. The Sri Lanka Muslim Congress (SLMC) is under immense pressure from its supporters to ensure that the Muslim cause should not be subsumed by the Tamil cause, and that their political grievances need to be addressed separately.[37] It must be realised that ignoring the SLMC will not do. It can play a dual role, i.e., it can either be a spoiler or a game changer in the government-TNA negotiations. On the one hand, it can be used by the vested interests to prevent the conclusion of any agreement that may devolve power to the Tamils; on the other, the Muslims can be co-opted to generate a broad consensus on the devolution of power to the Tamils. They are presently not a part of the Government's talks with the TNA. They also nurse a grievance vis-à-vis the Government as they feel that the Muslims were unfortunately caught in the Government-LTTE crossfire, and have an entirely different set of political issues with both, and yet they are not part of the dialogue.

The three-decade long ethnic conflict has played a big role in the evolution of the Tamil Muslims as a separate Muslim ethno-religious community. Over a period of time, they have acquired their separate identity and emerged as a distinct political group. There is a view that India has not been supportive of the emergence of Tamil Muslims as a third party to the complex conflict. There is a belief amongst some analysts in India that such fragmentation would only weaken the cause of both Tamils and Muslims. There is also a view that the Tamil Muslim youths are vulnerable to radicalisation, and that Pakistan may try to use SLMC to reduce India's role in the resolution of Tamil issue.

The TNA is also under pressure from the Tamil people to deliver a political solution.[38] It fears that it would lose its political constituency if it is unable to extract concessions from an unwilling government. The elections held to the northern provincial council showed that the TNA represents the legitimate political aspirations of the Tamils. However, the talks have reached a dead-end, as the Government does not want to make any concession on major issues. The TNA has now asked the Government 'to meaningfully define and state the Government's response to three issues: the structure of governance; the division of subjects and functions between the centre and the devolved units, and fiscal and financial powers', before the dialogue can be resumed.[39] The issue of persons who went missing during the war is also a pressing political problem. The conversion of Jaffna into a garrison town reflects the lingering mutual suspicion between the two communities. The Tamil people there feel they are being forced to sing the national anthem in Sinhala to attest their loyalty to the state. The attitude of the state representatives towards the Tamils is being perceived as one of patronisation, and not equality. The manner in which the war has ended has demoralised the Tamils, yet there is a simmering tension and hatred that is brewing under the surface.[40] The resettlement of the Sinhala population in Tamil-dominated areas may lead to further tension between the Tamil and Sinhala population in future.

There is a need for genuine reconciliation and such an initiative has to come from the Sinhala community. It would be important to think of new terms, other than 'federalism' and 'devolution' which are regarded as politically sensitive in Sri Lanka, to describe the future political arrangement. The Government needs to bring the Sinhala hardliners who are opposed to devolution to the negotiating table and assure them that it would mean a redistribution of powers and not separatism. To start with, Sri Lanka could adopt a model that favours strong central control over the provinces and then should slowly proceed to give Tamils more autonomy.

Reconciliation through the three-language formula, starting a dialogue with the Tamil community, and assuring it that the Government is committed to resolution of their problems would help. This should be accompanied by a resettlement programme for the people uprooted from their homes, providing them with employment opportunities, and reducing visible military presence in the civilian areas. Recruitment of Tamils in the Government services and promoting their culture will help the emergence of a confident and ethnically secure Sri Lanka that can put the decades of civil war behind. There is a need to build roads and schools and bring the northern part of the country to a certain degree of parity with the south.[41]

To some extent, without the resolution of the Tamil issue, the relationship between India and Sri Lanka will remain problematic. India faces the difficult task of making the Sri Lankan Government realise that the resolution of the issue is in its own interest. However, many in Sri Lanka (from both the Sinhala and Tamil communities) argue that India has to find means either to cajole, or coerce Sri Lanka to move forward to evolve a political solution which will meet Tamil aspirations within a unified Sri Lanka.

Sri Lanka has also to put its domestic political sensitivities aside to realise the full potential of economic relationship with India which will boost its economy. It has to understand that no country other than India is in a position to help Sri Lanka as much to realise its true economic potential. Economic integration with India will create a win-win situation for both the countries. Thus India needs to engage Sri Lanka proactively to make it overcome the political sensitivities over ethnic and economic issues.

INDIA-SRI LANKA RELATIONS IN 2030

The main drivers of India-Sri Lanka relations are: political management of the Tamil issue, economic opportunities and aspirations of Sri Lanka, and the role of external players.

Political Management

The end of the war may motivate the Government to put the ethnic issue on the back burner and concentrate on taking economic measures hoping that it would prevent the re-emergence of the separatist movement. Alternatively, the Government may also try and address the issue of provincial autonomy. To achieve that, it may attempt to hold talks with various stakeholders and try to reach a consensus. The main opposition political party has largely been ineffective and is mired in its internal problems. The ruling party and other political parties are trying to cash in on the victory. As a result, no one is willing to support the mitigation of political grievances of the Tamils out of fear of being branded as anti-national.

Over the next two decades it is unlikely that the Government of Sri Lanka will make any sort of political accommodation with the Tamil community to resolve the issue. The Tamil diaspora would continue to play a significant role in creating international public opinion against the Sri Lankan Government over human rights violations. Some LTTE sympathisers are internationally active even though they do not have the political muscle to raise a militia group in the near future. If the Government does not address the issue of the political alienation of Tamils and continues to rely excessively on fanning Sinhala nationalistic sentiments, it is likely that the Tamils may again take recourse to militancy. The Lesson Learnt and Reconciliation Commission (LLRC) report submitted in November 2011 recognised that 'despite the lapse of two years since the ending of the conflict, the violence, suspicion and sense of discrimination are still prevalent in social and political life' and hence '[d]elay in the implementation of a clearly focused post-conflict peace building agenda may have contributed to this situation.'[42]

A military approach to address political grievances would not help. The resettlement of the Sinhala population in the north and east would aggravate inter-ethnic cleavages. If the Government does not take political measures to establish internal stability, it would have a deleterious effect on security. This, in turn, would impinge on economy. It is unlikely that there would be recurrence of violence in short term. However, political turmoil cannot be ruled out over the long term, given the role of diaspora. It is likely that Sinhala triumphalism will make the resolution of the Tamil issue difficult. If substantial power is not devolved it is unlikely that peace would prevail.

In the absence of the LTTE, the Tamils feel that there is no pressure on the Government. The Tamil political parties are divided and thus they pin high hopes on India, the Tamil diaspora and the international community to put pressure on the Government for adequate devolution of power to make them feel safe and secure. The post-conflict political situation in Sri Lanka favours Rajapaksa's policy of procrastination. Since all the political parties want to derive mileage from the end of the war and elimination of LTTE, no one has any serious interest in taking up the issue of devolution for the Tamils. The LLRC report acknowledged that the 'culture of suspicion, fear, mistrust and violence needs to be removed and opportunities and space opened up in which people can hear each other and be heard.'[43]

If the Government continues to ignore the core political issue, it is likely that the cleavages between the communities would get sharpened, leading to societal and political instability by 2030. Relations with India would suffer as a result, and economic integration with India will not materialise.

ECONOMIC OPPORTUNITIES AND ASPIRATIONS

Sri Lanka has aspirations to replicate the economic success of Singapore. It wants to be a trans-shipment hub and an economic powerhouse because of its favourable geographic location and educated workforce. It would like to be economically engaged with all major economies of the world; at the same time, it recognises the importance of India to its economic prosperity. Its GDP has grown consistently at 8 per cent after the end of the ethnic war. Sri Lanka is also developing harbours, new commercial ports and attendant infrastructure to emerge as a major commercial hub. But this is too early to draw conclusions about the country's economic trajectory. It would need political stability and will have to overcome international pressure to investigate human rights violations during the war, in order to make sustainable economic progress and attract investments. This is important because the Government of Sri Lanka feels that economic prosperity would automatically bring peace dividends.

Sri Lanka has been trying to expand its trade relations with India. It has discussed and finalised a draft CEPA agreement in 2008. However, it has not yet signed this agreement with India, given the opposition of some political and economic vested interests who are apprehensive about getting closely integrated to the Indian market; this, they feel, will make Sri Lanka dependent on India; it may also provide India with the necessary leverage to pressurise the Government on the Tamil issue. This may also strengthen the bargaining position of the Tamils vis-à-vis the Government. The Rajapaksa Government has, therefore, sought to diversify Sri Lanka's economic relations and offered stakes to different countries like China, Russia and Pakistan to balance India. It hopes that this policy of engagement would help the country in international fora to ease political pressure on it over the Tamil issue. With regard to India, it is likely that Sri Lanka will adopt a sector-wise approach as an alternative to CEPA.

Role of External Players

China and Pakistan emerged as major suppliers of weapons to the Sri Lankan Army to fight the LTTE. Due to opposition from Tamil Nadu, India confined itself to providing intelligence and non-lethal weapons that changed the course of war. Sri Lanka recognises the help extended by India in the last phase of war and acknowledges centrality of India in its peace effort with Tamils. However, in popular perception, China and Pakistan have emerged as more reliable partners of Sri Lanka than India. Sri Lanka's economic engagement with China has also significantly increased in recent years. Though Sri Lanka's China policy is guided by the idea of marginalising India or reducing its importance in Sri Lankan politics, the country also realises the importance of having close relations with India since it has the capacity to emerge both as a spoiler and a benefactor.

It also realises that India's role would be crucial in dealing with international pressure on Sri Lanka to investigate war crimes. The Tamil diaspora is playing a major role in mobilising international opinion against human rights abuses committed during the last phase of the war. Should Sri Lanka feel tempted to use other external powers to balance India or deny legitimate rights to its minorities, its economic aspirations may be difficult to achieve. The direction of Sri Lankan policy in this regard is uncertain and is likely to remain so for a long time. Sri Lanka is yet to emerge as a self-confident nation and is still apprehensive of a likely emergence of Tamil terrorist organisations with the help of the diaspora. To avoid being pressurised by the international community, it is also possible that Sri Lanka will move slowly on the path to closer economic integration with India. However, it is likely to simultaneously engage China to balance India. Although the US and the EU would like to have greater direct influence in Sri Lanka, they may be amenable to synchronise their policy with that of India and allow it to play a lead role in Sri Lanka. China's considerations will be different.

The interplay of these drivers may lead to the following three broad scenarios.

Scenario I: Emerald Shines
Sri Lanka resolves the ethnic problem to the satisfaction of all the stakeholders. It also agrees to investigate the human rights violations that took place towards the end of the ethnic war and attempts genuine reconciliation by punishing the guilty. The Army is withdrawn from the northern and eastern provinces and a major push is given to economic regeneration of the country. There is a certain amount of disquiet in the Army and the Buddhist clergy but Sri Lanka manages to overcome the problem with a broad-based political consensus. It resettles the displaced people and establishes an inclusive political structure, including

substantial provincial autonomy that enables Tamils to play an important role in the governance of the country. The Government of Sri Lanka also recruits Tamils in administration and security forces to provide them with an even playing field. The Tamil diaspora makes important economic contribution by investing in and remitting money to Sri Lanka. India also contributes towards human resource development in Sri Lanka in a major way. Sri Lanka's major infrastructure projects are completed by 2020 and its trade volumes grow substantially. It implements the CEPA and major investments flow in from India. Although investments from China also grow simultaneously, the Government is sensitive towards India's security.

Scenario 2: Full Potential not Realised

Sri Lanka's economy improves and, due to investment in infrastructure, ports in Colombo and Hambantota become important hubs of trans-shipment. Its GDP rises at an average rate of 7-8 per cent. Its exports to the EU also rise as the latter's ban on exports is removed. It operationalises the CEPA hesitantly and Indian investments increase, which provide employment opportunities to Sri Lankans. Similarly Sri Lankan investors invest in India and economic dependency grows. Autonomy with land and police rights is ceded to the provincial governments but the Tamils still feel discriminated against in matters of entry into the civil service, police and military, and they continue to be distrusted. The Sinhala and Tamils remain suspicious of each other and economic inequality remains. Suspicions about India's role in supporting Tamils of Sri Lanka persist as a result of which Sri Lanka remains hesitant about integrating with Indian economy. However, Sri Lankan businessmen invest heavily in the Indian market. Trade between the two countries increases significantly. India tries to keep itself aloof from the ethnic problem and allows the Sri Lankan Government to address the issue while persuading it to arrive at an amicable solution despite occasional differences brought about by India's domestic political compulsions. In spite of political apprehensions about India's possible role the relations between the two countries remain on an even keel, given the economic linkages.

Scenario 3: Sri Lanka in Peril

The ethnic situation deteriorates as Sri Lanka refuses to address the political issue. Disaffected Tamils resort to demonstrations, which lead to severe crackdowns by Sri Lanka's security forces. Sporadic armed clashes start taking place between Tamil youths and the police. After a period of instability, the Government of Sri Lanka redeploys the Army in the Jaffna peninsula and the eastern province to prevent ethnic conflict from escalating. At the same time, the Tamil Muslims are instigated to fight the Tamils. The Tamil diaspora in European countries, Canada and the US influence the host governments to pressurise the Sri Lankan Government. Meanwhile, India's coalition government at the Centre, which is supported by regional parties from Tamil Nadu, is forced to come out openly against disproportionate use of force by Sri Lanka. There is large inflow of refugees to India. In view of the Sinhala nationalistic outpouring, the Sri Lankan Government decides not to pay heed to the international opinion and relies on continued support from China and Pakistan. This development externalises the issue and India, along with other Western countries, steps in effectively to force Sri Lanka to de-escalate the conflict. Anti-India sentiment grows exponentially in Sri Lanka and economic cooperation is withheld, thus diminishing India's leverage; this also harms Sri Lanka's economy. It resists economic integration and imposes a non-tariff barrier on Indian investment. India retaliates by taking similar action. China benefits from the situation and emerges as a major supporter of the Sri Lankan Government, increasing its strategic value for economic benefits.

RECOMMENDATIONS

- Sri Lanka's current relations with India are likely to be strengthened further. India must take certain steps to improve the atmospherics of economic relations before it can pursue CEPA. An enabling environment like visa on arrival, speedy customs clearance, facilitating opening of letters of credit and other banking facilities needs to be created in the short term. This would build trust between the two countries. India needs to take a closer look at the non-tariff barriers, establish quarantine facilities near the sea ports and airports besides speedy dispute settlement mechanisms that provide relief without much business loss. Under invoicing, the problem of quality control and standardisation also needs to be addressed.[44]

- India needs to invest in deep sea fishing and both countries can invest in packaging marine products. Investment in developing hotels and resorts is another potential area of cooperation. Labelling is required in three languages. Prior permission is required from Sri Lanka's standards institution for labelling. Certification, packaging requirement, rule of origin, and movement of labour and cost factor are some issues that would need a re-look.

- In the long term, development of infrastructure will boost trade ties. The private sectors of both countries have the potential to integrate the their economies, and they will invest if business facilities are provided. The two governments should try and facilitate the entry of private sector. These private players will, in the long run, create pressure on the Sri Lankan Government to implement CEPA. Sri Lanka's automobile market needs to be augmented further. India needs to take a long-term view of its investments in Sri Lanka. The economic investment needs to be looked at from a strategic perspective to prevent a repeat of Hambantota.

- The two countries, put together, account for 80 per cent of the world production of coir.[45] Joint investment and a joint marketing strategy between the Coir Boards of India and Sri Lanka should be taken up.
- It is unlikely that current Government will work towards credible devolution of power to the Tamils. Thus India's role in prodding the Sri Lankan Government to resolve the issue would be of paramount importance.
- The manner in which Tamil issue is resolved would impact on Indo-Sri Lanka relations, given the Tamil Nadu factor. Moreover, instability in Sri Lanka will bring in refugees and make Tamil Nadu a hotbed of ethnic politics, which is not conducive to India's security. Such tensions will hinder greater economic integration.
- Taking development initiatives in southern Sri Lanka where the Sinhala are in a majority would help India to be seen as a neutral actor genuinely concerned about the holistic development of Sri Lanka. This can help India to develop its stakes in the country in the long run.
- While economic engagement is important, India must persuade the Government of Sri Lanka to work towards a political solution which should be akin to core Indian interests. This would have a beneficial impact on India-Sri Lanka relations and keep the external forces away from India's neighbourhood. India also needs to expand its defence ties and strengthen sharing of intelligence. The general public are not aware of India's role in the defeat of the LTTE. A nuanced articulation of India's contribution would help.
- Many Tamils hold India responsible for the human rights violations indirectly because it was apathetic to their sufferings at a critical juncture and allowed the Sri Lankan Army to kill Tamils indiscriminately.[45] India should persuade the Sri Lankan Government to hold speedy trials and release Tamil people who have been in Army's custody for a long time. Non-resolution of Tamil issue is likely to cast its shadow on Indo-Sri Lanka relations, especially if the situation gets externalized due to diaspora intervention.

- The humanitarian issue has the potential to isolate the Sri Lankan Government. It is in need of India's support at this crucial juncture. India needs to use the international pressure to hold investigation into war crimes to bargain with the Rajapaksa Government.

- China is likely to distance itself from the human right abuse issue and would not like to take sides. However, if there is a need, it will prevent any international measure against the Sri Lankan Government to probe war crimes. China will bail out Sri Lanka as has it has done in the case of Myanmar, given China's own sensitivities towards human rights issue.

- India needs to engage the Sri Lanka Muslim Congress (SLMC). Attempts are being made by Pakistan to engage the party. But such engagement needs to be based on a long-term strategy. The Muslims would be an important factor in the resolution of the ethnic issue.

- To deal with the fishermen issue that threatens to derail the bilateral goodwill, the two countries need to undertake joint coast guard patrols.

- India needs to increase scholarships for the Sri Lankan students as they can become an important constituency in Sri Lanka and would help in bridging the gap between the Sinhala community and India. India should extend a helping hand in building schools and infrastructure in northern part of the country.

NOTES

1. *Sri Lanka: State of Economy 2010*, Colombo: Institute of Policy Studies, 2010, p.47.
2. For details see http://www.ft.lk/wp-content/uploads/file/11(62).jpg), accessed on January 11, 2012.
3. For details see http://www.lankabusinessonline.com/fullstory.php?nid=1167612783, accessed on January 11, 2012.
4. For details see http://www.reuters.com/article/idUSSGE70301F20110104, accessed on January 11, 2012.
5. For details on infrastructure projects undertaken by the Government of Sri Lanka, see *Sri Lanka: State of Economy 2010*, Colombo: Institute of Policy Studies, 2010, pp.133-140.
6. 'Mahinda Chintana: Vision for the Future', available at http://www.treasury.gov.lk/publications/mahindaChintanaVision-2010full-eng.pdf, accessed on January 11, 2012.
7. For details see 'Doing Business in Sri Lanka', the website of High commission of India, Colombo, at http://www.hcicolombo.org/index.php?option=com_pages&id=37, accessed on January 21, 2012.
8. For details see http://www.buildsrilanka.com/boi/boi-InvestOpp.htm.
9. Shirajiv Sirimane, 'Sri Lanka ranked eighth fastest growing economy – EIU', January 31, 2010, available at http://www.sundayobserver.lk/2010/01/31/new02.asp, accessed on February 22, 2012.

10. For details see http://www.tradechakra.com/economy/sri-lanka/fdi-in-sri-lanka-337.php.
11. For details see http://www.lankabusinessonline.com/fullstory.php?nid=1443769787.
12. According to the Central Bank of Sri Lanka, there was an increase in skilled labour migration from 61,321 in 2009 to 71,114 in 2010. Remittances rose by 23 per cent from $3.3 billion in 2009 to $4.1 billion in 2010. See http://www.lbr.lk/fullstory.php?nid=201106092054497818 and also http://www.cbsl.gov.lk/htm/english/02_prs/p_1.asp?yr=2011
13. For details see http://www.doingbusiness.org/data/exploreeconomies/sri-lanka/ accessed on January 9, 2012.
14. *Central Bank of Sri Lanka Annual Report-2011*, Government of Sri Lanka, p.91.
15. For details see http://www.statistics.gov.lk/samplesurvey/2010q3report.pdf.
16. Ministry of Economic Development, Government of Sri Lanka, 'Tourism Development Strategy 2011-2016',, p.4, available at http://srilanka.travel/catalog/view/theme/default/image/pdf/English.pdf, accessed on January 22, 2012.
17. For details see http://www.asiantribune.com/news/2011/04/26/india-was-leading-foreign-investor-sri-lanka-last-year.
18. For details see http://www.cbsl.gov.lk/pics_n_docs/10_pub/_docs/statistics/other/Pub_E&SS_2010.pdf.
19. See the Joint Study Group Report, 'Indo-Sri Lanka: Comprehensive Economic Partnership Agreement', October 2003, p. 91
20. Some of the industrialists opposed to the CEPA are WKH Wegapitiya of Laugfs, MP Wickramasinghe of Ceylon Biscuits, Asoka Siriwardane of Bitumix, Ruwan Edirisinghe of R&N Group, Dilith Jayaweera of Triad Advertising, Pubudu Wickrema of Wickrema Printers, Daya Dehigama of EPIC Lanka, Parakrama Perera of Sparklink Travels, and Rohith de Silva of IDEC.
21. Dushni Weerakoon and Jayanthi Thennakoon, 'India-Sri Lanka FTA: Lessons for SAFTA', CUTS International and Commonwealth Secretariat, undated, pp.12-15.
22. Interview with Secretary Finance, Dr P Jayasundara, on April 27, 2011.
23. Interview with one of the Advisers to the President Rajapaksa, interview held in Delhi on May 6, 2009, who did not want to be named.
24. Interview with Ajith Nivard Cabraal, the Governor, and B. D. W. A. Silva, Deputy Governor of the Central Bank of Sri Lanka, on April 27, 2011.
25. Interview with Dr. Anura Ekanayake, the then Chairman of Ceylon Chamber of Commerce and Industries, April 29, 2011.
26. Forty-four per cent of India's exports to Sri Lanka at the time of FTA negotiation were excluded from preferential market access in Sri Lanka, whereas for Sri Lanka it was 13.6 per cent of its export. By 2006, Sri Lanka's exports to India, which received preferential treatment, rose to 93 per cent. See Dushni Weerakoon and Jayanthi Thennakoon, n. 21, pp. 12 & 17.
27. Interviews with Ceylon Chamber of Commerce and Institute for Policy Studies, Colombo, April 29, 2011. Twenty-four Chinese companies are currently handling the Mirigama Special Economic Zone, a 1,000-acre Tapioca farm, Hambantota port, 900 MW coal fired Norochcholai power plant, Colombo-Katunayake Expressway, Palai-Kankasanthurai rail-line, Jaffna housing complex for the Army, and a host of other projects. The entire Hambantota project is expected to cost about $1.5 billion and a consortium of Chinese companies led by the China Harbour Engineering Company and the Sino Hydro Corporation are involved in the project's construction. China has provided $1million as humanitarian aid for internally displaced persons and

technical assistance for de-mining operations in Northern and Eastern provinces. Some 332 km of roads inclusive of the Kandy- Jaffna A9 highway will be developed and modernized with Chinese funding of US $355 million. China has employed 30,000 semi-skilled and unskilled workers displacing local labourers. See Bandula Sirimana, 'Chinese and Indian Companies Dominate Sri Lanka's Mega Project Business', available at http://sundaytimes.lk/100905/BusinessTimes/bt21.html.
28. Ibid.
29. Long-term borrowing from China at interest rates ranging from 2-3 per cent and 6-7 per cent under strict conditions laid down by Chinese lending institutions was the only option available to the Sri Lankan Government to implement post-war development projects in the north, east and the south. According to Finance Ministry sources, multilateral donor agencies such as the World Bank and the Asian Development Bank provide soft loans at a very low interest rates ranging from 0.25 per cent, 2 per cent or 3 per cent. But these agencies stipulate strict conditions. Sri Lanka has borrowed $306 million at 6.3 per cent for Phase I of the Hambantota Port Project. A one-year grace period is provided for on completion of the construction. The loan repayment period is 11 years with two instalments per annum. The Chinese Government has provided $891 million through the Exim Bank to finance Phase II of the Norochcholai Coal Power Plant Project in Puttalam District, under a Preferential Buyer's Credit Facility, at an interest rate of around 4 per cent. According to the terms and conditions of the Exim Bank, Chinese companies should be selected as the project contractor and for procurement projects and the equipment supply shall, in principle, come from a Chinese exporter. See Bandula Sirimana, 'Chinese Project Loans at High rate of Interest', *The Sunday Times*, June 19, 2011, available at http://sundaytimes.lk/110619/BusinessTimes/bt01.html, accessed on June 25, 2011.
30. Ravi Karunanayake, former Minister of Commerce, UNP. Interview held on April 26, 2011 in Colombo.
31. Interview with a civil society activist who would prefer to remain anonymous, April 25, 2011, Colombo.
32. 'Sri Lanka for Home Grown Solution, *Daily News*, February 25, 2012, available at http://www.dailynews.lk/2012/02/25/pol01.asp, accessed on February 28, 2012.
33. Interview with a human right activist, who would prefer to remain anonymous, on April 25, 2011 in Colombo.
34. Interview with Commander in Chief, Jaffna, Sri Lankan Army, on April 30, 2011 in Jaffna.
35. Interview with Foreign Secretary of Sri Lanka, April 27, 2011.
36. Interview with Basudeva Nanayakkara, Minister of Language and Social Integration, April 27, 2011, Colombo.
37. Interview with a Muslim leader of SLMC, who would prefer to remain anonymous, in Colombo on May 1, 2011.
38. Interview with Sampathan, President of the TNA in Colombo on May 1, 2011
39. Kumar David, 'As Expected TNA-Rajapakse Dialogue Collapse: Armageddon Inches Closer', *The Island*, August 11, 2011.
40. The observation is based on the author's interaction with Tamil people, Sri Lankan armed forces officials as well as interaction with the India Consul General in Jaffna, April 30, 2011.
41. Interview with academicians, civil society members, intellectuals and rights activists,

and government officials who would not like to be named. All the interviews held by the author between April 25, 2011 and May 1, 2011.
42. Report on Commission of Enquiry on Lesson Learnt and Reconciliation Commission, November 2011,, available at http://slembassyusa.org/downloads/LLRC-REPORT.pdf, p.369, accessed on January 14, 2012.
43. Report on Commission of Enquiry on Lesson Learnt and Reconciliation Commission, November 2011, available at http://slembassyusa.org/downloads/LLRC-REPORT.pdf, p.368, accessed on January 14, 2012.
44. Many buyers in Sri Lanka demand under-invoicing in order to save themselves from import duties. This causes exporters undue harassment.
45. *Business Line*, September 16, 2010.
46. Interviews with Tamils between April 23, 2011 and May 1, 2011.

Conclusion

The survey of India's relations with neighbouring countries leads to several broad conclusions regarding the future evolution of the neighbourhood, and the challenges and opportunities for India's foreign policy.

1. The Neighbourhood is Changing Rapidly

The pace of socio-economic and political change in India and its neighbourhood will accelerate. The South Asia of 2030 will differ significantly from that of today. In the next two decades, the geo-political situation in the region would be different. Some major changes anticipated are as follows:

    a. Demographic pressure would increase across South Asia. The population of the region would increase from about 1.6 billion to over 2 billion. This would create tremendous pressure on resources. Each country would be under severe pressure to provide for food, energy, employment, housing, education, and schools to its burgeoning population.

    b. The adverse consequences of climate change would come to the fore. The frequency of floods and droughts and extreme weather events would increase. Migrations due to sea level rise and other socio-economic reasons may pose a critical challenge to internal security.

    c. Pakistan and Afghanistan would become even more unstable and ungovernable. This could have implications for India's security. India would be required to have a more pro-active policy towards Pakistan.

    d. Nepal would be in the process of building and consolidating its new political and economic structures. The prospects of instability cannot be ruled out. India will have stakes in Nepal's stability but it cannot be seen as interfering in Nepal's internal affairs. India will need to address the anti-India feelings in Nepal. This can be tackled if India is seen as a disinterested party while focusing on the people and addressing their needs.

e. Bangladesh would face the problems of climate change. Its expanding population would put pressure on India's Northeast. India's approach should be to build connectivity and integrate the Bangladesh economy with its own, particularly in the Northeast. Bangladesh should become an important part of India's Look East Policy.

f. Sri Lanka's economy is likely to grow at a faster pace but it is not clear whether the ethnic issue would be resolved. Internal tensions in Sri Lanka would put pressure on the country's growth. India's relationship with Sri Lanka should be multifaceted. The process of integrating Sri Lanka's economy with that of India should be continued.

g. Maldives would be struggling with the adverse consequences of climate change and seeking closer ties with India to manage them. India should assist Maldives as comprehensively as possible.

h. Myanmar may be more democratic and more integrated with the rest of the world. India's should accelerate the process of economic cooperation with Myanmar and involve the latter in regional integration projects.

i. All these changes would be taking place in the backdrop of the rising influence of China in South Asia, Southeast Asia and Africa. Tibet could become restive. Developments there would have a destabilizing impact on the Himalayan countries. Competition with China is likely to intensify. India's most important challenge will be to deal with an assertive China.

j. On the positive side, South Asia could be better integrated, better connected, and more prosperous if the countries in the region realize the gravity of the situation and take urgent steps now to promote interdependence. Democratic institutions in many countries would have strengthened. Regional cooperation would have improved, with several sub-regional groupings having taken shape. There is so much untapped advantage of economic integration with ready markets within the region, which can sustain regional economies despite global economic uncertainties.

2. India's Foreign Policy Approach Will Need to be Broadened

In light of these changes, India's foreign policy would face several challenges and require a broader approach. Firstly, a clear articulation of the security and developmental objectives of the country will need to be done. The questions that arise are: what are India's primary security concerns? What is India's long-term strategy? What role does India seek in the immediate neighbourhood, in the extended neighbourhood, and at the global level? For this, a national debate and consensus would be required. Secondly, India would need to build the necessary institutions and capabilities to achieve these objectives. In particular, our decision-making structures will need to be revamped for greater transparency and effectiveness. Speedy decisions will be a must. Some specific challenges India' foreign policy will face are listed below.

a. India will need to have a strong, inclusive economy, a strong military, well-regulated borders and good governance to deal with the security and developmental challenges that it will face in the coming years.

b. India needs to develop comprehensive defence cooperation with friendly countries. This should include strategic linkages, training, capacity building, disaster management, etc. India could also fulfil the defence equipment needs of friendly countries. Defence diplomacy will assume importance in India's overall policy towards her neighbours.

c. There would be an increasing need to incorporate the human security concerns in foreign policy, which has traditionally been dominated by hard security concerns. The issues of water, food, energy, trade and investment, socio-economic and cultural contacts will assume greater salience in India's foreign policy. India would need to find abundant human, physical and financial resources to pursue a broad-based foreign policy with regard to its neighbours.

d. India will be faced with situations where it may be required to take unilateral steps to promote economic and social integration with the neighbours. Some of these may be in the area of trade and commerce while others may be extending concessions demanding and assistance of one kind or another.

e. Domestic factors will influence foreign policy increasingly. The various Indian states will come to play increase role in the making and formulation of India's foreign policy. The interests of the populations in the bordering states will need to be understood and addressed. The Central Government would need to evolve effective mechanisms for this. The governance model will also need to be fine-tuned to strengthen internal cohesion and achieve sustained economic growth in India.

f. Terrorism, organised crime, human trafficking, cyber security and WMD proliferation will continue to pose challenges to India's security. Dealing with these will require an effective counter-terrorism policy, a forward-looking approach on cooperation with the neighbours to manage the borders, and including several new areas in regional cooperation agenda such as cyber security, science and technology, agricultural development, education culture, capacity building, etc. Only by adopting a holistic approach in which its neighbours and the people are involved, will help India meet the challenges of terrorism and of non-traditional security.

g. Addressing the adverse consequences of the failure of governance in the region and even in parts of India will pose a formidable challenge to India's foreign policy. A combination of policies based on the broader understanding of security will be required. The use of force alone would not be enough to deal with these challenges.

h. India has faced several conflicts, wars and insurgencies over the last 65 years. There is a need to continue with the ongoing defence modernisation programme. The threat of nuclear weapons falling into non-state actors will increase. Nuclear security will become an important element in India's security policy.

i. Dealing with China will require an effective diplomatic and security approach, particularly in the post-Dalai Lama scenario. India's Tibet policy may require further fine-tuning. The best way to deal with China will be to build our military and economic capabilities. India will need to pay special attention to the development of the border regions. India's border development areas programmes would need to be improved manifold. Whereas rhetoric and undue provocation need to be avoided, articulating our concerns clearly, improving our deterrence capability, and leveraging the concerns of other powers vis-à-vis China are likely to moderate its behaviour.

j. Since India's foreign policy would become more people-centric, India will have to re-think its visa regime. The visa regime is a great tool of foreign policy. The movement of people from one country to another would have to be regulated but made less cumbersome and easier. Special attention will need to be paid to the populations sharing ethnic and cultural identities on either side of the border and due steps should be taken to facilitate regulated crossings by means of special permits. Modern approaches to border management and regulation would need to be adopted, especially because more migrations into India from neighbouring countries are expected to take place in the coming years.

k. India should become an educational hub for higher studies, skill development, vocational training and professional courses. The SAARC University is a step in the right direction. However, there is a need to develop high-quality institutions and facilitate students from the neighbourhood, who could be allowed to take up short-term research assignments. This will require changes in the visa regime.

l. India lacks the capabilities to deliver timely on promises made at highest levels. This is a sore point between India and its neighbours. A lot of this had to do with sorry state of coordination within the country. India will need to improve its project management skills, coordination mechanisms, and delivery capabilities to establish its credibility.

m. India will need to fine-tune its diplomatic and security apparatus to deal with neighbouring countries, keeping in view their sensitivities. For example, while diplomatic resources will have to be harnessed to deal with border-related issues, border guarding forces will also need to be trained to deal with the border problems in a sensitive manner.

n. Undoubtedly, India will need to remain a pre-eminent political, military and economic power in the region to safeguard its national interests. However, India would need to connect with the neighbouring countries and promote their integration with its rising economy. The flip side of this scenario is that a fall in India's economic growth could result in increase in problems with neighbours. Thus maintaining a sound inclusive growth rate and a broad consensus on foreign policy would be of paramount importance.

o. South Asia cannot remain immune from developments in the extended neighbourhood, and in the world in general. Thus, India's neighbourhood policy will be affected by developments elsewhere. India would need to connect with the Gulf, Central

Asia, Southeast Asia and the Indian Ocean region to ensure that its neighbourhood policy remains effective.

3. The Main Conclusion of the Study is that South Asia is at Crossroads

In view of the wide-ranging changes in India's neighbourhood, as has been suggested in the study, India will have to deal with a range of uncertainties over the next 20 years. The region can progress if the countries of the region create interdependencies and cooperate with each other to tackle common challenges. India has a responsibility to promote cooperation as this will be its own national interest. The action that India takes today will have profound impact on the developments in the next 20 years, not only within India but also in the neighbourhood. India cannot control every development but, as a pre-eminent power in the region, its actions will have consequences. While new challenges will arise undoubtedly, a progressive foreign policy approach towards its neighbours—which places emphasis on people-to-people ties—is likely to be more effective. India will have to harness both its soft and hard powers judiciously.

INDEX

Afghan National Security Forces (ANSF), 2, 7, 11
Afghanistan:
   Emerging Situation, 1
      India's Position and Challenges, 3
      A Balkanise, 11
      Fragile but Relatively Stable, 10
      Highly Destabilised, 8
      Issues likely to Shape Future Events, 5
      Likely Scenarios and India's Options, 1-18
Af-Pak frontier, 4
Ahmadiyas, 166
Al Qaeda, 6, 166, 177
anti-India feeling, 137
anti-Pakistan Afghan elements, 4
Automatic Message Handling System (AMHS), 115

Bangladesh
   Border Control Measures, 31
   Causes of Migrant Flow, 20
      Pull Factor, 20
      Push Factors Emanating from Bangladesh, 21
      Bangladesh Economy, 22
   Demographic Changes, Sectarian Discords, and Security Concerns, 20
      Statistics of Illegal Migrants, 20
   Economic Measures, 30
   Illegal Migration and Challenges for India, 19-34
   India's Response, 25
      Legal Mechanisms, 26
      Fencing, 27
   Long-term Measures, 32
   Population Growth Rate, 21
Behuria, Ashok K, 163
Bengal Initiative for Multi-Sectoral Technical and Economic Cooperation (BIMSTEC), 49, 123
Bhutan
   'Balances' India with China, 50
   Bhutan's Foreign Policy Engagement, 41
   India-Bhutan Relations in Next Two Decades, 35-54
   Limits of Democracy, 50
   Moves Further South, 49
   Potential Challenges, 44
      Bilateral Relations with non-SAARC Countries, 46
      Bilateral Relations with SAARC Countries, 46
      Boundary dispute between China and Bhutan, 48
      Democracy, 48
      Economic Model, 44
      Export-Import Imbalance in Hydel Trade, 44
      Nature of Democratisation, 45
      Non-Traditional Challenges, 46
      Drivers, 47
      State of the Economy, 47
Bhutan-Nepal relations, 42
Bilateral Investment Promotion and Protection Agreement (BIPPA), 142
Bisht, Medha, 35
BJP-led NDA Government, 20
Board of Investment (BOI) Act, 192
Brigade 313, 177

Ceylon Chamber of Commerce, 198
Chandra, Vishal, 1
Chaudhry, Iftikhar Muhammad, chief justice,, 178
China ebb, 65
China
   Fragile Stability, 83
   Himalayan Spring, 82
   Implications of Chinese Military Modernisation for India, 76
   Limits of Cooperation on Global Issues, 74
   Open Confrontation, 84
   Response to Post-Dalai Lama Scenario, 68
   Tibet, 65

Index

War with India (1962), 80
China's Strides in Myanmar, 116
    Air Connectivity, 117
    Hydropower, 117
    Hydrocarbon Resources, 117
    Railways, 116
    Roads, 116
China-Japan relationship, 57
China-Pakistan friendship, 72
Chure Bhawar Ekta Samaj (CBES), 145
climate refugees, 25
Climate Summit for Living Himalayas, 40
Coastal (Disaster) Management Centre, 105
Cold War, 66
Communist Party of Bhutan, 40
Communist Party of China (CPC), 63
Communist Party of Nepal-Maoist (CPN-M), 138-39
Comprehensive Economic Partnership Agreement (CEPA), 195, 197-99, 207
Congress-led UPA Government, 20
Constituent Assembly (CA), 138, 147
    elections, 139

Dahiya, Rumel, 55
Datta, Sreeradha, 19
Delhi High Level Conference on Climate Change: Technology Development and Transfer, 104
Deng Xiaoping, 62
drugs trafficking, 181
Druk Phuensum Tshogpa (DPT), 36

East Asia Summit (EAS), 74
Economic Development Policy 2010, 37
Economic Survey of Bangladesh, 23
European Union (EU), 98, 148

fake currencies, 181
Federal Investigative Agency (FIA), 177
Federally Administered Tribal Areas (FATA), 166, 177
Fiscal Incentives 2010, 37
Foreign Direct Investments (FDI), 51
    Policy 2010, 37
Free Trade Agreement (FTA), 196-98

Gandhi, Rajiv, 59
Glacial Lake Outburst Floods (GLOF), 52
good behaviour, 60
Gorkha Janamukti Morcha (GJM), 41
Gross National Happiness (GNH), 39

Illegal Migrants Determination by Tribunal (IMDT) Act, 1983, 26
India's Connectivity with Myanmar, 117
India's Foreign Policy Approach Will Need to be Broadened, 218
India's Look East Policy, 110, 123, 217
India's Policy Options and Recommendations, 14
India's Political Will and Capacity, 124
India-Bhutan Diplomatic Engagement, 38
India-Bhutan Friendship Treaty, 38
India-Bhutan partnership, 50
India-Bhutan relationship, 39
India-China Relations, 58, 75
    Border Dispute, 59
    in South Asian, Southeast Asian and East Asian Contexts, 69
    India-China Economic Relations, 56
    Managing, 55-94
Indian Military Training Team (IMTRAT), 39
Indian threat, 178
India-Nepal Relations
    Chronic Political Instability, 152
    Red Nepal, 153
    Future Scenarios, 149
    Drivers, 149
    Economic Opportunities and Aspirations, 150
    External Powers, 151
    Political Upheaval, 149
    Issues and Concerns in, 137-62
    Nepal Muddles Through, 152
    Win-Win Situation: Political Stability, 151
India-Pakistan relation, 182
India-Sri Lanka Bilateral Free Trade Agreement, 195
India-Sri Lanka Relations in 2030, 205
    Political Management, 205
Indo-US cooperation, 62
Indo-US relations, 62
Indo-US relationship, 60, 62
Integrated Check Post (ICP), 155
International Monetary Fund (IMF), 76

Joint Working Group (JWG), 59

Khyber Pakhtunkhwa (KP), 168
Koirala, Girija Prasad, 43
Korean War, 80
Kumar, Anand, 95
Kyoto Protocol, 97

Labour Force Survey 2005-06, 24

Laden, Osama bin
  killing of, 173
Lama, Dalai, 60, 62, 66-69, 80
Landslide Dam Outburst Floods (LDOF), 52
Lashkar-e-Jhangvi, 177
Lesson Learnt and Reconciliation Commission (LLRC), 206
Line of Actual Control (LAC), 82
loot-of-national-wealth, 58
LTTE, 200-07

Machine Readable Passport (MRP), 147
Maldives
  Debate over Climate Change, 96
    Green Development, 97
    Important Bilateral Engagements, 104
    Policy/Approach to Deal, 97
  Durban Climate Summit, 97
  Harmonising Efforts to Mitigate Adverse Impacts of Climate Change and Achieve Growth, 95-109
  Helping Growth without Endangering Survival, 101
  High Water Mark, 102
  Low Water Mark, 103
  Mitigating Adverse Impact through Bilateral and Multi-lateral Efforts, 98
  Muddled Waters, 103
  Vulnerabilities to Climate Change, 96
Maldivian Government
  Climate Mitigation and Adaptation Measures, 99
Malik, Mohan, 60
McMahon Line, 62, 66
Mekong-Ganga Cooperation (MGC) project, 119
Mekong-Ganga Cooperation Initiative (MGCI), 123
Memorandum of Understanding (MoU), 37
Miliband, David, 66
Multi National Companies (MNCs), 101
Musharraf, Pervez, 178
  departure of, 167
Myanmar
  East Looks Bright, 127
  External Environment, 125
  Inland Water Transport (Kaladan River), 122
  Kaladan Multimodal Project, 122
  Multilateral Fora, 123
  Myanmar is Too Far!, 127
  Need for Infrastructure Integration, 110-136
  Political and Security Situation within, 124
  Proposed Rail Network, 120
  Proposed Road Network, 129
  Road Transport (Paletwa to India-Myanmar Border), 122
  Security and Infrastructure in the Northeast, 124
  State of Infrastructure Development in Northeast Region of India, 111
    Air connectivity, 112
    Hydropower and Energy, 114
    Railways, 112
    Roads, 111
  State of Infrastructure in Myanmar, 114
    Air Connectivity, 115
    Hydroelectric Projects, 115
    Railways, 115
    Roads, 114
  Thus Far and No Further, 127
  Trade and Economic Investment in, 121
    Investment, 121
    Trade, 121
  Upgradation of Roads Linking Northeast India, 128

Natarajan, Jayanthi, 98
National Democratic Front of Bodoland (NDFB), 40
National Geographic, 25
National Human Rights Commission (NHRC), 26
National Hydroelectric Power Corporation (NHPC), 119
National League for Democracy (NLD), 125
National Thermal Power Corporation (NTPC), 196
national unity government, 151
NATO, 6
Nayak, Nihar, 137
Neighbourhood is Changing Rapidly, 216
Nepal
  Anti-India Sentiments in, 137
  Economic, 140
  Geographical Issues: The Case of Open Borders, 147
  Hydel Projects, 161
  Issue of Water and Hydropower Cooperation, 142
  Political, 138
  Project Development Agreement, 161
  Psychological, 149
  Role of External Forces, 146
  Social, 145
Nepali Congress (NC), 140, 145, 149
Nepal-India Maitri, 154

Index

Northeastern Region (NER), 110
Northern Distribution Network (NDN), 6

Official Development Assistance (ODA), 169
Official Languages Commission (OLC), 202
One China policy, 65
Operation Geronimo, 6

Pakistan Muslim League (PML-N), 163, 178
Pakistan Naval Station (PNS), 177
Pakistan occupied Kashmir (PoK), 71
Pakistan People's Party (PPP), 163
Pakistan Sunni Tehreek (PST), 165
Pakistan Tehrik-e-Insaf (PTI), 163
Pakistan
    Chronic Instability and India's Options, 163-90
    Civil-Military Relations, 178
    Ethnic Situation, 175
    Hybrid Jihadi State, 185
    Internal Contradictions and Socio-political Dynamics, 164
    Challenges, 171
    Economic Situation, 168
    Ethnic Faultlines in the Society, 167
    External Dependence, 169
    Grievances against Punjabi Dominance and Economic Disparity, 168
    Impact on Society, 174
    Inter and Intra-sectarian Faultlines to Widen, 164
    Radicalisation of the Deep State, 173
    Rising Radicalism and the Portents for Political Stability, 173
    System of Diarchy, 166
        Operation Midnight Jackal, 166
    Weak Fundamentals, 169
    Issue of Water, 180
        Indus Water Treaty of 1960, 180
        What should be India's Strategy?, 180
    Muddling Through: A Banana Republic?, 185
    ODA Received, 171
    Overall Impact on India, 181
        Equation among Different Actors, 183
        Relationship with India, 184
        Role of External Powers, 184
        Socio-economic Pressures, 183
    Pakistan of Jinnah's Dream, 185
    Prognosis, 186

Pakistan's Strategy in Afghanistan Durand Line and, 179
Pakistani economy, 171

Pakistani State
    Talibanisation and Stability, 177
Pandalai, Shruti, 110
Pattanaik, Smruti S, 191
People's Democratic Party (PDP), 45
People's Liberation Army (PLA), 63, 71, 153
Performance Based Navigation (PBS), 114
Population Research Bureau (PRB), 22
post-Cold War period, 66
post-Dalai Lama period, 82
post-Dalai Lama scenario, 69, 82
President Karzai, 2
President Nasheed of the Maldives, 95
Public Interest Litigation (PIL), 26

Rajapaksa Government, 200
Reconciliation through the three-language formula, 204

SAARC Development Fund (SDF), 42
Saran, Shyam, Ambassador, 104
Sareen, Sushant, 163
Security Force (SF), 140
Seventh National Finance Commission (NFC) Award, 168
Shahzad, Syed Saleem, journalist, 173
Shanghai Cooperation Organisation (SCO), 5, 74
Sharif, Nawaz, 182
Shimla Conference (1914), 66
Singh, Manmohan, Prime Minister of India, 60, 95
Singh, Prashant Kumar, 55
Singh, Udai Bhanu, 110
Sinhala nationalism
    rise of, 198
Sino-Indian relations, 55
Sino-Tibetan talks, 68
Small and Medium Enterprises (SMEs), 156
South Asia is at a Crossroads, 221
South Asian Association for Regional Cooperation (SAARC), 40, 75
    Sixteenth Summit, 42
South China Sea, 78
Special Accelerated Road Development Programme for North East (SARDP-NE), 118
Sri Lanka Freedom Party (SLFP), 197
Sri Lanka Muslim Congress (SLMC), 203-04
Sri Lanka
    Challenges and Opportunities for India, 191-215
    Doing Business in Sri Lanka
    Political Solution Key to Better Relations, 199

Economic Opportunities and Aspirations, 207
  Role of External Players, 207
  Emerald Shines, 208
  Foreign Finance Commitments, 193
  Full Potential not Realised, 209
  in Peril, 209
  Issue of Devolution/Autonomy, 203
  Trilingual Formula, 202
Sri Lankan Central Bank Report, 195
State Peace and Development Council (SPDC), 125
Status of Force Agreement (SoFA), 5
Stilwell Road (Ledo Road), 115

Taiwan Strait Crisis of 1996, 80
Tamil issue, 205
Tamil National Alliance (TNA), 199, 200, 203, 204
Tarai-Madhesh Loktantrik Party (TMLP), 145
Tehrik-e-Taliban Pakistan (TTP), 174, 177
Tibet Autonomous Region (TAR), 76
Tibetan Youth Congress (TYC), 62
Trailokya Raj Aryal, 149
Turkmenistan-Afghanistan-Pakistan-India (TAPI), 5

UML, 149

UNESCAP Trans Asian Railway (TAR) network, 117
United Liberation Front of Assam, (ULFA), 40
United National Party (UNP), 197
United Nations (UN), 98
United Nations Development Programme (UNDP), 101
United Nations Security Council (UNSC), 67, 95
Upendra Yadav, 145
US President Barack H. Obama, 1
US-led anti-China alliance, 82
US-Pakistan relations, 11

Vajpayee, Atal Bihari, 59, 66

Wangchuk, Jigme Singye, 43
war of necessity, 1
What after Karzai, 5
World Bank, 76
World Economic Forum (WEF), 172
World Food Programme (WFP), 148
World Trade Organisation (WTO), 57
World War II, 128

Young Communist League (YCL), 153

Zardari, 182
Zhou Enlai, 62